Portable Australian Authors

The 1890s

For my parents:
Alfred Emile and Patricia Pettit Cantrell

PORTABLE AUSTRALIAN AUTHORS

This series provides carefully selected volumes introducing major Australian writers and movements. The format is designed for compactness and for pleasurable reading. Each volume is intended to meet a need not hitherto met by any single book. Each is edited by an authority distinguished in his field, who adds an introductory essay and other helpful material.

General Editor: L.T. Hergenhan

Also in this series:

Marcus Clarke edited by Michael Wilding
Henry Lawson edited by Brian Kiernan
Five Plays for Stage, Radio, and Television
edited by Alrene Sykes

In Preparation:

Joseph Furphy edited by John Barnes
The Jindyworobaks edited by Brian Elliott
Rolf Boldrewood edited by Alan Brissenden

Portable Australian Authors

The 1890s
Stories, Verse, and Essays

Edited with an Introduction by
LEON CANTRELL

 University of Queensland Press

Published by University of Queensland Press,
St. Lucia, Queensland, 1977
Introduction © Leon Cantrell, 1977
This compilation © University of Queensland Press, 1977

Typeset by Academy Press Pty. Ltd., Brisbane
Printed and bound in Hong Kong

Distributed in the United Kingdom, Europe, the Middle East,
Africa, and the Caribbean by Prentice-Hall International,
International Book Distributors Ltd., 66 Wood Lane End,
Hemel Hempstead, Herts., England

*National Library of Australia
Cataloguing-in-Publication data*
The 1890s: stories, verse and essays.

(Portable Australian authors).
Bibliography.
ISBN 0 7022 1037 4.
ISBN 0 7022 1038 2 Paperback.

1. Australian Literature. I. Cantrell, Leon
Nicolas, 1943 —, ed. (Series).

A820.8002

Contents

THE CITY OR THE BUSH?

UP THE COUNTRY

Acknowledgments

Acknowledgment is made to Angus & Robertson Publishers for permission to include works by Barbara Baynton, Christopher Brennan, Edward Dyson, Miles Franklin, Mary Gilmore, Hugh McCrae, John Shaw Neilson, Will Ogilvie, A.B. "Banjo" Paterson, and Roderic Quinn; to Lothian Publishing Company for permission to include poems by Bernard O'Dowd; to Whitcoulls Publishing Division for permission to include poems by Arthur Adams; to Mr. Eric Davis for permission to include stories by "Steele Rudd"; and to the literary executors of A.G. Stephens. Details of the original book publication for each work are given in the Textual Sources section at the back of this anthology.

Introduction

The decade of the 1890s has meant many different things as Australians have tried to come to terms with their past. Perhaps there is always an aura of nostalgia and sentiment hanging over a period which seems to mark a watershed between an old way of life and a new. And when that period marks the closing years of a century, especially the first full century of a country's recorded history, something special seems to attach to it. Certainly this has long been the case with the 1890s in Australia. There is a persistent romantic interpretation of the decade which sees it as through the hazy glow of a golden afternoon. To the generation of the First World War and the 1920s the earlier age seemed to contain a potential and a promise which had been lost. Early volumes of reminiscences, taking their cue from the *fin de siècle* tone of the English decadents, emphasized the nineties' free-and-easy, devil-may-care bohemianism as both attractive and liberating. They spoke of its principal figures as creative giants, the like of whom we would be lucky to see again. George Taylor's wistfully titled *Those Were the Days* (1918) heralded the beginning of a steady stream of articles and books which saw the literary achievements of the 1890s as central to the Australian experience. A few years later Arthur Jose refered to "the romantic years" of the nineties and told legendary tales of Christopher Brennan's "Casuals" and of Victor Daley's "Dawn and Dusk" group as centres of cultural and creative ferment. Even up-country, Jose wrote, young men's minds were "working as if some super-baker had permeated them with a spiritual yeast."[1]

Oddly enough, however, the period itself seemed to be unaware of its mythical proportions. Certainly there was a feeling of opportunity and achievement in the air, but it was viewed in essentially modest terms, quite lacking the note of euphoria later writers ascribed to it. Desmond Byrne's *Australian Writers* (1896), for instance, lamented the absence of a literature with "something of a national savour in it"[2] yet chose to ignore the work of such *Bulletin* writers as Henry Lawson and "Banjo" Paterson because it was seen as somehow inferior. Though H.G. Turner's and Alexander Sutherland's *The Development of Australian Literature* (1898) mentions Lawson and Paterson, it similarly concentrates on such earlier figures as Clarke, Gordon, and Kendall. The principal aim of this anthology is to provide enough of the evidence for us to make our own judgments as to the nature and quality of the decade's writing. I have tried to include those works which are now recognized as the indubitable masterpieces of the period (or extracts from them, in the case of novels) as well as a representative cross-section of minor works and authors. In addition, I have isolated the major concerns of writers to show a variety of approaches to similar themes: writing in Australia, city life, lyricism, politics and nationalism, the city versus the bush, and life up the country. In this way we can see something of the wholeness of the period: how its preoccupations persisted or were modified, how different writers responded to common issues and pressures. It is my contention that the variety of Australian nineties' writing has been underestimated. We have been too prone to accept the generalizations and stereotypes which criticism and literary history have spawned. Like Byrne, eighty years ago, we have been reluctant to look at the evidence. The editorial principle of this anthology is that a full appreciation of any period's achievement can only come through a consideration of its representative as well as its greatest products.

But why the 1890s? What features of Australian writing from that decade warrant an anthology such as this? Were the nineties so very different from the 1880s or the first decade of this century? Certainly there is a tradition among our literary critics and historians of treating the nineties as a special case, though there is widespread disagreement as to what its special features were. The one indisputable point of agreement is that the nineties saw a proliferation in the writing and publication of verse and prose. A glance through the pages of the *Annals of Australian Literature* shows that collections of stories, especially, became increasingly common—so much so that the short story or sketch has come to be regarded as the nineties' most characteristic literary product. The reading public's interest in Australian books also grew so that, for the first time, it was not uncommon for a local volume to sell by the thousands. G.A. Wilkes has pointed out that the first collection of Lawson's stories, *While the Billy Boils* (1896) sold 32,000 copies within twenty years and that his verse collection of the same year, *In the Days When the World was Wide*, had cleared 20,000 copies by 1914. The nineties' writers were also the mainstay of "the first successful paperbacks in Australian publishing—the Commonwealth series from Angus and Robertson, which had sold over 140,000 copies by 1908, and the N.S.W. Bookstall series, advertised at the same time as 'selling in thousands'."[3] Ethel Turner's children's novel, *Seven Little Australians* (1894), though published in London, rapidly became an Australian bestseller and "Steele Rudd"'s *On Our Selection* (1899) was perhaps the most popular of all books of the time, selling 20,000 copies in four years. Paterson's verse, *The Man From Snowy River* (1895) outstripped even Lawson in sales. It had been reprinted twelve times in Australia and twice in England by the end of the century and had sold 35,000 copies by 1906.

But what of the quality of this literature, being so swiftly written and so widely read? Earlier critics, such as Nettie Palmer, sifting through the pages of the *Bulletin* of the nineties in search of material for her *Australian Story Book* (1928),[4] complained of an uninspired sameness in many of the short stories. To read through the great mass of nineties' ballads can be equally tedious. But we mistake the achievement of the age if we do not consider its diversity, if we see it solely in terms of its most characteristic forms. For local writing of the 1890s covered a wide range of styles and subjects. Byrne complained that city and political themes were virtually non-existent in Australian literature, but this anthology shows such not to have been the case. At its best, local writing of the period can hold its own with much that was being written elsewhere and even in its more characteristically minor phases it has a native vigour which helps us define our concept of the society from which it arose and to which it spoke. Self-consciousness about Australian writing, a fear that it may not be "good enough", is still with us, and one of its most obvious legacies is a general underestimation of the nineteenth century's achievement. Though the decade of the nineties has suffered less from this neglect than have earlier decades, because of the obvious stature of such writers as Lawson and Joseph Furphy, there persists a reluctance to view its achievement as a whole. Certainly the bush, and life "up-country", provided the inspiration for many of the best nineties' stories and verses. But, contrary to the common view, outback themes were far from being the only ones explored. And the image of the age as one which simply celebrated the Australian landscape and character will not hold up before the evidence.

One reason for these common misconceptions is the emphasis which has been placed upon the nineties as the great nationalist phase of our history. This view sees the decade's social, political, and cultural achievements as the summation of a uniquely Australian way of life. It emphasizes the local content of nineties' writing. In the ballads and stories of bush life, as on the canvases of Roberts, Streeton, and McCubbin, it locates the "true Australia": a golden age of achievement and progress, a definition and a consolidation of the Australian experience. Our major literary historian, H.M. Green, thus writes of "a mood of confidence and romantic optimism" as a hallmark of the nineties. He sees the "spirit" of the times as "a fervent democratic nationalism" which finds its "most characteristic expression in Lawson's doctrine of mateship."[5] Such an interpretation stresses another side of the nineties' alleged uniqueness. It sees the period as marking virtually a new beginning for local writing. Jose wrote of "rather a naissance than a renaissance".[6] Other writers too have seemed at times quite happy to cast aside Australian writing before 1890 as somehow misdirected or artificial. Nettie Palmer felt that too much "attention has been concentrated on novels like *Geoffry Hamlyn* and *For the Term of His Natural Life* to the exclusion of more indigenous work",[7] which may have been true; but such a position could easily lead to excesses in the opposite direction. Certainly the view that the 1890s marks the first full flowering of a native-born literature, as it marks the growth to a united nationhood by the Australian people, has been hard to dislodge. Writers and artists of the period learned to portray the country as it really is, we have been told. They learned to characterize the quality of the local landscape (which landscape?); to capture, for the first time, the essence of Australian life (whose life?). The legend of the nineties has insisted that their triumph was to throw off the shackles of an imported vision, which had recoiled from the strangeness of the local scene, to show us ourselves and our land, whole and clear.

This interpretation of the period has been a potent force for conservatism in Australian literature and culture generally. During the early decades of this century the popular styles and themes of the nineties came to be regarded by many as the natural and appropriate norms for Australian writers and artists. For a period of some fifty years the local cultural scene was notoriously conservative and resisted departure from these earlier models. Yet such a view of its achievement would have surprised the nineties. Many keen observers of the time stressed the roads Australian writers and artists had yet to travel before they could rest on their laurels. A.G. Stephens, surveying in 1901 the short stories of the 1880s and 1890s, emphasized the potential of the future rather than the successes of the past. "We take the goods the gods provide", he wrote, "and are properly grateful while striving for better and best."[8] The nineties could speak meaningfully of "Australian literature" as a rapidly growing body of work but it tended to be diffident about the nature of acknowledged success. Many writers and artists, such as Lawson in 1899, felt they were not receiving their due in this country and travelled elsewhere in search of recognition and reward. Others, such as R.H. Croll, suggested Australian writers were not adventurous enough in exploiting material to hand:

> Whalers, damper, swag and nosebag, Johnny-cakes and billy-
> tea,
> Murrumburrah, Meremendicoowoke, Yoularbudgeree,
> Cattle-duffers, bold bushrangers, diggers, drovers, bush
> racecourses.
> And on all the other pages horses, horses, horses, horses.[9]

To find the origins of the legend of the decade as a golden era, as the summation of a peculiarly and admirably Australian way of life, we have to turn to the period between the two world wars. Perhaps Australians then were searching for a notion of nationhood—a sense of identity—they could not find in their immediate lives. The impact of the First World War and the great depression caused many to feel a sense of betrayal of earlier ideals. It was natural to look back then to the work of the decade before federation for defini-tion and purpose. The writings of Lawson, Paterson, and Furphy, disparate though they are, were hailed as enshrining an Australian way of looking at the world. Concepts of mateship, democracy, and nationalism, deriving their basic stimulus from life in the bush, were seen as integral and necessary parts of the Australian ethic. From the vantage point of thirty or forty years it was easy to cite the weekly *Bulletin*, which had begun publication in 1880, as the prin-cipal polemical organ of the nineties' legend. It was widely suggested that the pictures of up-country life, frequently en-countered in its pages, contained all that was representative-ly and generically Australian, that the *Bulletin*'s balladists and short story writers established our literature as Parkes and Deakin established our commonwealth. In 1933 Jose observed that "for most people nowadays the eighteen-nineties are the birth years of Australian literature".[20] If historians saw the decade as establishing our basic social and political groupings it seemed natural for the argument to spill over to literary history and criticism as well. As late as 1965 the last of the volumes of nineties' nostalgia, Norman Lindsay's *Bohemians of the Bulletin*, could speak of the period's creation of "a national literature in prose and poetry".[11]

By the 1950s, however, other writers had begun to ques-tion the legend of the nineties. The idea of the forceful homogeneity of the age came increasingly under attack as its complexities and contradictions were explored. The so-called "Lawson tradition" in fiction no longer seemed an adequate model. The ballad form had clearly outstayed its welcome and purpose. Patrick White castigated the "dreary, dun-coloured realism"[12] of much contemporary Australian prose. Older writers, such as Vance Palmer, suggested that the strength of the nineties lay less in the absolute literary value of its products than in their symbolic function. He saw such characters as Lawson's Joe Wilson, Paterson's Clancy, and Furphy's Tom Collins as representing a "national figure ... (and) the habit of regarding it as the literary norm." Their creators had principally succeeded in establishing a "special quality" in Australian writing which "might be called a democratic quality."[13] Russel Ward's important book endorsed this view. *The Australian Legend* (1958) singled out the "noble frontiersman" as the major figure in our nineties' writing and the central character in our national life and literature. Within the last decade Ian Turner too has spoken of the period as marking "a decisive turn in the way Australians thought about themselves and their future."[14]

Throughout this continuing debate on the nature and importance of the nineties there have been two major assumptions which have not been spelt out and adequately discussed. As they both have a good deal of bearing upon how we view nineties' writers and writing I propose to outline them here. The first is the assumption that there was a radicalization of Australian life during the period: the belief that concepts of nationalism and democracy suddenly took on new and more vital meanings and that they were (perhaps necessarily) reflected in the literature of the time.

Evidence for this political view has been seemingly easy to find. The 1880s in Australia had been a period of economic boom, so that the depression which gripped most of the country by 1892 marked a decisive change in general standards of prosperity. By the middle of that year many banks had failed and several large development companies had closed their books amid rumours of fraud and corruption. Country people were at least as hard hit as those in the cities. Wool especially, the staple commodity, now seemed heavily overproduced. It has been estimated that something like a quarter of the Australian work force was unemployed at the worst stages of the depression.[15] Naturally, people began to look elsewhere, to different philosophies, for a solution to the country's ills. The American Henry George's *Progress and Poverty*, with its theory of a single, land tax, as well as doctrines of socialism, was widely discussed. George himself visited Australia in 1890 and held many meetings. The young Henry Lawson was one of his avid listeners. But the trade unions, which had become increasingly powerful during the 1880s, were now also hit by financial difficulties as many members were unemployed. Such organizations were thus ill-prepared for the great strikes of the years 1890–94. These disputes, especially on the waterfront and in the shearing sheds, the first major testings of organized labour in Australia, were generally resolved in the employers' favour. In times of economic depression and uncertainty only they could afford to name their own terms. The important result was a wave of working class feeling against the efficacy of militant action. Throughout the country the nineties saw the labour parties emerge as powerful political groups, which seemed to promise success through parliament rather than through strikes. But the initial gains and programmes of labour now seem rather less impressive than they once did. More by design than misjudgment, they left the basic social and economic anomalies of the country virtually unscathed. Real power is not to be found in the ballot box but through the control of property and profits. Far from establishing a democratic decade, labour policies can be seen as consolidating the foundations of the increasingly undemocratic conduct of Australian political life.

If then we must qualify our concept of the political radicalization of Australia in the 1890s we must also look again at the literature, which, we have been told, enshrines the spirit of the decade. There is a common view, for instance, that the *Bulletin* was a radical newspaper, espousing egalitarian views. Its literary policy has thus been seen as an expression of its political stand: akin to Furphy's (ironical?) description of *Such is Life*: "temper, democratic; bias, offensively Australian". But if we look closely at the social and political platforms on which the *Bulletin* stood, it is hard to see it as other than a bourgeois-reformist journal which was in no way equipped to instigate a radicalization or democratization of Australian society. Week after week it declared its intention to bring about a number of political and administrative changes but it failed to direct attention to other than superficial anomalies. "The more equitable distribution of wealth is a good thing", it conceded in 1901, "but unless it is first made certain that the country has a reasonable amount of wealth of its own to distribute more equitably, it is not so good as it looks. 'Socialism in our Time' has its advantages, but 'Solvency in our Time' needs to come first."[16]

Like the labour parties which shared so many of its views, the *Bulletin* failed to support social and political restructuring in any other than a narrowly liberal-bourgeois sense principally because it lacked any coherent ideological basis or interests. The doctrines of scientific socialism, widely disseminated in Europe by this time, had no popular platform in this country. The *Bulletin*'s principal political concern was for the preservation and furtherance of middle-class self-help and capital. Its reputation as a radical, democratic weekly can only be understood in the context of our present undemocratic and un-radical society. By 1894 it was clear that so-called radical thought in Australia was expedient rather than ideologically revolutionary. In the Anglo-Saxon manner it sought to prop up or disguise the injustices of the present system rather than to take a leaf or two from the book of European socialism and attempt the overthrow of the established hierarchy. Only William Lane among nineties' activists saw the necessity for a new beginning and he tried it in South America, not Australia. Lane's departure in 1893 marked the effective end of any dream of Utopia in the Australian colonies.[17]

The second assumption underlying much of the debate on the 1890s is that Australian writing of the period can be regarded as a reflection of Australian life: that its importance as literature can somehow be measured by the accuracy with which it reflects the nineties' world. Thus Lawson, for so long hailed as the "apostle of mateship", has been cited as the most representatively Australian writer because his work supposedly reveals the essential truths of our egalitarian, democratic tradition. Such a view is far from accurate. The need to believe in a democratic tradition has been the principal distorting factor in our understanding of writing from the 1890s. It has led to an exaggerated emphasis upon certain features to the virtual exclusion of more important ones. We may well ask: should we even anticipate that literature will enshrine the popular concept of a national ethos, as Russel Ward suggests? Indeed, can we now regard Vance Palmer's "democratic quality" as a unique or even outstanding aspect of our writers of the period? Is it possible that in a search for a national identity we have seized upon particular aspects of an age and have given them a centrality which they never really had? And what of the writers themselves? Were they deliberate social chroniclers? Noble frontiersmen? Or were they, consciously or unconsciously, mythmakers themselves, creating a legend which has passed for substance? It seems an odd coincidence that most of those whose work has been cited as enshrining the tradition were, in fact, city-dwellers; urbanites, whose lives were often a rejection of a rural past. Paterson was a well-to-do Sydney solicitor and journalist: a "city bushman", as Lawson sneeringly called him. But Lawson himself was a city down-and-out for almost his entire writing career. "Steele Rudd"'s life in Brisbane was made possible by his accounts of the harshness of bush life. Barbara Baynton, later Lady Headley, was an Anglo-Australian socialite and a highly successful businesswoman. Even Furphy found Shepparton, with its proximity to the Melbourne public library, more congenial than the Riverina of which he wrote. The truth is that bush life is most frequently depicted in our literature of the 1890s as harsh and destructive of all but the basic urge to survive. Or, if Arcadian, as belonging to a bygone age, now lost. Egalitarian mateship is less common than loneliness and betrayal. Failure is more real than success.

My view of the 1890s sees a sense of alienation and loss as a principal literary hallmark. In the selection and arrangement of material for this anthology I have sought to show how much of the best writing of the period recoils from those very features which the nationalist interpretation holds to be most characteristic and most affirmatively Australian: mateship, egalitarian democracy, the celebration of bush life. The stories of Lawson, Baynton, Albert Dorrington, and Edward Dyson reprinted here are emphatic in their emphasis upon the horrors of outback life, on the dehumanizing qualities of the frontier existence. The poetic "debate" between Lawson and Paterson in the *Bulletin* of 1892,[18] where the latter seemed to suggest that Lawson was merely being pessimistic about the bush, can now be seen as a major watershed in our writing. For what was at stake, for Lawson at least, was the whole notion of the relationship of a writer to his society. Should the writer attempt to fabricate and idealize his experience in the interests of a national ideal? Or should he try to depict the world as he saw it, in spite of the hurt to himself and his readers? The path he took was unequivocal:

> I believe the Southern poets' dream will not be realised
> Till the plains are irrigated and the land is humanised.
> ("Up the Country")

Even when Paterson himself writes of the present, such as in parts of "Clancy of the Overflow", it is with a similar sense of disbelief in its humanizing potential.

In those writers more exclusively concerned with the city, or even with more philosophical themes, we can frequently detect a similar thread of disillusionment. Indeed, by the 1890s Australia was already one of the most urbanized nations and the pattern was reinforced by the drift of population to the cities during the lengthy period of recession and unemployment. For writers like Lawson and William Lane the urban landscape was as bleak and inhuman as the poorest place up-country. Christopher Brennan, our finest poet from the period, composed a sequence of poems around a search for ultimate meaning and value. But it remained a search. Even in those pieces where the task seemed most immediately fruitful (such as "We sat entwined an hour or two together") the tone of loss and resignation predominates at the end:

> lost in the vast, we watched the minutes hasting
> into the deep that sunders friend from friend;
> spake not nor stirr'd but heard the murmurs wasting
> into the silent distance without end.

Indeed, Brennan's affinities with other Australian writers of the nineties have not been sufficiently drawn out. He has been seen as something of an exotic, writing in a European tradition at a level far above the local balladists and versifiers. But his images of loneliness, of deeply-felt alienation and despair, suggest links with Baynton's *Bush Studies*, with "The Union Buries its Dead", and with those parts of *Such is Life* which reveal a forcefully jaundiced view of many of the values we regard as integral to the myth of a democratic tradition. Yet there is one passage in Furphy's novel which seems to offer an almost apocalyptic vision of the Australia of the future:

> It is not in our cities or townships, it is not in our agricultural or mining areas, that the Australian attains full consciousness of his own nationality; it is in places like this, and as clearly here as at the centre of the continent. To me the monotonous variety of this interminable scrub has a charm of its own; so grave, subdued, self-centred; so alien to the genial appeal of more winsome landscape, or the assertive grandeur of mountain and gorge. To me this wayward diversity of spontaneous plant life bespeaks an unconfined, ungauged potentiality of resource; it unveils an ideographic prophecy, painted by Nature in her Impressionist mood, to be deciphered aright only by those willing to discern through the crudeness of dawn a promise of majestic day.[19]

But here too the vision lies in the uncertain future: in the world of "potentiality" and "promise". The force of the present is much more assertive: it is "monotonous" and "interminable", "grave" and "alien". Indeed, the major impetus of the novel, its picture of life, is much more in the direction of loneliness, betrayal, physical and mental suffering, and injustice than critics have generally allowed. Perhaps it is "offensively Australian" in a sense which has not been sufficiently emphasized. Its sense of the present as a denial of that which was rightly and properly anticipated in the past suggests similarities with many other works of the period. Two of the nineties' most popular verses, "The Man From Snowy River" and "In the Days When the World Was Wide", speak of a golden age which has passed and which can only be recreated through the memory of the deeds of yesteryear. They celebrate a way of life and spirit which have vanished. Lawson's sense of betrayal at the hands of middle-class capital, which we see in the bitterly titled "'Pursuing Literature' in Australia", is given the edge of moral outrage in his lament for the passing of the "roaring days":

> But golden days are vanished,
>   And altered is the scene;
> The diggings are deserted,
>   The camping-grounds are green;
> The flaunting flag of progress
>   Is in the West unfurled,
> The mighty bush with iron rails
>   Is tethered to the world.

The decade's interest in political events as literary themes reveals a similar dichotomy between the awareness of the shortcomings of the achieved present and the inspiration and hope to be derived from a sense of the past and the future. Though the short stories of "Price Warung" deal with the convict days of Australia's past they are finely tuned to the world of the 1890s in their interest in the dehumanizing tendency of organized authority. Some, such as Brunton Stephens and William Gay, may have seen the political events of the period, leading to federation, as the crowning glory of the colonial experience. Others were unconvinced. They suspected that federation, like labour politics (and unionism?), was simply the old game under new rules. The flatulent style of Brunton Stephens's "Fulfilment" and George Essex Evans's "Federal Song" has to be measured against the indignant energy of Victor Daley and the heavily qualified sense of achievement (and even of potential) in Bernard O'Dowd's "Australia" and "Young Democracy". O'Dowd's first book, published by the *Bulletin* in 1903, was dedicated "to young democracy", but its title—*Dawnward?*—was far from confident or celebratory.

G.A. Wilkes has recently pointed out how, in emphasizing certain aspects of our nineties' writing, earlier critics have given a false sense of discontinuity to our literary history. Marcus Clarke, he suggests, saw the scenery not so very differently from Lawson. The sense of the future potential of Australia, as opposed to the harshness of its present, "also appealed to Harpur and Kendall: it was by no means the invention of the 1890s."[20] Similarly, developments in our writing this century have emphasized continuity with the view of the nineties I have been advancing. The poetry of James McAuley and A.D. Hope shares many affinities with that of Brennan. The landscape of *Voss* would have been recognized by Lawson. The prevailing tone of the 1890s, an uneasy acceptance of a world which seems to offer more than it can give, is the major tradition of Australian writing.

The selection of texts which follows necessarily omits many pieces worthy of inclusion. For instance, in keeping almost exclusively to creative writing I have been unable adequately to represent the essay form. There were many social, political, and polemical essays published during the nineties which contribute richly to our understanding of the forces which shaped the decade. Ian Turner's *The Australian Dream* (1968) offers a good selection, especially of those which attempted to define the unique nature of Australian society. I am aware too that some writers who established considerable reputations during the nineties are here omitted: Louis Becke, Ernest Favenc, and E.J. Brady, for example. But Brady's ballads of the sea and Becke's and Favenc's tales of life in the exotic tropics, though they fill out our picture of the literary achievement of the period, are somewhat removed from the spirit of the nineties I have attempted to capture. Similarly, in a larger anthology it would have been possible to represent the novels and stories of three further women writers, Jessie Couvreur ("Tasma"), Mrs. Campbell Praed, and Ada Cambridge, though "Tasma" left Australia in 1873 and Mrs. Campbell Praed three years later. "Tasma"'s first two novels, *Uncle Piper of Piper's Hill* (1889) and *In Her Earliest Youth* (1890), contain full and vigorous accounts of middle-class city life, an aspect of Australian society uncommon in the literature of the time. Yet the lives and books of all three writers were removed from the spirit of the decade which this anthology seeks to define. They belong to an earlier generation in our literature. Finally, I have omitted to represent the work of such a popular writer as Rolf Boldrewood on the grounds that his talent had spent itself by the nineties. None of his later books approaches the interest or energy of *Robbery Under Arms* (1888).

Leon Cantrell
Brisbane
March 1977

Notes to Introduction

1. Arthur Jose, *The Romantic Nineties* (Sydney: Angus and Robertson, 1932), p. 32.
2. Desmond Byrne, *Australian Writers* (London: Bentley, 1896), p. 24.
3. G.A. Wilkes, *Australian Literature: A Conspectus* (Sydney: Angus and Robertson, 1969), p. 32.
4. Nettie Palmer, *Fourteen Years: Extracts From a Private Journal, 1925–1939* (Melbourne: Meanjin Press, 1948), p. 22.
5. H.M. Green, *A History of Australian Literature* (Sydney: Angus and Robertson, 1961), pp. 347–48.
6. *Romantic Nineties*, p. 28.
7. From the introduction to C. Hartley Grattan, *Australian Literature* (Seattle: University of Washington Bookstore, 1929), p. 8.
8. From A.G. Stephens's introduction to *The Bulletin Story Book* (Sydney: *Bulletin* Newspaper Company, 1901), p. v.
9. *Bookfellow*, 5 May 1899, p. 21.
10. *Romantic Nineties*, p. 21.
11. (Sydney: Angus and Robertson, 1965), p. 7.
12. Patrick White, "The Prodigal Son", *Australian Letters* 1 (1958): 37–40.
13. Vance Palmer, *The Legend of the Nineties* (Melbourne: Melbourne University Press, 1963), p. 170.
14. Ian Turner, *The Australian Dream* (Melbourne: Sun Books, 1968), p. xvi.
15. B.K. de Garis, "1890–1900", in F.K. Crowley, ed., *A New History of Australia* (Melbourne: Heinemann, 1974), p. 225.
16. *Bulletin*, 18 May 1901, p. 6.
17. This view of the *Bulletin* is outlined more fully in my essay "A.G. Stephens, *The Bulletin*, and the 1890s", in Leon Cantrell, ed., *Bards, Bohemians, and Bookmen: Essays in Australian Literature* (St. Lucia: University of Queensland Press, 1976), pp. 98–113.
18. See Bruce Nesbitt, "Literary Nationalism and the 1890s", *Australian Literary Studies* 5 (1971): 3–17.
19. *Such is Life* (Sydney: *Bulletin* Newspaper Company, 1903), p. 65.
20. G.A. Wilkes, "Going Over the Terrain in a Different Way", *Southerly*, 35 (1975): 147.

Writing in
Australia

EDITOR'S NOTE

When considering Australian writing of the 1890s it is hard to overestimate the importance of the Sydney *Bulletin*. It had begun weekly publication in 1880 and within a few years had become the most widely read and one of the most influential local magazines. It encouraged versifiers and story-tellers of all kinds, though it showed a marked preference for bush themes. Its irreverent nationalism, heralded by the catch-cry "Australia for the Australians", encouraged many to put their experiences of this land into ballads or sketches and to submit them to the "Bully". "Every man with brains has at least one good story to tell", declared editor J.F. Archibald each week; and the stories and verses, good or not, rolled in. The regular "Answers to Correspondents" column offered criticism, praise, or advice as needed. Much of the best literature of the nineties first appeared in the *Bulletin*'s pages where it was eagerly read. Miles Franklin, in later life, wrote of her memories of *Bulletin* writing:

> It is hardly possible to overstate how much indigenous ballading and versifying meant in the nineties to those in and below their teens, and on up to grizzled old men too. Each fresh expression of the land and its activities had the stimulation of news. Lawson, Paterson and Ogilvie ably filled the places of the film's favourites today, being of handsome physical appearance and winning personality. The poems of these men and others were recited by everybody, whether he had gifts that way or not. Around camp fires or in huts rival self-expressionists grew truculent as to who should come first with "The Man From Snowy River" or "When the World as Wide".[1]

A.G. Stephens joined the *Bulletin* in 1894 and took charge of its literary activities. He edited the Red Page until 1906, establishing it as the preeminent spot for literary discussion and debate in the country. In addition, he controlled the *Bulletin*'s book publishing division and saw numerous

1. Miles Franklin, *Laughter, Not for a Cage* (Sydney: Angus and Robertson, 1956), p.106.

volumes (including "Steele Rudd"'s *On Our Selection* and Joseph Furphy's *Such is Life*) through the press. *The Bulletin Story Book* and *The Bulletin Reciter* (both 1901) were also the products of Stephens's editorial hand. Other publishers (especially Angus and Robertson in Sydney) were at least equally concerned to place the work of Australian writers before the public. But the life of a writer in the 1890s was not an easy one. Lawson's bitter lament, "'Pursuing Literature' in Australia" (1), sets out the problems clearly enough: they boil down to the lack of a large enough audience for a writer to live from the proceeds of his writing. Yet Lawson's belief that his lot in England would be a better one proved sorely untrue. He was back in Australia by mid 1902 and the remaining twenty years of his life were wretched. Certainly his best work was completed by this date. As Victor Daley indicated (2, 3, and 6) material enough for local writers was near at hand. The centre of the literary world may have seemed to lie in London, and Lawson was not the only local writer to seek its favour, but the impetus and audience for Australian writing was at home. "Heaven forbid that I should think of treating with an English publisher", wrote Furphy to Stephens in 1897, during the protracted negotiations over the publication of *Such is Life*. "Aut Australia aut nihil."[2]

This sense of literary nationalism among our writers is a feature of the period. Lawson (5) lamented the "niggard recognition" he felt his fellow countrymen paid to talent in their midst, but he came to recognize that his place lay in the ranks of "Southern writers" and not in the pages of "Northern magazines". Stephens's image of Australian writing as a branch of the tree of life (8) indicates the nature of the achievement of our literature as well as an attempt to see it in a larger perspective.

2. John Barnes, ed., *The Writer in Australia: A Collection of Literary Documents, 1856 to 1964* (Melbourne: Oxford University Press, 1969), p.121.

1. HENRY LAWSON

"Pursuing Literature" in Australia

In the first fifteen years of my life I saw the last of the Roaring Days on Gulgong goldfield, N.S.W. I remember the rush as a boy might his first and only pantomime. "On *our* selection" I tailed cows amongst the deserted shafts in the gullies of a dreary old field that was abandoned ere Gulgong "broke out". I grubbed, ring-barked, and ploughed in the scratchy sort of way common to many "native-born" selectors round there; helped fight pleuro and drought; and worked on building contracts with "Dad", who was a carpenter. Saw selectors slaving their lives away in dusty holes amongst the barren ridges: saw one or two carried home, in the end, on a sheet of bark; the old men worked till they died. Saw how the gaunt selectors' wives lived and toiled. Saw elder sons stoop-shouldered old men at 30. Noted, in dusty patches in the scrubs, the pile of chimney-stones, a blue-gum slab or two, and the remains of the fence—the ultimate result of 10 years', 15 years', and 20 years' hard, hopeless graft by strong men who died like broken-down bullocks further out. And all the years miles and miles of rich black soil flats and chocolate slopes lay idle, because of old-time grants, or because the country carried sheep—for the sake of an extra bale of wool and an unknown absentee. I watched old fossickers and farmers reading *Progress and Poverty* earnestly and arguing over it Sunday afternoons. And I wished that I could write.

The droughts of the early eighties, coming with the pleuro, the rabbits, crop and vine diseases and other troubles, burst a lot of us round there. Some old selectors did pick-and-shovel work in the city, or drove drays, while their wives took in washing. I worked for subcontractors in coach-factories, painting; tramped the cities in search of work; saw the haggard little group in front of the board outside the *Herald* office at 4 o'clock in the morning, striking matches to run down the 'Wanted" columns; saw the slums and the poor—and wished that I could write, or paint.

I heard Tommy Walker, and Collins, and the rest of 'em and, of course, a host of Yankee free-thought and socialistic lecturers. I wore the green in fancy, gathered at the rising of the moon, charged for the fair land of Poland, and dreamed of dying on the barricades to the roar of the "Marseillaise" —for the Young Australian Republic. Then came the unexpected and inexplicable outburst of popular feeling (or madness)—called then the Republican riots—in '87, when the Sydney crowd carried a disloyal amendment on the Queen's Jubilee, and cheered, at the Town Hall, for an "Australian Republic". And I had to write then—or burst. The *Bulletin* saved me from bursting.

"Youth: the first four lines are the best. Try again." Answers to Correspondents, *Bulletin*, June 18, 1887.

The first four lines were printed. I haven't felt so excited over a thing since. The fire blazed too fiercely to last; but it burned for ten years.

"H.L.: Will publish your 'Song of the Republic.'"

I was up at daylight every publishing morning and down to the earliest news-agent's, but "The Song of the Republic" was held over for a special occasion—Eight Hours' Day (Oct. 1887). Democracy and Unionism were alive those times, and Eight Hours' Day was called "The Carnival of Labour".

I was a coach painter's improver at 5s per day, with regular work, and only needed to practise "lining", or tracing, to be master of the trade. I helped write, machine, and publish a flyblister called the *Republican*. I wrote some verses called "The Song of the Outcasts", or "The Army of the Rear"; also "Golden Gully", "The Wreck of the Derry Castle", and one or two others (rejected). I took the parcel down to the old *Bulletin* office, in Pitt-street, after dusk, intending to slip it surreptitiously into the letter-box; but the charwoman, broom in hand, opened the door suddenly, and gave me a start. I thrust the screed into her hands and made off.

In Dec., '87, I was coach-painting at Windsor, Melb., for 6s a day, when I got *my* first Xmas *Bulletin*. I tore it open, tremblingly; glanced through it, to make sure I was there;

and hid it in a hearse I was "rubbing-down"—for the boss
was a fierce Wesleyan. I rubbed hard with the pumice-stone
till my heart didn't thump so much, and I felt calmer. I stole
glances, behind the hearse, at "Golden Gully" and "The
Wreck of the Derry Castle", and the kindly editorial note to
the effect that I was a mere lad (aged 19), earning a living,
under difficulties, at house-painting, and that my education
was as yet unfinished (N.B.—I couldn't spell), and that my
talent spoke for itself in the following poem. I was in print,
and in the Xmas number of a journal I had worshipped, and
devoured every inch of, for years. I felt strong and proud
enough to clean pigsties, if need be, for a living for the rest
of my natural life—provided the *Bulletin* went on publishing
the poetry. Varnish on old hearses is hard as flint; but I
made a good job of that one, and a quick job—for I "rubbed down" on air if I didn't walk on it. It was the shortest
eight hours' graft I ever did.

When house-painting on Mt. Victoria early in '88 (8s a
day—trade was good then) I got my first cheque, £1 7s from
the *Bulletin*. It was totally unexpected, for, being in constant
work and getting what I thought such a grand outlet for my
thoughts and feelings, I hadn't dreamed of receiving pay-
ment for literary work—which might be a hard fact for the
present cashier of the *Bulletin* to swallow. But before that I
had written and worked, and I have written and worked
since, for Australian unionism and Democracy—for
nothing. I had a strong, deep-down feeling against taking
money for anything I wrote in the interest of "the Cause" I
believed in; and I felt red-hot about—

> I hate the wrongs I read about! I hate the wrongs I see!
> The marching of that Army is as music unto me!
>
> —"The Army of the Rear", '87.

And I went a bit mad over—

> We'll make the tyrants feel the strength
> Of those that they would throttle!
> They need not say the fault is ours
> If blood should stain the wattle!
>
> —"Freedom on the Wallaby", '92.

But I believed what I wrote was true.

When out of graft awhile in Sydney I helped turn the old *Republican* machine, and wrote "Faces in the Street", for which I received a guinea. Along in these times I wrote bush ballads for the *T. and C. Journal*, but only got an occasional half-sovereign. I tried "Tom" Butler of the *Freeman's Journal*, of whom I have kindly recollections. He told me when I first saw him that they didn't pay for poetry, but I might bring something round to him; and if it was fairly good and suitable for his readers, he would see what he could do. I wrote a few bush rhymes for him; whenever I brought one round he reminded me that they didn't pay for verse—except, perhaps, at Xmas, and by special arrangement or for special stuff; and whenever he wrote me a cheque he never failed to draw my attention to the fact that the *Freeman's Journal* didn't pay for poetry. The *T. and C.* proprietary treated me a little better later on—but only took Xmas matter; and, when I got "finally" hard-up in Sydney, contributed £1 towards my fare to Maoriland.

But it was before that—in '89—that I went to Albany, W.A. I painted; and wrote articles at a penny a line for a local paper. Came back, and hung out for the best part of '90 in a third-rate hash-house in Sydney, where I got some good "copy". Up-country again, and started house-painting at 8s or 9s a day, with every prospect of a good run of work; but one day, as I was painting a ceiling, I got a telegram to say that Brisb. *Boomerang* offered £2 per week and a position on the staff. I was doubtful of my abilities, and wired to an old friend in Sydney for advice. He advised accept; so I accepted.

It was the first, the last, and only chance I got in journalism. I wrote pars, sketches, and verse for six months for the £2; and barracked, spare times, for Democracy, in the Brisbane *Worker*, for nothing. I got very fond of the work, and was with difficulty kept out of the office on Sundays, publishing days, Saturday afternoons, and other holidays. I might have been an experienced journalist today, with a good "screw" and no ambition, but the *Boomerang* "ghost" was fading fast. We hashed up a couple of columns of pars from the country papers every week, with the names of the papers attached—to curry favour with the country press; and I conceived an idea of *rhyming* this "Country Crumbs" column, and having it set as prose, and kept two columns a week going for a couple of months. You can rhyme anything if you stare at it long enough between whiles of walking up and down and scratching your head.

Perhaps the "Country Crumbs" in prosy rhyme had the same effect on the readers as at first on the comps; anyway the spectre grew less and less discernible, and deputations of comps went up oftener to the sanctum to discuss the inadvisability of their taking shares in the paper in part-payment of wages. A piece I wrote, called the "Cambaroora Star", was the *Boomerang*'s own epitaph.

I came south, steerage, with £2. It wasn't the first time I went saloon and came back steerage, so to speak. I got as far as Bathurst once, during an unemployed period, and came back in charge of the guard.

I hung out (with difficulty) in a restaurant in Sydney, getting an occasional guinea from the *Bulletin*, and painting for nigger-driving bosses at 5s a day. Hard times had come to Sydney, and it took a good, all-round tradesman to be sure of seven or even six "bob" and fairly constant graft. When the trade failed me I used to write a column of red-hot socialistic and libellous political rhymes for *Truth*. I still believed in revolutions, and the spirit of righteousness upheld me. *Truth*'s "ghost" was eccentric, and the usual rates for outside contributions were from 5s upwards; but John Norton gave me 15s to £1, for special stuff. He cursed considerably; and there were times when it wasn't advisable to curse back; but he saw that I, and one or two other poor devils of scribblers on their uppers, were paid—even before the comps. I haven't forgotten it.

Toward the end of '92 I got £5 and a railway ticket from the *Bulletin* and went to Bourke. Painted, picked-up in a shearing-shed, and swagged it for six months; then came back to Sydney "in charge of five trucks of cattle". Bourke people will understand that dodge. (Most of my hard-up experiences are in my published books, disguised but not exaggerated.)

Most of the matter in *While the Billy Boils* (and some of what my reviewers considered the best) was written for Syd. *Worker* for 12s 6d a column. During one of the frequent interregnums I edited the *Worker* a while gratis, on the understanding that I should get the permanent editorship—for "the Cause" didn't loom so big in my eyes as it used to, and I was only then beginning to find out that others had not been quite so enthusiastic as I was. But that mysterious inner circle, the trustees and their friends, brought an editor from another province.

Towards the end of '93 I landed in Wellington with a pound in my pocket—just in time to see the women vote for the first time. Got a little painting to do now and then, and a guinea (5s "out of the editor's pocket", I understood) from the *NZ Mail* for a 1½ col. rhyme called "For'ard". And I wrote some steerage sketches at the rate of 5s a col. Did a three-months unemployed "perish", and then went with a mate to a sawmill in the Hutt Valley, for a boss who had contracted to supply the mill with logs. We two bullocked in a rough, wet gully for a fortnight—felling trees, making a track for the bullocks, and 'jacking" logs to it over stumps and boulders. But we were soft and inexperienced, and at the end of the fortnight the boss said we weren't bushmen— which, strange to say, hurt me more than any adverse criticism on my literary work could have done at the time. The boss had no cash; and my mate was only restrained from violence by the fact that he was a big man and the boss a little one. He gave us each an order for our wages on the owner of the sawmill in Wellington, and, as we had no money for railway fares, we "tramped it"—twenty miles, without tucker or tobacco. Those orders have not been cashed yet.

I house-painted a bit; then got on with a ganging lineman on a telegraph line in South Island. It has hard graft at first, through rough country, in the depth of winter, and camping-out all the time—humping poles some times where the trace-horses couldn't go. The boss was a bit of a driver, with a fondness for "hazing" the gang when his liver went wrong; but it's better to be driven to the benefit of your muscles, general health, and consequent happiness, than to be brain-sweated in the city to the danger of your reason through brooding over it. In four or five months I was too healthy to read or write, or bother about it, or anything, or to hate anybody except the cook when "duff" didn't even- tuate at reasonable intervals. But there came a letter from the *Worker* people to say that a *Daily Worker* had been success-fully floated, and there was a place for me on it. I said, "Get behind me, Literature!" but she didn't; so I threw up the billet, and caught a steamer that touched the coast to deliver poles. I arrived in Sydney three days after the *Daily Worker* went bung.

After a deal of shuffling humbug, I was put on the *Weekly Worker* as "provincial editor", but in a month I received a notice, alleged to come from the trustees, to the effect that, on account of the financial position of the Workers' Union, they were regretfully obliged to dispense with my ser-vices—"for the present, at least". No one was responsible for the *Daily Worker*, nor for the thousand pounds sunk in it, nor the crowded staff, exorbitant "screws" and gross mis-management of the *Weekly Worker*, nor for me—except, perhaps, the "last committee".

House-painting was dead; clerical work was always out of the question— I couldn't add a column of figures without hanging on like grim death till I got to the top, and two trips with poor results utterly demoralized me. Deafness stood in the way of a possible Government billet.

My two books published by Angus and Robertson, *In the Days When the World was Wide* and *While the Billy Boils*, are advertised as in their seventh thousand and eighth thousand respectively. The former is sold to the public at 5s; the latter has been sold in various editions at from 5s to 2s 6d. My total receipts from these books have been something over £200; and I have sold the entire rights. The books represent the cream of twelve years' literary work. I estimate my whole literary earnings during that period at £700.

I went to W.A. again, painted houses, and wrote a little for the *Western Mail* people—who, by the way, didn't treat me so badly. Came back, went to Maoriland again, and taught school. I had a wife by this time. When I came back to Sydney last year there were three in the party.

Up to a couple of years ago the *Bulletin* paid me at the fixed rate of a guinea a column; but advances written off and special prices for special matter brought it nearer 30s per col. all through. The only thing I have to complain about with regard to the *Bulletin* is that the paper is unable to publish the sketches and stories within reasonable time.

Some of mine published lately were written and paid for as far back as '91. While the publication of *W.B.B.* was being arranged for, the *Bulletin* held some stories and sketches which were to complete the "Steelman" and "Mitchell" series; and, as the *Bulletin* could not rush them through, an idea of having the matter arranged with an eye to sequences had to be abandoned. Which explains the apparently haphazard appearance of the order of the stories and sketches in the volume, and will be responsible for the same thing in my next prose volume—which will contain some *introductory* sketches to others in *W.B.B.*

There are, perhaps, a score of Australian writers known to the *Bulletin*, and most of them little more than lads, who could write better stuff than has been appearing in the shoal of popular English magazines lately (no offence intended); but they have no scope, and, as far as I can see, no hope of future material encouragement from the "great" and wealthy Australasian weeklies and dailies, only one or two of which (excepting the *Sunday Times*) that I know of have, up to date, offered even the most niggardly assistance to purely Australian writers, and this only after the *Bulletin* had introduced them and established their Australian reputations. Many papers, notably in Maoriland, clip their racy Australian sketches from the *Bulletin*; and in at least one of these offices that I know, and have a hearty contempt for, it would be thought an act of charity to offer a hard-up *Bulletin* writer 5s per col.; while in another it would be a mark of special favour to offer him a chair. I have stood (and walked up and down and boiled over) for two hours in the passage outside the office of a paper which has been "clipping" my work for years, and this because they knew I was hard up and wanted them to pay for a contribution by way of a change.

Meanwhile, our best Australian artists and writers are being driven to England and America—where the leaders are making their mark, and a decent living; and the rest would follow in a lump if *they* got the show.

The work of some of those who have gone brightened Australia for years, yet no one asked how they lived, and no one, in all the wide Australias, stood up and asked whether a native-born artist or writer went aboard the boat with a decent suit to his back, or a five-pound note in his pocket. And they talk about our "cheap", "unhealthy" or "affected pessimism!" The fools!

A last word for myself. I don't know about the merit or value of my work; all I know is that I started a shy, ignorant lad from the Bush, under every disadvantage arising from poverty and lack of education, and with the extra disadvantage of partial deafness thrown in. I started with implicit faith in human nature, and a heart full of love for Australia, and hatred for wrong and injustice. I taught myself a trade—the first years in Sydney I rose at five o'clock in the morning to go to work with a rough crowd in the factory of a hard taskmaster; and learnt the little I did at a night-school; and I worked even then, before I could write, for a cause I believed in. I sought out my characters and studied them; I wrote of nothing that I had not myself seen or experienced; I wrote and re-wrote painfully, and believed that every line was true and for the right. I kept steady and worked hard for seven years, and that work met with appreciation in Australia and a warm welcome in London. When desperately hard up and with a wife to provide for, I at last was forced to apply to the Govt. for temporary work. I was kept hanging about the office for weeks; and when, as a last resource, I applied for a railway-pass for a month to enable me to find work in the country and gather new material for literary work, I did not receive a reply. I was obliged to seek the means of earning bread and butter from the Govt. of a province (M.L.) in whose people's interests I had never written a line.

My advice to any young Australian writer whose talents have been recognized, would be to go steerage, stow away, swim, and seek London, Yankeeland, or Timbuctoo—rather than stay in Australia till his genius turned to gall, or beer. Or, failing this—and still in the interests of human nature and literature—to study elementary anatomy, especially as applies to the cranium, and then shoot himself carefully with the aid of a looking-glass.

2. VICTOR DALEY

WHEN LONDON CALLS

They leave us — artists, singers, all —
　　When London calls aloud,
Commanding to her Festival
　　The gifted crowd.

She sits beside the ship-choked Thames,
　　Sad, weary, cruel, grand;
Her crown imperial gleams with gems
　　From many a land.

From overseas, and far away,
　　Come crowded ships and ships —
Grim-faced she gazes on them; yea,
　　With scornful lips.

The garden of the earth is wide;
　　Its rarest blooms she picks
To deck her board, this haggard-eyed
　　Imperatrix.

Sad, sad is she, and yearns for mirth;
　　With voice of golden guile
She lures men from the ends of earth
　　To make her smile.

The student of wild human ways
　　In wild new lands; the sage
With new great thoughts; the bard whose lays
　　Bring youth to age;

The painter young whose pictures shine
　　With colours magical,
The singer with the voice divine —
　　She lures them all.

But all their new is old to her
　　Who bore the Anakim;
She gives them gold or Charon's fare
　　As suits her whim.

Crowned Ogress — old, and sad, and wise —
    She sits with painted face
And hard, imperious, cruel eyes
    In her high place.

To him who for her pleasure lives,
    And makes her wish his goal,
A rich Tarpeian gift she gives —
    That slays his soul.

The story-teller from the Isles
    Upon the Empire's rim,
With smiles she welcomes — and her smiles
    Are death to him.

For Her, whose pleasure is her law,
    In vain the shy heart bleeds —
The Genius with the Iron Jaw
    Alone succeeds.

And when the Poet's lays grow bland,
    And urbanised, and prim —
She stretches forth a jewelled hand
    And strangles him.

                    * * *

She sits beside the ship-choked Thames
    With Sphinx-like lips apart —
Mistress of many diadems —
    Death in her heart!

3. VICTOR DALEY

CORREGGIO JONES

Correggio Jones an artist was
 Of pure Australian race,
But native subjects scorned because
 They were too commonplace.

The Bush with all its secrets grim,
 And solemn mystery,
No fascination had for him:
 He had no eyes to see

The long sad spectral desert-march
 Of brave Explorers dead,
Who perished — while the burning arc
 Of blue laughed overhead;

The Solitary Man who stares
 At the mirage so fair,
While Death steals on him unawares
 And grasps him by the hair;

The Lonely Tree that sadly stands,
 With no green neighbour nigh,
And stretches forth its bleached, dead hands,
 For pity to the sky;

The Grey Prospector, weird of dress,
 And wearied overmuch,
Who dies amidst the wilderness —
 With Fortune in his clutch;

The figures of the heroes gone
 Who stood forth undismayed,
And Freedom's Flag shook forth upon
 Eureka's old stockade.

These subjects to Correggio Jones
 No inspiration brought;
He was an ass (in semitones)
 And painted — as he thought.

"In all these things there's no Romance,"
 He muttered, with a sneer;

"They'd never give C. Jones a chance
    To make his genius clear!"

"Grey gums," he cried, "and box-woods pale
    They give my genius cramp —
But let me paint some Knights in Mail,
    Or robbers in a camp.

"Now look at those Old Masters — they
    Had all the chances fine,
With churches dim, and ruins grey,
    And castles on the Rhine,

"And Lady Gay in miniver,
    And hairy-shirted saint,
And Doges in apparel fair —
    And things a man might paint!

"And barons hold and pilgrims pale,
    And battling Knight and King —
The blood-spots on their golden mail —
    And all that sort of thing.

"Your Raphael and your Angelo
    And Rubens, and such men,
They simply had a splendid show.
    Give me the same — and then!"

*   *   *

So speaks Correggio Jones — yet sees,
    When past is Night's eclipse,
The dawn come like Harpocrates,
    A rose held to her lips.

The wondrous dawn that is so fair,
    So young and bright and strong,
That e'en the rocks and stones to her
    Sing a Memnonic song.

He will not see that our sky hue
    Old Italy's outvies,
But still goes yearning for the blue
    Of far Ausonian skies. . .

*   *   *

He yet is painting at full bat —
    You'll say, if him you see,
"His body dwells on Gander Flat,
    His soul's in Italy."

4. HENRY LAWSON

AUSTRALIAN BARDS AND BUSH REVIEWERS

While you use your best endeavour to immortalise in verse,
The gambling and the drink which are your country's greatest
    curse,
While you glorify the bully and take the spieler's part —
You're a clever southern writer, scarce inferior to Bret Harte.

If you sing of waving grasses when the plains are dry as bricks,
And discover shining rivers where there's only mud and sticks;
If you picture "mighty forests" where the "mulga" spoils the
    view —
You're superior to Kendall, and ahead of Gordon too.

If you swear that there's no country like the land that gave you
    birth,
And its sons are just the noblest and most glorious chaps on
    earth;
If in every girl a Venus your poetic eye discerns,
You are gracefully referred to as the "young Australian Burns."

But if you should find that bushmen — spite of all the poets
    say —
Are just common brother-sinners, and you're quite as good as
    they —
You're a drunkard, and a liar, and a cynic, and a sneak,
Your grammar's simply awful and your intellect is weak.

5. HENRY LAWSON

A SONG OF SOUTHERN WRITERS

Southern men of letters, vainly seeking recognition here —
Southern men of letters, driven to the Northern Hemisphere!
It is time your wrongs were known; it is time you claimed
    redress —
Time that you were independent of the mighty Northern press.
Sing a song of Southern writers, sing a song of Southern fame,
Of the dawn of art and letters and your native country's shame.

Talent goes for little here. To be aided, to be known,
You must fly to Northern critics who are juster than our own.
You may write above the standard, but your work is seldom
    seen
Till it's noticed and reprinted in an English magazine.
O the critics of your country will be very proud of you,
When you're recognized in London by an editor or two.

In the land where sport is sacred, where the labourer is a god,
You must pander to the people, make a hero of a clod!
What avail the sacrifices of the battles you begin
For the literary honour of the land we're living in?
Print a masterpiece in Melbourne, and it will be lost, I ween,
But your weakest stuff is clever in a London magazine.

Write a story of the South, make it true and make it clear,
Put your soul in every sentence, have the volume published
    here,
And 'twill only be accepted by our critics in the mist
As a "worthy imitation" of a Northern novelist.
For the volume needs the mighty Paternoster Row machine,
With a patronizing notice in an English magazine.

What of literary merit, while the Southern reader glories
In "American exchanges", with their childish nigger-stories;
In the jokes that ancient Romans chuckled over after lunch;
In the dull and starchy humour of the dreary London *Punch*?
Here they'll laugh at Southern humour — laugh till they are
    out of breath —
When it's stolen from the papers that Australia starves to death!

Do we ask why native talent — art and music cannot stay?
Why Australian men of letters emigrate and keep away?

Do we ask why genius often vanishes beyond recall?
From the wrecks of honest journals comes the answer to it all.
Over Southern journalism let the epitaph be seen:
"Starved by cheap imported rubbish! — an Australian
    Magazine!"

Southern men of letters, seeking kinder fields across the wave,
Tell a shameful tale entitled "Deniehy's Forgotten Grave".
Ask the South of Charlie Harpur! Seek the bitter truth, and tell
Of the life of Henry Kendall, in the land he loved so well!
Sing the songs he wrote in vain! Touch the South with bitter
    things;
Take the harp he touched so gently; show the blood upon the
    strings!

It was kind of Southern critics. it was very brave to mouth
At the volume of his boyhood, that was published in the
    South;
Kendall knew it all — he knew it; and the tears were very near
When he spoke about the sorrows of "the man of letters here".
(And his cry of "O My Brother!" came again to one who went
To his grave before "his brothers" mocked him with a
    monument.)

Banish envy, Southern writer! Strike with no uncertain hand,
For the sound of Gordon's rifle still is ringing through the land!
Ah! the niggard recognition! Ah! the "fame" that came in vain
To the poor dead poet lying with a bullet through his brain!
"Gone, my friends!" (he thought it better to be gone away
    from here).
Gone, my friends, with "last year's dead leaves . . . at the
    falling of the year".

Pleasant land for one who proses, pleasant land for one who
    rhymes
With the terrible advantage of a knowledge of hard times:
To be patronized, "encouraged", praised for his contempt of
    "pelf",
To be told of greater writers who were paupers, like himself;
To be buried as a pauper; to be shoved beneath the sod —
While the brainless man of muscle has the burial of a god.

We have learned the rights of labour. Let the Southern writers
    start
Agitating, too, for letters and for music and for art,
Till Australian scenes on canvas shall repay the artist's hand,
And the songs of Southern poets shall be ringing through the
    land,
Till the galleries of Europe have a place for Southern scenes,
And our journals crawl no longer to the Northern magazines.

6. VICTOR DALEY

THE MUSES OF AUSTRALIA

She plays her harp by hidden rills,
    The sweet shy Muse who dwells
In secret hollows of the hills,
    And green untrodden dells.

Her voice is as the voice of streams
    That under myrtles glide;
Our Kendall saw her face in dreams,
    And loved her till he died.

At times, by some green-eyelashed pool,
    She lies in slumber deep;
Her slender hands are white and cool
    As are the hands of sleep.

And, when the sun of Summer flaunts
    His fire the hills along,
She keeps her secret sunless haunts,
    And sings a shadowy song.

She weaves a wild, sweet magic rune,
    When o'er the tree-tops high
The silver sickle of the moon
    Shines in a rose-grey sky.

But in the dawn, the soft red dawn,
    When fade the stars above,
She walks upon a shining lawn,
    And sings the song of Love.

*   *   *

But, lo, the Muse with flashing eyes,
    And backward-streaming hair!
She grips her steed with strong brown thighs,
    Her panting breasts are bare.

In trances sweet, or tender dreams,
    She has not any part —
Her blood runs like the blood that streams
    Out of the mountain's heart.

Her lips are red; the pride of life
 Her heart of passion thrills;
She is the Muse whose joy is strife,
 Whose home is on the hills.

Her voice is as a clarion clear,
 And rings o'er the hill and dell;
She sings a song of gallant cheer —
 Dead Gordon knew her well.

She checks her steed upon a rise —
 The wind uplifts his mane —
And gazes far with flashing eyes
 Across the rolling plain.

* * *

Who comes in solemn majesty
 Through haze of throbbing heat?
It is the Desert Muse, and she
 Is veiled from head to feet.

Yet men the Mountain Muse will leave,
 And leave the Muse of Streams,
To follow her from dawn to eve —
 And perish with their dreams.

She passes far beyond their ken,
 With slow and solemn pace,
Over the bleaching bones of men
 Who died to see her face.

Her secrets were to some revealed
 Who loved her passing well —
But death with burning fingers sealed
 Their lips ere they could tell.

In silence dread she walks apart —
 Yet I have heard men say
The song that slumbers in her heart
 Will wake the world some day.

She is the Muse of Tragedy,
 And walks on burning sands;
The greatest of the Muses Three
 In our Australian lands.

7. HENRY LAWSON

THE UNCULTURED RHYMER TO HIS CULTURED CRITICS

Fight through ignorance, want, and care —
    Through the griefs that crush the spirit;
Push your way to a fortune fair,
    And the smiles of the world you'll merit.
Long, as a boy, for the chance to learn —
    For the chance that Fate denies you;
Win degrees where the Life-lights burn,
    And scores will teach and advise you.

My cultured friends! you have come too late
    With your bypath nicely graded;
I've fought thus far on my track of Fate,
    And I'll follow the rest unaided.
Must I be stopped by a college gate
    On the track of Life encroaching?
Be dumb to Love, and be dumb to Hate,
    For the lack of a college coaching?

You grope for Truth in a language dead —
    In the dust 'neath tower and steeple!
What know you of the tracks we tread?
    And what know you of our people?
"I must read this, and that, and the rest,"
    And write as the cult expects me? —
I'll read the book that may please me best,
    And write as my heart directs me!

You were quick to pick on a faulty line
    That I strove to put my soul in:
Your eyes were keen for a "dash" of mine
    In the place of a semi-colon —
And blind to the rest. And as it for such
    As you I must brook restriction?
"I was taught too little?" I learnt too much
    To care for a pedant's diction!

Must I turn aside from my destined way
    For a task your Joss would find me?
I come with strength of the living day,
    And with half the world behind me;
I leave you alone in your cultured halls
    To drivel and croak and cavil:
Till your voice goes further than college walls,
    Keep out of the tracks we travel!

8. A. G. STEPHENS

Introduction to The Bulletin Story Book

In collating these stories and literary sketches from the files of *The Bulletin*, the aim has been to make an interesting book. It has not been attempted to choose the best examples of literary style. Judged by a high canon, our most talented story-writers are still only clever students of the art of writing. A mere two or three have been able to earn a living by the profession of literature, and even these have been obliged to make the perilous compromise with journalism. So the stories and sketches which follow are usually the literary dreams of men of action, or the literary realisation of things seen by wanderers. Usually they are objective, episodic, detached—branches torn from the Tree of Life, trimmed and dressed with whatever skill the writers possess (which often is not inconsiderable). In most of them still throbs the keen vitality of the parent stem: many are absolute transcripts of the Fact, copied as faithfully as the resources of language will permit. Hence many of them, remaining level with Nature, remain on the lower plane of Art—which at its highest is not imitative, but creative—making anew the whole world in terms of its subject. What is desiderated is that these isolated impressions should be fused in consciousness, and re-visualised, re-presented with their universal reference made clear—yes! with the despised Moral, but with a moral which shines forth as an essence, is not stated as an after-thought. In other words, the branch should be shown growing upon the Tree, not severed from it; the Part should imply the Whole, and in a sense contain it, defying mathematics. Every story of a man or woman should be a microcosm of humanity; every vision of Nature should hold an imagination of the Universe. These be counsels of perfection which it is easier to teach than to practise, though many writers in other lands have practised them. So we take the good the gods provide, and are properly grateful, while striving for better and best.

Further, in this book it has not been attempted to choose examples of work characteristically Australian. The literary work which is Australian in spirit, as well as in scene or incident, is only beginning to be written. The formal establishment of the Commonwealth has not yet crystallised the floating elements of national life. Australia is still a suburb of Cosmopolis, where men from many lands perpetuate in a new environment the ideas and habits acquired far away. Our children bow instinctively to the fetishes of their fathers, for the heredity of centuries is not eliminated in a generation, or in half-a-dozen generations. Only here and there we receive hints and portents of the Future. Australian Nationality today is like an alchemist's crucible just before the gold-birth, with red fumes rising, and strange odours, and a dazzling gleam caught by moments through the bubble and seethe. Yet, without a deliberate choice, a few examples of Australian work—of work which could not have been conceived or written anywhere but in Australia—have naturally included themselves in the following pages. These are often sad or tragic: because, first, the fierce intensity of Tragedy makes more poignant, profounder literature than Comedy can make; because, second, our pioneering stage of civilisation is necessarily a stage of hard struggle, often of individual defeat, and the shadow of Tragedy lowers heavily over men who are fighting in a doubtful battle. Yet there are not wanting abumbrations of the Beauty of Australia— glimpses of the secret enchantment in which this strange, feline land—half-fierce, half-caressing—holds those who have listened to the gum-trees' whispered spells or drunk the magic philter of landscapes flooded with Nature's opiate-tints.

Verlaine's cult of Faded Things, extolling the hinted hue before the gross colour, finds a natural home in Australia—in many aspects a Land of Faded Things—of delicate purples, delicious greys, and dull, dreamy olives and ochres. Yet we have been content to let strangers foist upon us the English ideals of glaring green or staring red and orange; we have permitted them to denounce our grave harmonies of rock and vegetation, with shadow laid on tender shadow, light on dusky light. This, though the chief English art-magazine passes by all the English emeralds and flaunting autumn tints to bind itself in dull Australian green! This, though intelligent Englishmen themselves revolt against their tradition of crude colouring, and declare, like returning Morley Roberts, that "there was one thing that struck me in England as very strange, not to say painful, and that was the vivid colour of the pastures. We are quite proud of our perpetual verdure; but, to tell the truth, the tint of the grass after the soberer dull greys and greens and browns of Australia was extremely unpleasant to my eye. I thought the colour glaring, not to say inartistic; it certainly was not unnatural, and yet it struck me as being as nearly that as if someone had deliberately painted the fields. It took me months to get reconciled to it."

And the typical English beauty often looks as painted as the fields, with her coarse contrast of carmine and white; yet we permit Englishmen to come here and decry the divine pallor of Australians ruddied like a capricious coral! Englishmen have been permitted even to denounce the gum-tree, the most picturesque tree that grows, always at ease and unconventional. To see the many-bosomed gum-tree moving in a breeze (that gum-tree shaped like a soaring parachute made of a score of minor parachutes which lift and strain as if eager to be off and up); to watch the shifting interspaces of sky when amber days or purple nights play hide-and-seek among the wayward branches, and to listen to the birdlike murmur of the leaves, almost a twittering;—this is to receive an aesthetic education. Yet Englishmen persist in bringing hither their dense, sombre trees which defy even an Australian sun-ray, which almost disdain to ruffle in an Australian breeze—trees with the heavy magnificence of an English dinner, and often as dull; —and they call upon us to admire these unnatural exotics! Englishman Marcus Clarke has even called our gum-tree "melancholy," our forests "funereal". He knew nothing of this country beyond Victoria and Tasmania; but he multiplied a Wimmera station by the literary imagination and called the product Australia—actually winning quasi-Australian praise for the misrepresentation!

The grotesque English prejudice against things Australian, founded on no better reason than that they are unlike English things, still remains to vitiate the local sense of local beauty; but every year is teaching us wisdom. We have learnt to laugh at the ridiculous and reiterated fiction that our flowers have no scent and our birds no song. Why, the whole Bush is scented; in no land is there a greater wealth of aromatic perfume from the tree and shrub and blossom—making the daisied meadows of England, as honest Henry Kingsley suggests, tame and suburban by comparison. And when you go up beyond the tropic-line, and walk out of your tent at dawn, the air in many places is literally weighed down with the fragrance of a hundred brilliant flowers. What would they not give in England for ten acres of wattle-blossom on Wimbledon Common? and how many nightingales would they exchange for a flight of crimson lories at sunset?—a shower of flaming rubies. Did Marcus Clarke never hear the fluting of an Australian magpie?—so mellow, so round, so sweet. If the little brown English birds sing better than our vari-plumaged parrakeets, is not the strife at least equal? Does not fine colour yield as much pleasure to the artist eye as fine song to the artist ear? When will Englified city critics realise that Australia is a country which extends through forty degrees of latitude and thirty-five of longitude, and comprehends all climates, all scenery—snow-capped mountain and torrid desert, placid lake and winding river, torrent and brook, charm as well as grandeur, garden and homely field as well as barren solitude?

It is heredity and custom which again betray us. The rose is a beautiful flower, but the most beautiful only because thousands of years of care and cultivation have been lavished to bring it to perfection, because thousands of lovers have breathed its perfume, thousands of poets have apostrophised its exquisite form. Give the same care and cultivation to a hundred modest bush flowers, draw them from obscurity as the rose has been drawn from the parent wilderness, let them be worshipped and adored through centuries of sentiment—and we have here the rivals of the rose herself. Cluster the associations of the oak and yew around the yarran or the cedar (all the cedars of Lebanon were not more stately than those of the Herberton scrub), and the oak and yew will shrink, not indeed into insignificance, but into their proper proportion as regarded from Australia. In a word, let us look at our country and its fauna and flora, its trees and streams and mountains, through clear Australian eyes, not through bias-bleared English spectacles; and there is no more beautiful country in the world.

It will be the fault of the writers, not of the land, if Australian literature does not by-and-by become memorable. In the field of the short sketch or story, for example,—the field which includes this book—what country can offer to writers better material than Australia? We are not yet snug in cities and hamlets, moulded by routine, regimented to a pattern. Every man who roams the Australian wilderness is a potential knight of Romance; every man who grapples with the Australian desert for a livelihood might sing a Homeric chant of victory, or listen, baffled and beaten, to an Aeschylean dirge of defeat. The marvels of the adventurous are our daily commonplaces. The drama of the conflict between Man and Destiny is played here in a scenic setting whose novelty is full of vital suggestion for the scrub; in the spectacle of the Westralian prospector tramping across his mirage-haunted waste; in the tropic glimpse of the Thursday Island pearling fleet, manned by men of a dozen turbulent races—the luggers floating so calmly above a search so furious;—here, and in a hundred places beside, there is wealth of novel inspiration for the writers who will live Australia's life and utter her message. And when those writers come, let us tell them that we will never rest contented until Australian authors reach the highest standards set in literature, in order that we may set the standards higher and preach discontent anew.

City Life

EDITOR'S NOTE

Though Australia was an urbanized country by the 1890s, most writers continued to derive their inspiration from the bush. Whatever was unique or important about the Australian experience seemed more likely to be found in the backblocks than in the city streets. Certainly there was a huge demand for tales of up-country life. But there was also a growing body of verse and fiction about life in the cities and towns. The great strikes and the economic recession of the early nineties had forced many country people off the land into the ranks of the urban unemployed. The most frequent picture of city life in Australian writing of the period stresses this poverty of the down and outs (12 and 16). Lawson's best known early poem, "Faces in the Street" (1888), set the tone for the ensuing decade with its images of loneliness and misery:

> Drifting on, drifting on,
> To the scrape of restless feet;
> I can sorrow for the owners of the faces in the street.

Other writers, such as Bernard O'Dowd (10), developed a complex argument which saw the present state of cities, with their slums, poverty and "whey-faced crowd", as a temporary state which would be overturned when "the outcast sons of Art and Want" had laid the seeds of revolution. Indeed, throughout much of our writing of the nineties there runs this belief in a golden future. Though William Lane's novel *The Workingman's Paradise* deals with the breaking of the strikes, it makes an impassioned plea for a socialist future where the distress and suffering we see in "Saturday Night in Paddy's Market" will be swept aside (15).

Arthur Adams and Victor Daley (9, 13, and 14), however, were two writers (neither born in Australia, incidentally) who wrote of the great natural beauty of Sydney. Adams saw that the "graceful domes from squalor stagger up" but he saw also the "golden beauty" of lights reflected in the harbour and the attractiveness of the city's parks. It is not until such later writers as Kenneth Slessor (1901–71) that we find a similar fascination with the grimy beauty of our cities.

9. ARTHUR ADAMS

SYDNEY

In her grey majesty of ancient stone
She queens it proudly, though the sun's caress
Her piteous cheeks, ravished of bloom, confess,
And her dark eyes his bridegroom-glance have known.
In mantle of her parks, serene, alone,
She fronts the East; and with the tropic stress
Her smooth brow ripples into weariness —
Yet hers the sea for footstool, and for throne
A continent predestined. Round her trails
The turbid tumult of her streets, and high
Her graceful domes from squalor stagger up;
Her long, lean fingers, with their grey old nails,
Straining to passionate lips that thirsty sigh
The cool, bronze beauty of her harbour's cup.

10.   BERNARD O'DOWD

THE CITY

The City crowds our motley broods,
    And plants its citadel
Upon the delta where the floods
    Of evil plunge to Hell.

Through fogs retributive, that steam
    From ooze of stagnant wrongs,
The towers satanically gleam
    Defiance at our throngs.

It nucleates the land's Deceit;
    Its slums our Lost decoy;
It is the bawdy-house where meet
    Lewd Weath and venal Joy.

Grim wards are here, where Timour Trade
    His human cairns uprears:
There, Silent Towers, where girls betrayed
    Unseen rot through their years.

The City curbs the wrath that bays
    Rebellious in our souls,
By soothing fumes, and pageant days,
    And sweet Circean bowls.

With Saturnalia of the Serf
    Our discontent it cures;
Its Fraud, to dalliance of the Turf,
    Hysteric Folly lures.

The Babylonian Venus sways
    In every city park;
Her idiot niece, Abortion, plays
    Beside her in the dark.

Here, Office fawns fidelity
    When stroked by gilded hands;
In bramble of chicanery
    Belated Justice stands.

Glib Sophistry our mobs deludes,
    As showman does his beast,
By serving up their whims as foods
    From wholesome Wisdom's feast:

From craze to crime they bleating rage,
    Pursue what least is wise,
And, stoning the unselfish sage,
    Imposters canonise.

At times in free-lance echelons,
    Or called, at times, "The State,"
Ubiquitous its myrmidons
    Our foison desolate.

Exactions on its counters perch;
    Our marts Commission raids;
Sleek Simony, behind the Church,
    Prepares his ambuscades.

Dame Rumour, organised, the Press,
    Spirts slander — for a fee;
Or, masked in Public Welfare's dress,
    She gags or dirks the Free.

Great spider intellects here lurk
    In band and in exchange;
And through the feebler folds of Work
    Hyaena sweaters range.

Debt's gargoyles 'neath each eave grimace;
    Debt's mildews sour the soil;
At all there grins a Shylock face:
    Round all, Debt's suckers coil.

Here Thrift, with Art obscene endowed,
    A sterile haven finds
Where Malthus-Onan's whey-faced crowd
    Sink from the genial winds.

The Dead's miasma o'er us creeps;
    Their mandates dull our brains;
Inheritance, their steward, keeps
    The tithes of our demesnes.

Phylacteried ascetics brood
    On their precedence here;
There, Science tampers with our food,
    Or taints our atmosphere;

And Art spurns Poverty, her spouse,
    To be the courtesan
Of ogre of the counting-house
    Or ribonned Caliban;

And o'er that hovel-burdened waste
    Where Indigence is pent,
The Huns of Property have raced ·
    Of withering hoofs of Rent.

*   *   *

Yet not all black our horoscope,
    For, urged by Guardian Fates,
On hoyden Disobedience, Hope
    Rebellions procreates;

And awful Exorcists contrive
    The potion and the thong
That from the City's breast will drive
    Its incubus of Wrong.

Ripe knowledge of our ill and good,
    In fellowship of woe,
Makes fertile streams of Brotherhood
    From Ego's glacier flow.

The outcast sons of Art and Want
    Tyrtaean songs prepare,
To nerve us 'gainst the guns that daunt
From bastioned Mammon's lair.

Self-sacrifice averts His frown,
    When, angry, God at last
Our Gadarenian droves adown
    Disaster's cliff would cast;

And those Bohemians of the mist,
    Arrayed 'gainst Law, 't would seem,
Are cleansing for the Harmonist
    The City of His Dream.

11. ARTHUR ADAMS

SYDNEY NOCTURNES

FROM THE NORTH SHORE

To day she would not show her charms;
    But now the Night beseeches,
A white reproach of wistful arms
    Over the bay she reaches.
Upon her gleaming bosom, wet
    With tears and quivering,
In ropes of golden beauty set
    Her vivid jewels swing.

Upon the pathway of the night
    She, pausing often, paces;
About her body waves gleam white
    Like froth of filmy laces;
And to her pleasure hurrying,
    Their torches holding high,
On molten waters smouldering
    The ferry-boats flame by.

KING STREET

A morn, a sallow lamp-lit morn,
    A dawn that never breaks to day!
Old, old the faces, and forlorn;
    The hearts look out, so seared, so grey!
It is as if some upturned stone
    Had flung to light a vermin rout —
For things misfeatured, souls unknown,
    Stagger in blind amaze about.

Along their gleaming lines of light
    The charging trams go, head to ground;
Out from the drifting pathways, white
    The faces flash — like faces drowned!
And there with painted features drear,
    And eyes whose pathos still is sweet,
The hunted hunters prowl and peer —
    Their lair the long, slow-surging street.

IN HYDE PARK

The white mist walks between the trees
 In silver gown;
Her mystic floating draperies
 The branches drown;
And lurking there with eager leer
 And wonder new,
The lamps inquisitively peer
 Their fingers through.

The world sighs wearily, with pain
 Drawing tired breath;
The stars are like a silver rain;
 And down beneath
On Night's smooth garment running o'er
 In sullen flood,
The city, like a festering sore,
 Oozes warm blood.

12. HENRY LAWSON

"Dossing Out" and "Camping"

At least two hundred poor beggars were counted sleeping out on the pavements of the main streets of Sydney the other night—grotesque bundles of rags lying under the verandahs of the old Fruit Markets and York-street shops, with their heads to the wall and their feet to the gutter. It was raining and cold that night, and the unemployed had been driven in from Hyde Park and the bleak Domain—from dripping trees, damp seats, and drenched grass—from the rain, and cold, and the wind. Some had sheets of old newspapers to cover them—and some hadn't. Two were mates, and they divided a *Herald* between them. One had a sheet of brown paper, and another (lucky man!) had a bag—the only bag there. They all shrank as far into their rags as possible—and tried to sleep. The rats seemed to take them for rubbish, too, and only scampered away when one of the outcasts moved uneasily, or coughed, or groaned—or when a policeman came along.

One or two rose occasionally and rooted in the dust-boxes on the pavement outside the shops—but they didn't seem to get anything. They were feeling "peckish", no doubt, and wanted to see if they could get something to eat before the corporation carts came along. So did the rats.

Some men can't sleep very well on an empty stomach—at least, not at first; but it mostly comes with practice. They often sleep for ever in London. Not in Sydney as yet—so we say.

Now and then one of our outcasts would stretch his cramped limbs to ease them—but the cold soon made him huddle again. The pavement must have been hard on the men's "points", too; they couldn't dig holes nor make soft places for their hips, as you can in camp out back. And then, again, the stones had nasty edges and awkward slopes, for the pavements were very uneven.

The Law came along now and then, and had a careless glance at the unemployed in bed. They didn't look like sleeping beauties. The Law appeared to regard them as so much rubbish that ought not to have been placed there, and for the presence of which somebody ought to be prosecuted by the Inspector of Nuisances. At least, that was the expression the policeman had on his face.

And so Australian workmen lay at two o'clock in the morning in the streets of Sydney, and tried to get a little sleep before the traffic came along and took their bed.

The idea of sleeping out might be nothing to bushmen, not even an idea; but "dossing out" in the city and "camping" in the bush are two very different things. In the bush you can light a fire, boil your billy, and make some tea—if you have any; also fry a chop (there are no sheep running round in the city). You can have a clean meal, take off your shirt and wash it, and wash yourself—if there's water enough—and feel fresh and clean. You can whistle and sing by the camp fire, and make poetry, and breathe fresh air, and watch the everlasting stars that keep the mateless traveller from going mad as he lies in his lonely camp on the plains. Your privacy is even more perfect than if you had a suite of rooms at the Australia; you are at the mercy of no policeman, there's no one to watch you but God—and He won't move you on. God watches the "dossers-out", too, in the city, but He doesn't keep them from being moved on or run in.

With the city unemployed the case is entirely different. The city outcast cannot light a fire and boil a billy—even if he has one—he'd be run in at once for attempting to commit arson, or create a riot, or on suspicion of being a person of unsound mind. If he took off his shirt to wash it, or went in for a swim, he'd be had up for indecently exposing his bones—and perhaps he'd get flogged. He cannot whistle or sing on his pavement bed at night, for, if he did, he'd be violently arrested by two great policemen for riotous conduct. He doesn't see many stars, and he's generally too hungry to make poetry. He only sleeps on the pavement on sufferance, and when the policeman finds the small hours hang heavily on him, he can root up the unemployed with his big foot and move him on—or arrest him for being around with the intention to commit a felony; and, when the wretched "dosser" rises in the morning, he cannot shoulder his swag and take the track—he must cadge a breakfast at some back gate or restaurant, and then sit in the park or walk round and round, the same old hopeless round, all day. There's no prison like the city for a poor man.

Nearly every man the traveller meets in the bush is about as dirty and ragged as himself, and just about as hard up; but in the city nearly every man the poor unemployed meets is a dude, or at least, well dressed, and the unemployed *feels* dirty and mean and degraded by the contrast—and despised.

And he can't help feeling like a criminal. It may be imagination, but every policeman seems to regard him with suspicion, and this is terrible to a sensitive man.

We once had the key of the street for a night. We don't know how much tobacco we smoked, how many seats we sat on, or how many miles we walked before morning. But we do know that we felt like a felon, and that every policeman seemed to regard us with a suspicious eye; and at least we began to squint furtively at every trap we met, which, perhaps, made him more suspicious, till finally we felt bad enough to be run in and to get six months' hard.

Three winters ago a man, whose name doesn't matter, had a small office near Elizabeth Street, Sydney. He was an hotel broker, debt collector, commission agent, canvasser, and so on, in a small way—a very small way—but his heart was big. He had a partner. They batched in the office, and did their cooking over a gas lamp. Now, every day the man-whose-name-doesn't-matter would carefully collect the scraps of food, add a slice or two of bread and butter, wrap it all up in a piece of newspaper, and, after dark, step out and leave the parcel on a ledge of the stonework outside the building in the street. Every morning it would be gone. A shadow came along in the night and took it. This went on for many months, till at last one night the man-whose-name-doesn't-matter forgot to put the parcel out, and didn't think of it till he was in bed. It worried him, so that at last he had to get up and put the scraps outside. It was midnight. He felt curious to see the shadow, so he waited until it

came along. It wasn't his long-lost brother, but it was an old
mate of his.

Let us finish with a sketch:—

The scene was Circular Quay, outside the Messageries
sheds. The usual number of bundles of misery—covered
more or less with dirty sheets of newspaper—lay along the
wall under the ghastly glare of the electric light.
Time—shortly after midnight. From among the bundles an
old man sat up. He cautiously drew off his pants, and then
stood close to the wall, in his shirt, tenderly examining the
seat of the trousers. Presently he shook them out, folded
them with great care, wrapped them in a scrap of newspaper, and laid them down where his head was to be. He
had thin, hairy legs and a long grey beard. From a bundle of
rags he extracted another pair of pants, which were all
patches and tatters, and into which he engineered his way
with great caution. Then he sat down, arranged the paper
over his knees, laid his old ragged grey head back on his
precious Sunday-go-meetings—and slept.

13. VICTOR DALEY

AFTER SUNSET

Dusk-dark against grave red,
   The little hills of the harbour stand:
A black pine lifts its head,
   Like an old chief grim and grand,
   The last to yield in a conquered land.

And darkly against the sky,
   Stand rows of tall green trees,
Like warriors doomed to die,
   Who ask no elegies,
But lean on their spears, and wait
The swift, sure steps of Fate.

Behold, where a soft light shows
   Over a hill-top near,
   Delicate, pure and clear
As the ghost of a golden rose —
   A gum-tree gently sways,
Sways in the breeze and swings;
And to itself it sings —
   "This is not the last of days —
This is not the End of Things!"

For the gum-tree brave was born
   Beneath Australian skies,
In Australia's earliest morn,
And knows that its own bright Sun,
When the long dark hours are done,
   Will again in the East arise.

And now
Each dark hill's breast and brow
   Are flashing with jewels bright
That seem — so shining there —
Like diamonds in dark hair,
   Or eyes that in the night
Gleam in a lion's den —
   But each is a kindly light
From street-lamps shining fair,
And the kindly homes of men.

And from many a wharf and quay,
    And many an anchored barque,'
The long reflections shine,
Quivering tremulously,
    On the waters velvet-dark —
And those shining spirals seem to be
Tall golden columns Byzantine
Of palaces under the sea.

But, seen in another mood,
    They seem unto mine eyes
The swords of the seraphs who stood
    By the Gate of Paradise.

The ferries flash to and fro —
    Marvellous mortal-carrying sprites,
    Genii of the Arabian Nights —
For they are alive, and aglow
    From stem to stern, and they make —
    Each with its shining wake,
And its light and its life in the night —
A music of sound and sight,
A melody of delight.

The moon's cold virgin face
Looks down with a brighter grace,
    As once she gazed upon
    The young Endymion;
For though, from her ear impearled,
She sees strange sights and rare,
    And Beauty and Mystery —
    She sees no sight more fair,
More fair in all the world,
    Than Sydney by the Sea.

14. VICTOR DALEY

THE CALL OF THE CITY

There is a saying of renown —
"God made the country, man the town."
Well, everybody to his trade!
But man likes best the thing he made.
The town has little space to spare;
The country has both space and air;
The town's confined, the country free —
Yet, spite of all, the town for me.

For when the hills are grey and night is falling,
*   And the winds sigh drearily,*
I hear the city calling, calling, calling,
*   With a voice like the great sea.*

I used to think I'd like to be
A hermit living lonesomely,
Apart from human care or ken,
Apart from all the haunts of men:
Then I would read in Nature's book,
And drink clear water from the brook,
And live a life of sweet content,
In hollow tree, or cave, or tent.

This was a dream of callow Youth
Which always overleaps the truth,
And thinks, fond fool, it is the sum
Of things that are and things to come.
But now, when youth has gone from me,
I crave for genial company.
For Nature wild I still have zest,
But human nature I love best.

I know that hayseed in the hair
Than grit and grime is healthier,
And that the scent of gums is far
More sweet than reek of pavement-tar.
I know, too, that the breath of kine
Is safer than the smell of wine;
I know that here my days are free —
But, ah! the city calls to me.

Let Zimmerman and all his brood
Proclaim the charms of Solitude,
I'd rather walk down Hunter-street
And meet a man I like to meet,
And talk with him about old times,
And how the market is for rhymes,
Between two drinks, than hold commune
Upon a mountain with the moon.

A soft wind in the gully deep
Is singing all the trees to sleep;
And in the sweet air there is balm,
And Peace is here, and here is Calm.
God knows how these I yearned to find!
Yet I must leave them all behind,
And rise and go — come sun, come rain —
Back to the Sorceress again.

For at the dawn or when the night is falling,
    Or at noon when shadows flee,
I hear the city calling, calling, calling,
    Through the long lone hours to me.

15. WILLIAM LANE

Saturday Night in Paddy's Market (*from* The Workingman's Paradise)

Paddy's Market was in its glory, the weekly glory of a Sydney Saturday night, of the one day in the week when the poor man's wife has a few shillings and when the poor caterer for the poor man's wants gleans in the profit field after the stray ears of corn that escape the machine-reaping of retail capitalism. It was filled by a crushing, hustling, pushing mass of humans, some buying, more bartering, most swept aimlessly along in the living currents that moved ceaselessly to and fro. In one of these currents Ned found himself caught, with Nellie. He struggled for a short time, with elbows and shoulders, to make for himself and her a path through the press; experience soon taught him to forego attempting the impossible and simply to drift, as everybody else did, on the stream setting the way they would go.

He found himself, looking around as he drifted, in a long low arcade, brilliant with great flaring lights. Above was the sparkle of glass roofing, on either hand a walling of rough stalls, back and forward a vista of roofing and stalls stretching through distant arches, which were gateways, into outer darkness, which was the streets. On the stalls, as he could see, were thousands of things, all cheap and most nasty.

What were there? What were not there? Boots and bootlaces, fish and china ornaments, fruit, old clothes and new clothes, flowers and plants and lollies, meat and tripe and cheese and butter and bacon! Cheap music-sheets and cheap jewellery! Stockings and pie-dishes and bottles of ink! Everything that the common people buy! Anything by which a penny could be turned by those of small capital and little credit in barter with those who had less.

One old man's face transfixed him for a moment, clung to

his memory afterwards, the face of an old man, wan and white, grey-bearded and hollow-eyed, that was thrust through some hosiery hanging on a rod at the back of a stall. Nobody was buying there, nobody even looked to buy as Ned watched for a minute; the stream swept past and the grizzled face stared on. It had no body, no hands even, it was as if hung there, a trunkless head; it was the face of a generation grown old, useless and unloved, which lived by the crumbs that fall from Demos' table and waited wearily to be gone. It expressed nothing, that was the pain in it. It was haggard and grizzled and worn out, that was all. It knew itself no good to anybody, knew that labouring was a pain and thinking a weariness, and hope the delusion of fools, and life a vain mockery. It asked none to buy. It did not move. It only hung there amid the dark draping of its poor stock and waited.

Would he himself ever be like that, Ned wondered. And yet! And yet!

All around were like this. All! All! All! Everyone in this swarming multitude of working Sydney. On the faces of all was misery written. Buyers and sellers and passers-by alike were hateful of life. And if by chance he saw now and then a fat dame at a stall or a lusty huckster pushing his wares or a young couple, curious and loving, laughing and joking as they hustled along arm in arm, he seemed to see on their faces the dawning lines that in the future would stamp them also with the brand of despair.

The women, the poor women, they were most wretched of all; the poor housewives in their pathetic shabbiness, their faces drawn with child-bearing, their features shrunken with the struggling toil that never ceases nor stays; the young girls in their sallow youth that was not youth, with their hollow mirth and their empty faces, and their sharp angles or their unnatural busts; the wizened children that served at the stalls, precocious in infancy, with the wisdom of the Jew and the impudence of the witless babe; the old crones that crawled along—the mothers of a nation haggling for pennies as if they had haggled all their lives long. They bore baskets, most of the girls and housewives and crones; with some were husbands, who sometimes carried the basket but not always; some even carried children in their arms, unable even for an hour to escape the poor housewife's old-man-of-the-seas.

The men were absorbed, hidden away, in the flood of wearied women. There were men, of course, in the crowd, among the stallkeepers—hundreds. And when one noticed them they were wearied also, or sharp like ferrets; oppressed, overborne, or cunning, with the cunning of those who must be cunning to live; imbruted often with the brutishness of apathy, consciousless of the dignity of manhood, only dully patient or viciously keen as the ox is or the hawk. Many sottish-looking, or if not sottish with the beery texture of those whose only recreation is to be bestially merry at the drink-shop. This was the impression in which the few who strode with the free air of the ideal Australian workman were lost, as the few comfortable-seeming women were lost in the general weariness of their weary sex.

Jollity there was none to speak of. There was an eager huckling for bargains, or a stolid calculation of values, or a loud commendation of wares, or an oppressive indifference. Where was the "fair" to which of old the people swarmed, glad-hearted? Where was even the relaxed caution of the shopping-day? Where was the gay chaffering, the boisterous bandying of wit? Gone, all gone, and nothing left but care and sadness and a careful counting of hard-grudged silver and pence.

Ned turned his head once or twice to steal a glance at Nellie. He could not tell what she thought. Her face gave no sign of her feeling. Only it came home to him that there were none like her there, at least none like her to him. She was sad with a stern sadness, as she had been all day, and in that stern sadness of hers was a dignity, a majesty, that he had not appreciated until now, when she jostled without rudeness in this jostling crowd. This dark background of submissive yielding, of hopeless patience, threw into full light the unbending resolution carved in every line of her passionate face and lithesome figure. Yet he noticed how on her forehead two faint wrinkles showing, and in the corners of her mouth an overhanging fold; and this he saw as if reflected in a thousand ill-made mirrors around, distorted and exaggerated and grotesqued indeed but nevertheless the self-same marks of constant pain and struggle.

They reached the end of the first alley and passed out to the pavement, slippery with trodden mud. There was a little knot gathered there, a human eddy in the centre of the pressing throng. Looking over the heads of the loiterers, he could see in the centre of the eddy, on the kerb, by the light that came from the gateway a girl whose eyes were closed. She was of an uncertain age—she might be twelve or seventeen. Beside her was a younger child. Just then she began to sing. He and Nellie waited. He knew without being told that the singer was blind.

It was a hymn she sang, an old-fashioned hymn that has in its music the glad rhythm of the "revival", the melodious echoing of the Methodist day. He recollected hearing it long years before, when he went to the occasional services held in the old bush schoolhouse by some itinerant preacher. He recalled at once the gathering of the saints at the river; mechanically he softly hummed the tune. It was hardly the tune the blind girl sang though. She had little knowledge of tune, apparently. Her cracked discordant voice was unspeakably saddening.

This blind girl was the natural sequence to the sphinx-like head that he had seen amid the black stockings. Her face was large and flat, youthless, ageless, crowned with an ugly black hat, poorly ribboned; her hands were clasped clumsily on the skirt of her poor cotton dress, ill-fitting. There was no expression in her singing, no effort to express, no instinctive conception of the idea. The people only listened because she was blind and they were poor, and so they pitied her. The beautiful river of her hymn meant nothing, to her or to them. It might be; it might not be; it was not in question. She cried to them that she was blind and that the blind poor must eat if they would live and that they desire to live despite the city by-laws. She begged, this blind girl, standing with rent shoes in the sloppy mud. In Sydney, in 1889, in the workingman's paradise, she stood on the kerb, this blind girl, and begged—begged from her own people. And in their poverty, their weariness, their brutishness, they pitied her. None mocked, and many paused, and some gave.

They never thought of her being an imposter. They did not pass her on to the hateful charity that paid parasites dole out for the rich. They did not think that she made a fortune out of her pitifulness and hunt her with canting harshness as a nuisance and a cheat. Her harsh voice did not jar on them. Her discords did not shock their supersensitive ears. They only knew that they, blinded in her stead, must beg for bread and shelter while good Christians glut themselves and while fat law-makers white-wash the unpleasant from the sight of the well-to-do. In her helplessness they saw, unknowing it, their own helplessness, saw in her Humanity wronged and suffering and in need. Those who gave gave to themselves, gave as an impulsive offering to the divine impulse which drives the weak together and aids them to survive.

Ned wanted to give the blind girl something but he felt ashamed to give before Nellie. He fingered a half-crown in his pocket, with a bushman's careless generosity. By skilful manoeuvring and convenient yielding to the pressure of the crowd he managed to get near the blind girl as she finished her hymn. Nellie turned round, looking away—he thought afterwards: was it intentionally?—and he slipped his offering into the singer's fingers like a culprit. Then he walked off hastily with his companion, as red and confused as though he had committed some dastardly act. Just as they reached the second arcade they heard another discordant hymn rise amid the shuffling din.

There were no street-walkers in Paddy's Market, Ned could see. He had caught his foot clumsily on the dress of one above the town-hall, a dashing demi-mondaine with rouged cheeks and unnaturally bright eyes and a huge velvet-covered hat of the Gainsborough shape and had been covered with confusion when she turned sharply round on him with a "Now, clumsy, I'm not a door-mat." Then he had noticed that the sad sisterhood were out in force where the bright gas-jets of the better-class shops illuminated the pavement, swaggering it mostly where the kerbs were lined with young fellows, fairly-well dressed as a rule, who talked of cricket and race horses and boating and made audible remarks concerning the women, grave and gay, who passed by in the throng. Nearing the poorer end of George-street, they seemed to disappear, both sisterhood and kerb loungers, until near the Haymarket itself they found the larrikin element gathered strongly under the flaring lights of hotel-bars and music hall entrances. But in Paddy's Market itself there were not even larrikins. Ned did not even notice anybody drunk.

He had seen drinking and drunkenness enough that day. Wherever there was poverty he had seen viciousness flourishing. Wherever there was despair there was a drowning of sorrow in drink. They had passed scores of public houses, that afternoon, through the doors of which workmen were thronging. Coming along George-street, they had heard from more than one bar-room the howling of a drunken chorus. Men had staggered by them, and women too, frowsy and besotted. But there was none of this in Paddy's Market. It was a serious place, these long dingy arcades, to which people came to buy cheaply and carefully, people to whom every penny was of value and who had none to throw away, just then at least, either on a brain-turning carouse or on a painted courtesan. The people here were sad and sober and sorrowful. It seemed to Ned that here was collected, as in the centre of a great vortex, all the pained and tired and ill-fed and wretched faces that he had been seeing all day. The accumulation of misery pressed on him till it sickened him at the heart. It felt as though something clutched at his throat, as though by some mechanical means his skull was being tightened on his brain. His thoughts were interrupted by an exclamation from Nellie.

"There's a friend of mine," she explained, making her way through the crowd to a brown-bearded man who was seated on the edge of an empty stall apparently guarding a large empty basket in which were some white cloths. The man's features were fine and his forehead massive, his face indicating a frail constitution and strong intellectuality. He wore an apron rolled up round his waist. He seemed very poor.

"How d'ye do, Miss Lawton?" said he getting off the stall and shaking hands warmly. "It's quite an age since I saw you. You're looking as well as ever." Ned saw that his thin face beamed as he spoke and that his dark brown eyes, though somewhat hectic, were singularly beautiful.

"I'm well, thanks," said Nellie, beaming in return. "And how are you? You seem browner than you did. What have you been doing to yourself?"

"Me! I've been up the country a piece trying my hand at farming. Jones is taking up a selection, you know, and I've been helping him a little now times aren't very brisk. I'm keeping fairly well, very fairly, I'm glad to say."

"This is Mr. Hawkins, Mr. Sim," introduced Nellie; the men shook hands.

"Come inside out of the rush," invited Sim, making room for them in the entrance-way of the stall. "We haven't got any armchairs, but it's not so bad up on the table here if you're tired."

"I'm not tired," said Nellie, leaning against the doorway. Ned sat up on the stall by her side; his feet were sore, unused to the hard paved city streets.

"I suppose Mr. Hawkins is one of us," said Sim, perching himself up again.

"I don't know what you call 'one of us,'" answered Nellie, with a smile. "He's a beginner. Some day he may get as far as you and Jones and the rest of the dynamiters."

Sim laughed genially. "Do you know, I really believe that Jones would use dynamite if he got an opportunity," he commented. "I'm not joking. I'm positively convinced of it."

"Has he got it as bad as that?" asked Nellie. Ned began to feel interested. He also noticed that Sim used book-words.

"Has he got it as bad as that! 'Bad' isn't any name for it. He's the stubbornest man I ever met, and he's full of the most furious hatred against the capitalists. He has it as a personal feeling. Then the life he's got is sufficient to drive a man mad."

"Selecting is pretty hard," agreed Nellie, sadly.

"Nellie and I know a little about that, Mr. Sim," said Ned.

"Well, Jones' selection is a hard one," went on Sim, good-humouredly. "I prefer to sell trotters, when I sell out like this, to attempting it. The soil is all stones, and there is not a drop of water when the least drought comes on. Poor Jones toils like a team of horses and hardly gets sufficient to keep him alive. I never saw a man work as he does. For a man who thinks and has ideas to be buried like that in the bush is terrible. He has no one to converse with. He goes mooning about sometimes and muttering to himself enough to frighten one into a fit."

"Does he still do any printing?" asked Nellie, archly.

"Oh, the printing," answered Sim, laughing again. "He initiated me into the art of wood-engraving. You see, Mr. Hawkins"—turning to Ned—"Jones hasn't got any type, and of course he can't afford to buy it, but he's got hold of a little second-hand toy printing press. To print from he takes a piece of wood, cut across the grain and rubbed smooth with sand, and cuts out of it the most revolutionary and blood-curdling leaflets, letter by letter. If you only have patience it's quite easy after a few weeks' practice."

"Does he print them?" asked Ned.

"Print them! I should say he did. Every old scrap of paper he can collect or get sent him he prints his leaflets on and gets them distributed all over the country. Many a night I've sat up assisting with the pottering little press. Talk about Nihilism! Jones vows that there is only one way to cure things and that is to destroy the rule of Force."

"He's a long while starting," remarked Nellie with a slight sneer. "Those people who talk so much never do anything."

"Oh, Jones isn't like that," answered Sim, with cheerful confidence. "He'll do anything that he thinks is worth while. But I suppose I'm horrifying you, Mr. Hawkins? Miss Lawton here knows what we are and is accustomed to our talk."

"It'll take considerable to horrify me," replied Ned, standing down as Nellie straightened herself out for a move-on. "You can blow the whole world to pieces for all I care. There's not much worth watching in it as far as I can see."

"You're pretty well an anarchist," said the brown-bearded trotter-seller, his kindly intellectual face lighted up. "It'll come some day, that's one satisfaction. Do you think that many here will regret it?" He waved his hand to include the crowd that moved to and fro before them, its voices covered with the din of its dragging feet.

"That'll do, Sim!" said Nellie. "Don't stuff Ned's head with those absurd anarchistical nightmares of yours. We're going; we've got somewhere to go. Good-bye! Tell Jones you saw me when you write, and remember me to him, will you? I like him—he's so good-hearted, though he does rave."

"He's as good-hearted a man as there is in New South Wales," corroborated Sim, shaking hands. "I'm expecting to meet a friend here or I'd stroll along. Good-bye! Glad to have met you, Mr. Hawkins."

He re-mounted the stall again as they moved off. In another minute he was lost to their sight as they were swallowed up once more in the living tide that ebbed and flowed through Paddy's Market.

After that Ned did not notice much, so absorbed was he. He vaguely knew that they drifted along another arcade and then crossed a street to an open cobble-paved space where there were shooting-tunnels and merry-go-rounds and try-your-weights and see-how-much-you-lifts. He looked dazedly at wizen-faced lads who gathered round ice-cream stalls, and at hungry folks who ate stewed peas. Everything seemed grimly and frayed and sordid; the flaring torches smelt of oil; those who shot, or ate, or rode, by spending a penny, were the envied of standers-by. Amid all this drumming and hawking and flaring of lights were swarms of boys and growing girls, precocious and vicious and foul-tongued.

Ten o'clock struck. "For God's sake, let us get out of this, Nellie!" cried Ned, as the ringing bell-notes roused him.

"Have you had enough of Sydney?" she asked, leading the way out.

"I've had enough of every place," he answered hotly. She did not say any more.

As they stood in George-street, waiting for their 'bus, a high-heeled, tightly-corsetted, gaily-hatted larrikiness flounced out of the side door of a hotel near by. A couple of larrikin acquaintances were standing there, shrivelled young men in high-heeled pointed-toed shoes, belled trousers, gaudy neckties and round soft hats tipped over the left ear.

"Hello, you blokes!" cried the larrikiness, slapping one on the shoulder. "Isn't this a blank of a time you're having?"

It was her ideal of pleasure, hers and theirs, to parade the street or stand in it, to gape or be gaped at.

16. MARY GILMORE

CHILD NEWSVENDORS

We know that always, somewhere, earth
   Is warm and grass is green; that skies
Are blue; that hours go by where none
   Turn slowly dayward, languid eyes

That wish themselves deceived and ask
   To find the dawn no nearer than
The night! We know that in the long
   Cold hours before the daylight can

Creep out across the world, within
   Their mother's arms lie children such
As we, so warm, ah God! so warm,
   It seems that if we could but touch

Them as they slept, to us might come
   Some faintly kindred throb, that might
Have power to warm us through the strange
   And pallid hours that follow night.

*   *   *

And when the summer comes, and night
   Draws, panting, back before the day,
We scarcely fall asleep before
   We must awake, and out away,

Across the silent city while
   Its people sleep. O, mothers, think
Upon us as you sit and dream,
   And turn towards us where we shrink

Before the hardship of our lives.
   O help us! We, who know not how,
Who have no power to help ourselves,
   O mothers we are asking here, and now.

Lyrical Verse

EDITOR'S NOTE

Though the ballad of bush life was the common and most widely read form of Australian verse during the nineties, considerable quantities of lyrical poetry were also published. Much of this lacked the vigour and relevance of the ballads and was palely imitative of contemporary English poetry. But the work of some, especially Christopher Brennan, was outstanding. Brennan introduced a new note of literary excellence and sophistication into local writing. Having studied in Europe, he was influenced by the French symbolist poets, though the degree to which the themes of his work are alien to other Australian writing of the nineties has been over-estimated. Brennan was attracted to the idea of the *livre composé*: a sequence of poems intended to be read as a whole. He came to view his total output in this way, but most of the lyrics included here (28–37) are from a particular sequence called "Towards the Source", where he writes of the passing of the potential of youth and love and of the never-ending search for "days of azure".

It is true, however, that the Australian lyric has flourished more this century than during the 1890s. Three poets in particular spring to mind: John Shaw Neilson, Hugh McCrae, and Mary Gilmore. All began publishing in the nineties and are represented here by some of their earliest pieces (18, 21, and 23). On the other hand, Victor Daley, John le Gay Brereton, and Roderic Quinn produced their best work during this period. These lyricists may not reflect the local landscape in the manner of Lawson or Furphy but in their tone, and in their general concern with unfulfilled promise, they are frequently closer to the bush writers than has been generally recognized. Barcroft Boake's "Where the Dead Men Lie" (27) is an unusual instance of a specifically outback lyric.

17. ARTHUR BAYLDON

CRABS

(Written on the Queensland Beach)

Poisonous, bloated, crab-like shapes
Crawl in gangs around these capes —
Stopping here and feeding there;
Listening, crawling everywhere;
Searching every rotten weed
With a frothing, wild-eyed greed;
Fighting o'er a lump of scurf,
Or a red boil of the earth;
Thrusting up their writhing claws
To their grinning, fiend-like maws.
And these horrid creatures wet
With a thick, unwholesome sweat
Have most hideous banquets here
On the poor drowned marineer.
Down they hurry eagerly,
Chittering all the way with glee;
They have smelt the tainted air
From that body festering there.
How they twitch their claws and pry
Into each distorted eye;
How they spit on him with spite
As their nippers pinch and bite;
How they strip him clean and bare,
Leaving not a morsel there,
Till they're gorged and all squat near
Fleshless remnants with a leer.
When the billows near them roll,
Each will scoop himself a hole
In the mudbank and therein
Sleep like a embodied sin.

In the world so crass and blind
Human crabs feed on their kind —
Glutted creatures that devour
All that fall into their power;
Skulking near their dismal holes,
They sniff out poor wretched souls
Thrown by life's unpitying sea
On the beach of misery.

18. JOHN SHAW NEILSON

MARIAN'S CHILD

First we thought of the river,
    But the body might be found;
And it did not seem so cruel
    To bury in the ground.
So small it seemed, so helpless —
    I hardened my heart like stone —
She kissed it over and over,
    And then I heard her groan.

I took it out of her bosom:
    It cried, and cried, and cried;
I carried it down the garden —
    The moon was bright outside.
I dug a hole with a shovel
    And laid the baby down;
I shovelled the sand upon it —
    The sand was soft and brown.

But, ah! its cry was bitter —
    I scarce could cover it in,
And when at last 't was hidden
    I sank beneath my sin.
Down at the foot of the garden,
    Where the moon-made shadows fell,
I sold myself to the Devil,
    And bought a home in hell.

Down at the foot of the garden,
    Where the weeds grew rank and wild,
Under the shivering willows
    I murdered Marian's child;
My heart was wildly beating,
    My eyes and cheeks were wet,
For I heard the baby crying —
    O God! I hear it yet.
I hear it crying, crying,
    Just as I heard it cry
In Marian's arms in the morning
    When I knew that it must die.

Neither of us was woman —
   I was the younger one;
And we strove to tell each other
   What a wise thing we had done.
Why should it live to plague us?
   Why should it ever begin
Travelling roads of trouble
   Soiling its soul with sin?

Marian! ah, she remembers!
   In spite of all her tears
Sweet children call her mother
   These many, many years.
Yet when I saw my darling,
   Her blue eyes seemed to swell:
"Annie!" she said, "do you hear it?
   Listen! I hear it well!

"In the night I hear it calling
   With a muffled, plaintive wail,
And my heart stands still to count its sobs,
   And ever I try and fail;
For I think the depth of my baby's grief
   Will never fathomed be
Till the fires are lit in the bottomless pit
   To blast eternity."

Once in a southern city
   Joy came into my life —
He loved me, kissed me, thought me
   Worthy to be his wife. . .

No I will never marry.
   God! I had rather die —
If ever I had a baby
   'T would curse me with its cry!
For down at the foot of the garden,
   Where the moon-made shadows fell,
I sold myself to the Devil
   And bought a home in hell.

19. VICTOR DALEY

DREAMS

I have been dreaming all a summer day
Of rare and dainty poems I would write;
Love-lyrics delicate as lilac-scent,
Soft idylls woven of wind, and flower, and stream,
And songs and sonnets carven in fine gold.

The day is fading and the dusk is cold;
Out of the skies has gone the opal gleam,
Out of my heart has passed the high intent
Into the shadow of the falling night —
Must all my dreams in darkness pass away?

I have been dreaming all a summer day;
Shall I go dreaming so until Life's light
Fades in Death's dusk, and all my days are spent?
Ah, what am I the dreamer but a dream!
The day is fading and the dusk is cold.

My songs and sonnets carven in fine gold
Have faded from me with the last day-beam
That purple lustre to the sea-line lent,
And flushed the clouds with rose and chrysolite;
So days and dreams in darkness pass away.

I have been dreaming all a summer day
Of songs and sonnets carven in fine gold;
But all my dreams in darkness pass away;
The day is fading, and the dusk is cold.

20. JOHN LE GAY BRERETON

IN CAMP

My floor the turfy ground, the open sky
Well-wrought with stars the ceiling of my room,
My walls the trees receding into gloom,
Beside my resinous-scented fire I lie.
Below, the creek is pattering merrily;
The air is heavy with a thick perfume
Of ghostly native-jasmine full of bloom,
And down the gully sounds the mopoke's cry.

My soul is on the breast of night. I fly
Motionless, tossed by neither space nor time,
Sustained by knowledge of a Truth sublime.
I realise the infinite Love. Can I,
Knowing the Life that is my being, die,
An automatic complex daub of slime?

21. HUGH McCRAE

THE MURDER-NIGHT

The tree-frogs sing in the rain,
  The stars are caught in the pines,
The wind has fled up the lane,
  And a sick man's window shines.

A loose horse neighs at the night,
  A housed horse stamps in his stall;
A swallow flutters with fright,
  And dies at the top of the wall.

The paddocks are striped with flood,
  And under the barn-door creeps
A silent gutter of blood
  In queer little jerks and leaps.

And the nested rain-drops plash
  And mix with the sinful stream
That writhes in the lightning flash,
  Like a snake in a fearsome dream.

And up on the bald wet hill
  A gibbering madman stands,
And sniffs his horrible fill
  Of the rose in his shaking hands.

22. JOHN LE GAY BRERETON

ROUGE ET NOIR

Why should I be thus shaken by a dream,
Than which a baby's babble has more meaning,
Unless the tedious thoughts that I have traced
Of late to where they lose themselves in the sea
Have wronged my sense? And that my friendship, too,
Should lay the spell on me. To think that love
Like mine should send a clap of misery
To cling upon me like a shadowy plague
That baffles grappling!
                Under a sloping roof
Of twining branches, as I thought, I lay
And read, and in among the perfect green
Of new-burst leaves the sunlight pierced and threw
Round splashes of lilac colour on the book,
Twinned circles wavering to the sleepy sigh
Of noontide, and the gladioles were stirred
To half-heard rustlings in their yellowing blades
And light seed-bearing wands; the lizard sunned
His grace of bronze beside the crisping leaves
That the last storm had torn from the trees; afar
The steam-boat panted on the river. While
I lay with fettered senses, lazily
Following Gautama's golden words and deeds,
I heard a sound of slowly-wending feet
Approaching, so I rose and thrust apart
The boughs and looked; a sad-faced company
Of men and maids and children walked adown
The hillside with its rust of perished ferns,
And each of them was clad in spotless white
And crowned with faded leaves, and in their midst
Four young men bare a coffin, over which
Was spread a blood-red pall. There as they went
The shrubs and flowers drooped behind them. Then
With reverent head I stood, and while they passed
I plucked the hindmost by the sleeve to ask
Whose body lay beneath yon crimson pall;
For answer came two whispered words that struck
My soul to dullness, but I watched them go,
With one thought in my heart, and on my lips
One single phrase — "He was my friend, my friend!"
Before the words had died away, the bush
Had vanished, but the thought remained unchanged.

Now I was in my sleeping-room, and there
With a keen knife I pierced a purple vein
Within my arm, and lay awaiting death,
And listening to the dripping of the blood
That redly marked the passing time.   I heard
The bees at work in the blossoming tree before
My window, and I heard a lumbering cart
Toil up the road with picnickers, and still
My blood flowed and my strength ebbed, but I thought
Of him, the boy I loved, and was content
To die, for we might meet beyond the bourne,
Or, though we met not, dreamless sleep were better
Than waking misery.   A distant clock
Tolled out the hour, and a cow lowed far away,
And farther still it seemed to me, my ears
Being blunted so that the sound of ruddy drops
Scarce entered, and my strength was almost null;
All will or power to move had faded out,
Till I was ripe for the end.   Then suddenly
Before the darkness fell I heard a laugh
Out in the sunshine, and my name was cried
In joyous tones; his foot scattered the gravel
As he ran through the garden, but I lay
Powerless, and the horror beats amain
At my temples as I write; I crushed my force
Into a single knot for one last cry,
To shout his name, and, with the effort, woke.

23. MARY GILMORE

THE TRUEST MATE

I don't know whether 'tis well to love,
    Or whether 'tis well to hate,
But I know this well, that the man who has sinned
    Is ever the truest mate.

For the man who has sinned his sins himself,
    And learned what a man may learn,
Is wiser than he who has lived untried
    By the fires that make, or burn.

He knows the needs of the human heart,
    The want in another's will,
And sees excuse where the untried man
    Sees only the love of ill.

He sees the good, and he sees the bad,
    And judges these two between,
And he knows the thing that counts for most,
    Is seldom the thing that's seen.

For one may know what a man has done,
    But who, how a man has tried?
And who shall say if a man go straight
    For purity's sake, or pride?

And who shall say if a sinner sin
    For love of the sin or no;
Or whether he drift in ignorance
    Of the things that a man should know?

I don't know whether 'tis well to love,
    Or whether 'tis well to hate,
But I know this well, that the man who has sinned
    Is ever the truest mate.

24. VICTOR DALEY

HIS SOUL

Once from the world of living men
I passed, by a strange fancy led,
To a still City of the Dead,
To call upon a citizen.

He had been famous in his day;
Much talked of, written of, and praised
For virtues my small soul amazed —
And yet I thought his heart was clay.

He was too full of grace for me:
His friends said, on a marble stone,
His soul sat somewhere near the Throne:
I did not know; I called to see.

His name and fame were on the door —
A most superior tomb indeed,
Much railed, and gilt, and filagreed;
He occupied the lower floor.

I knocked — *a worm crawled from its hole:*
I looked — *and knew it for his soul.*

25. RODERIC QUINN

THE HIDDEN TIDE

Within the world a second world
    That circles ceaselessly:
Stars in the sky and sister stars —
    Turn in your eyes and see!

Tides of the sea that rise and fall,
    Aheave from Pole to Pole —
And kindred swayings, veiled but felt,
    That noise along the soul.

Yon moon, noon-rich, high-throned, remote,
    And pale with pride extreme,
Draws up the sea, but what white moon
    Exalts the tide of Dream?

The Fisher-Folk who cast their nets
    In Vision's golden tide
Oft bring to light misshapen shells,
    And nothing worth beside.

And so their worn hands droop adown,
    Their singing throats are dumb;
The Inner-Deep withholds its pearls
    Till turn of tide be come.

But patience! wait — the good tide turns,
    The waters inward set;
And lo, behold! aleap, alive
    With glowing fish the net!

O Toilers of the Hidden Seas!
    Ye have strange gain and loss,
Dragging the Deeps of Soul for pearls,
    And oft-times netting dross.

Flushed to the lips with golden light,
    And dark with sable gloom;
Thrilled by a thousand melodies,
    And silent like a tomb.

Fierce are the winds across your realm,
    As though some Demon veiled
Had tossed the gales of Spirit-land
    To ravage ways unsailed.

But still sweet hours befall at times,
    Rich lit and full of ease;
The afterglow is like the light
    Of sunset on tired seas.

And worse, perhaps, may be the lot
    Of those whose fate is sleep;
The sodden souls without a tide,
    Dense as a rotten deep.

Pain paves the way for keener joy,
    And wondrous thoughts uproll
When the large moon of Peace looks down
    On high tide in the Soul.

26. VICTOR DALEY

THE OLD BOHEMIAN

The world was in my debt,
    I was the Friend of Man,
When, years ago, I met
    The Old Bohemian.

His hat was shocking bad,
    He wore a faded tie,
And yet, withal, he had
    A moist and shining eye.

And though his purse was lean,
    And though his coat was dyed,
He had a lordly mien
    And air of ancient pride.

We sat in a hotel,
    And drank the amber ale;
And as I touched the bell
    I listened to his tale.

He told me that some day
    In his place I would be;
But all the world was gay —
    No use in warning me.

He spoke of high Desire
    And aspirations true;
And flamed again the fire
    In eyes of faded blue.

"By God!" the old man said,
    "The days of old were grand;
I painted cities red,
    I owned the blessed land.

"I loved, when I was young,
    The girls in all the bars;
And, coming home, I hung
    My hat upon the stars.

"And O, the times were glad!
        Such times you never knew;
And O, the nights we had!
        And O, the jolly crew!

"Where are the songs — the talk —
        The friends that used to be;
I with my shadow walk
        At last for company.

"We dreamt in those old days
        That Poets we would be;
And though we missed the bays
        We *lived* our Poetry!

"We talked and talked and talked,
        And slowly, one by one,
My old companions walked
        Into the setting sun."

The old Bohemian said,
        "The world owes nought to me,
I lie upon the bed
        Which I made — carefully.

"There is one way to play
        The mad Bohemian game,
I found and took the way —
        And you will do the same."

Ah, that was years ago,
        When skies were bright and blue,
And now, alas, I know
        His prophecy was true.

Yet fill the glass once more,
        Bohemians and sing —
Upon another shore
        There waits another Spring!

27. BARCROFT BOAKE

WHERE THE DEAD MEN LIE

Out on the wastes of the Never Never —
  That's where the dead men lie!
There where the heat-waves dance for ever —
  That's where the dead men lie!
That's where the Earth's loved sons are keeping
Endless tryst: not the west wind sweeping
Feverish pinions can wake their sleeping —
  Out where the dead men lie!

Where brown Summer and Death have mated —
  That's where the dead men lie!
Loving with fiery lust unsated —
  That's where the dead men lie!
Out where the grinning skulls bleach whitely
Under the saltbush sparkling brightly;
Out where the wild dogs chorus nightly —
  That's where the dead men lie!

Deep in the yellow, flowing river —
  That's where the dead men lie!
Under the banks where the shadows quiver —
  That's where the dead men lie!
Where the platypus twists and doubles,
Leaving a train of tiny bubbles;
Rid at last of their earthly troubles —
  That's where the dead men lie!

East and backward pale faces turning —
  That's how the dead men lie!
Gaunt arms stretched with a voiceless yearning —
  That's how the dead men lie!
Oft in the fragrant hush of nooning
Hearing again their mothers' crooning,
Wrapt for aye in a dreamful swooning —
  That's how the dead men lie!

Only the hand of Night can free them —
   That's when the dead men fly!
Only the frightened cattle see them —
   See the dead men go by!
Cloven hoofs beating out one measure,
Bidding the stockman know no leisure —
That's when the dead men take their pleasure!
   That's when the dead men fly!

Ask, too, the never-sleeping drover:
   He sees the dead pass by;
Hearing them call to their friends — the plover,
   Hearing the dead men cry;
Seeing their faces stealing, stealing,
Hearing their laughter pealing, pealing,
Watching their grey forms wheeling, wheeling
   Round where the cattle lie!

Strangled by thirst and fierce privation —
   That's how the dead men die!
Out on Moneygrub's farthest station —
   That's how the dead men die!
Hardfaced greybeards, youngsters callow;
Some mounds cared for, some left fallow;
Some deep down, yet others shallow;
   Some having but the sky.

Moneygrub, as he sips his claret,
   Looks with complacent eye
Down at his watch-chain, eighteen-carat —
   There, in his club, hard by:
Recks not that every link is stamped with
Names of the men whose limbs are cramped with
Too long lying in grave mould, camped with
   Death where the dead men lie.

28. CHRISTOPHER BRENNAN

We sat entwined an hour or two together
(how long I know not) underneath pine-trees
that rustled ever in the soft spring weather
stirr'd by the sole suggestion of the breeze:

we sat and dreamt that strange hour out together
fill'd with the sundering silence of the seas:
the trees moan'd for us in the tender weather
we found no word to speak beneath those trees

but listen'd wondering to their dreamy dirges
sunder'd even then in voiceless misery;
heard in their boughs the murmur of the surges
saw the far sky as curv'd above the sea.

That noon seem'd some forgotten afternoon,
cast out from Life, where Time might scarcely be:
our old love was but remember'd as some swoon;
Sweet, I scarce thought of you nor you of me

but, lost in the vast, we watched the minutes hasting
into the deep that sunders friend from friend;
spake not nor stirr'd but heard the murmurs wasting
into the silent distance without end:

so, whelm'd in that silence, seem'd to us as one
our hearts and all their desolate reverie,
the irresistible melancholy of the sun,
the irresistible sadness of the sea.

29. CHRISTOPHER BRENNAN

Sweet silence after bells!
deep in the enamour'd ear
soft incantation dwells.

Filling the rapt still sphere
a liquid crystal swims,
precarious yet clear.

Those metal quiring hymns
shaped ether so succinct:
a while, or it dislimns,

the silence, wanly prinkt
with forms of lingering notes,
inhabits, close, distinct;

and night, the angel, floats
on wings of blessing spread
o'er all the gather'd cotes

where meditation, wed
with love, in gold-lit cells,
absorbs the heaven that shed

sweet silence after bells.

30. CHRISTOPHER BRENNAN

Autumn: the year breathes dully towards its death,
beside its dying sacrificial fire;
the dim world's middle-age of vain desire
is strangely troubled, waiting for the breath
that speaks the winter's welcome malison
to fix it in the unremembering sleep:
the silent woods brood o'er an anxious deep,
and in the faded sorrow of the sun,
I see my dreams' dead colours, one by one,
forth-conjur'd from their smouldering palaces,
fade slowly with the sigh of the passing year.
They wander not nor wring their hands nor weep,
discrown'd belated dreams! but in the drear
and lingering world we sit among the trees
and bow our heads as they, with frozen mouth,
looking, in ashen reverie, towards the clear
sad splendour of the winter of the far south.

The grand cortege of glory and youth is gone
flaunt standards, and the flood of brazen tone:
I alone linger, a regretful guest,
here where the hostelry has crumbled down,
emptied of warmth and life, and the little town
lies cold and ruin'd, all its bravery done,
wind-blown, wind-blown, where not even dust may rest.
No cymbal-clash warms the chill air: the way
lies stretch'd beneath a slanting afternoon,
the which no piled pyres of the slaughter'd sun,
no silver sheen of eve shall follow: Day,
ta'en at the throat and choked, in the huge slum
o' the common world, shall fall across the coast,
yellow and bloodless, not a wound to boast.
But if this bare-blown waste refuse me home
and if the skies wither my vesper-flight,
'twere well to creep, or ever livid night
wrap the disquiet earth in horror, back
where the old church stands on our morning's track,
and in the iron-entrellis'd choir, among
rust tombs and blazons, where an isle of light
is bosom'd in the friendly gloom, devise
proud anthems in a long forgotten tongue:
so cozening youth's despair o'er joy that dies.

32. CHRISTOPHER BRENNAN

Under a sky of uncreated mud
or sunk beneath the accursed streets, my life
is added up of cupboard-musty weeks
and ring'd about with walls of ugliness:
some narrow world of ever-streaming air.

My days of azure have forgotten me.

Nought stirs, in garret-chambers of my brain,
except the squirming brook of miseries
older than memory, while, far out of sight
behind the dun blind of the rain, my dreams
of sun on leaves and waters drip thro' years
nor stir the slumbers of some sullen well,
beneath whose corpse-fed weeds I too shall sink.

33. CHRISTOPHER BRENNAN

The yellow gas is fired from street to street
past rows of heartless homes and hearths unlit,
dead churches, and the unending pavement beat
by crowds — say rather, haggard shades that flit

round nightly haunts of their delusive dream,
where'er our paradisal instinct starves: —
till on the utmost post, its sinuous gleam
crawls in the oily water of the wharves;

where Homer's sea loses his keen breath, hemm'd
what place rebellious piles were driven down —
the priestlike waters to this task condemn'd
to wash the roots of the inhuman town! —

where fat and strange-eyed fish that never saw
the outer deep, broad halls of sapphire light,
glut in the city's draught each nameless maw:
— and there, wide-eyed unto the soulless night,

methinks a drown'd maid's face might fitly show
what we have slain, a life that had been free,
clean, large, nor thus tormented—even so
as are the skies, the salt winds and the sea.

Ay, we had saved our days and kept them whole,
to whom no part in our old joy remains,
had felt those bright winds sweeping thro' our soul
and all the keen sea tumbling in our veins,

had thrill'd to harps of sunrise, when the height
whitens, and dawn dissolves in virgin tears,
or caught, across the hush'd ambrosial night,
the choral music of the swinging spheres,

or drunk the silence if nought else — But no!
and from each rotting soil distil in dreams
a poison, o'er the old earth creeping slow,
that kills the flowers and curdles the live streams,

that taints the fresh breath of re-risen day
and reeks across the pale bewilder'd moon:
— shall we be cleans'd and how? I only pray,
red flame or deluge, may that end be soon!

34. CHRISTOPHER BRENNAN

The years that go to make me man
this day are told a score and six
that should have set me magian
o'er my half-souls that struggle and mix.

But wisdom still remains a star
just hung within my aching ken,
and common prudence dwells afar
among contented homes of men.

In wide revolt and ruin tost
against whatever is or seems
my futile heart still wanders lost
in the same vast and impotent dreams.

On either hand life hurries by
its common joy, its common mirth;
I reach vague hands of sympathy,
a ghost upon this common earth.

35. CHRISTOPHER BRENNAN

The pangs that guard the gates of joy
the naked sword that will be kist,
how distant seem'd they to the boy,
white flashes in the rosy mist!

Ah, not where tender play was screen'd
in the light heart of leafy mirth
of that obdurate might we ween'd
that shakes the sure repose of earth.

And sudden, 'twixt a sun and sun,
the veil of dreaming is withdrawn:
lo, our disrupt dominion
and mountains solemn in the dawn;

hard paths that chase the dayspring's white,
and glooms that hold the nether heat:
oh, strange the world upheaved from night,
oh, dread the life before our feet!

36. CHRISTOPHER BRENNAN

My heart was wandering in the sands,
a restless thing, a scorn apart;
Love set his fire in my hands;
I clasped the flame unto my heart.

Surely, I said, my heart shall turn
one fierce delight of pointed flame;
and in that holocaust shall burn
its old unrest and scorn and shame:

surely my heart the heavens at last
shall storm with fiery orisons,
and know, enthroned in the vast,
the fervid peace of molten suns.

The flame that feeds upon my heart
fades or flares, by wild winds controll'd:
my heart still walks a thing apart,
my heart is restless as of old.

37. CHRISTOPHER BRENNAN

What of the battles I would win?
alas! their glory is unheard:
the wind of song wakes not their din
wandering in shadowy glens unstirr'd.

— And the great sorrows that I dream'd?
not all unscathed I thought to rise
high in the dateless dawn, redeem'd,
and bare before eternal eyes.

— And is it then the end of dream?
O heart, that long'd for splendid woe,
our shame to endure this dire extreme
of joy we scorned so long ago!

Nationalism, Politics, and Society

EDITOR'S NOTE

Politics and concepts of nationhood were major topics of interest in the 1890s for several reasons. One was the growing pressure for a federation of the Australian states. A sense of Australian nationalism had grown steadily during the nineteenth century and by 1890 the time seemed ripe for it to be enshrined in political reality. A National Australasian Convention was held in Sydney in 1891 and prepared a draft constitution. Though the economic and industrial upheavals of the time made progress slow, they also underlined some of the disadvantages of the present state of disunity. Further conventions and referendums later in the decade established the popular nature of federation. The Commonwealth of Australia came into being as a single nation on the first day of the twentieth century, 1 January 1901.

Some writers, such as William Gay (49), George Essex Evans (52), and James Brunton Stephens (53) saw federation as the crowning achievement of Australian nationalism. Others were less sure, pointing out that social and economic anomalies remained whatever forms political structures took. Daley, Lawson, and O'Dowd at various times suggested that Australia as a republic would be a more equitable place than as a British dominion. Indeed, the relationship between the colonies and the mother country had been a topic of literary interest throughout the decade. At the time of the Sudan War in the late 1880s John O'Hara had called upon his countrymen to hasten to England's aid. "In the hour of Britain's peril / Shall we falter", he asked (42). John Farrell too stressed the necessity of continuing strong links between colonies and home country (44). Daley and Lawson, on the other hand, pointed out that both England and Australia were class-ridden societies where the lot of working people left much to be desired (45 and 46).

Indeed, if the federation debate caused Australians to pause and consider their character and role as a nation, the nineties also marked an increased interest in politics generally. The failure of the strikes of 1890–94 led to an upsurge of support for the labour parties and a widespread belief in the efficacy of social and economic change through the actions of elected parliaments. Yet the strikes, and the ensuing political action, stressed the underlying class hostility of Australian society. "Price Warung"'s stories of the early convict days (40) were seen by many as a reflection of a basic class division in Australia which the years since the abolition of transportation had done little to erase. Lawson and O'Dowd (41 and 50) were sceptical of the potential achievement of political action and spoke of a struggle still to come. In "The Union Buries Its Dead" (51), one of the major pieces from the nineties, Lawson suggested that mateship and unionism were vulnerable loyalties, even in the bush.

38. BERNARD O'DOWD

AUSTRALIA

Last sea-thing dredged by sailor Time from Space,
Are you a drift Sargasso, where the West
In halcyon calm rebuilds her fatal nest?
Or Delos of a coming Sun-God's race?
Are you for Light, and trimmed, with oil in place,
Or but a Will o' Wisp on marshy quest?
A new demesne for Mammon to infest?
Or lurks millennial Eden 'neath your face?

The cenotaphs of species dead elsewhere
That in your limits leap and swim and fly,
Or trail uncanny harp-strings from your trees,
Mix omens with the auguries that dare
To plant the Cross upon your forehead sky,
A virgin helpmate Ocean at your knees.

39. ARTHUR ADAMS

THE AUSTRALIAN

Once more this Autumn-earth is ripe.
Parturient of another type.

While with the Past old nations merge
His foot is on the Future's verge;

They watch him, as they huddle pent,
Striding a spacious continent.

Above the level desert's marge
Looming in his aloofness large.

No flower with fragile sweetness graced —
A lank weed wrestling with the waste.

Pallid of face and gaunt of limb,
The sweetness withered out of him.

Sombre, indomitable, wan,
The juices dried, the glad youth gone.

A little weary from his birth;
His laugh the spectre of a mirth.

Bitter beneath a bitter sky.
To Nature he has no reply.

Wanton, perhaps, and cruel. Yes,
Is not his sun more merciless?

Joy has such niggard dole to give,
He laughs, a child, just glad to live.

So drab and neutral is his day
He gleans a splendour in the grey,

And from his life's monotony
He lifts a subtle melody.

When earth so poor a banquet makes
His pleasures at a gulp he takes.

The feast is his to the last crumb:
Drink while he can . . . the drought will come.

His heart a sudden tropic flower,
He loves and loathes within an hour.

Yet you who by the pools abide,
Judge not the man who swerves aside.

He sees beyond your hazy fears;
He roads the desert of the years.

Rearing his cities in the sand.
He builds where even God has banned.

With green a continent he crowns.
And stars a wilderness with towns.

His gyves of steel the great plain wears:
With paths the distances he snares.

A child who takes a world for toy,
To build a nation, or destroy.

His childish features frozen stern,
A nation's task he has to learn.

From feeble tribes to federate
One splendid peace-encompassed State.

But if there be no goal to reach?
The way lies open, dawns beseech!

Enough that he lay down his load
A little further on the road.

So, toward undreamt-of destinies
He slouches down the centuries.

40. "PRICE WARUNG"

A Day with Governor Arthur*

Colonel George Arthur is sitting in an arm-chair in his study. The deep whirr of a clock (by Dent, London: you can see it, if not hear it, today in a Hobart public office) as it strikes the hour of ten is audible. He is always punctual is Governor Arthur, Lieutenant-Governor of Vandemonia— always has been—always will be. There are some men whose past unerringly foretells their future. Arthur is one of these men. When, as representative of British Majesty, he flogged a woman in his West Indian principality, he concluded his order for the punishment with the word "punctually". When he signs a death-warrant now, he hands it to the Clerk of Council with the remark, "Let the warrant be obeyed punctually". When his doctor tells him in the course of a few years that Death will wait upon him after the expiration of an hour, you may depend upon it Sir George, as he will be then, will simply request the medical man to present his compliments to the gentleman with the scythe, and desire him to be punctual. And as he is in precept so he is in practice.

At the first stroke of ten, then, His Excellency sits him down, and begins the day's routine. It is an "off-day"—that

* This narrative is mainly founded upon conversations with a prominent official—he died only the other day—who was for some years immediately associated with Colonel Arthur. Documentary evidence is, in addition, extant for nearly every statement made in the course of the tale, and the words put into the mouth of the characters are mere paraphrases of utterances of their originals. The "police reports" and convict "records" quoted are authentic in every particular; "Longden's" letter is that of a veritable convict. In the wording of the Executioner's Oath, the author has followed his informant instead of transcribing another form which he has in his possession, which, however, does not differ very materially from the former. "The Sheriff's bidding", which concludes the administration of the oath, was uttered, it is asserted, on as recent an occasion in England as the appointment of that late honoured servant of the State, Calcraft.

is to say, His Excellency does not this morning propose to do his Executive Councillors the pleasure of going through the form of conferring with them upon points as to which he has already made up his mind. Consequently, there being no Executive Council to bother him, he proceeds to act as the Executive.

We are going to spend the day with him. It is very rude of us, no doubt, as we have not been invited. And particularly rude, inasmuch as we know that on the rare occasions that the Governor departs from his repose of manner it is to consign all scribblers to the nethermost abode of lost souls. Frank Goddard, convict, otherwise, "Frank the Poet", peopled hell with penal officials. Governor Arthur peopled *his* hell with journalists.

❅   ❅   ❅

It is a spare-framed, thin-faced, medium-sized man who sits in the Governor's chair; clean-shaven, save for a tinge of greyish whisker; with steely-grey eyes that look with a critical disbelief in everything except the System; with a rasp in the voice. The lines at the corners of the drawn-down lips spell "Martinet"; the wrinkles of the brow and the crevices between the eyebrows tell that he is a precisian. At this present moment he is supreme over the destinies of 32,000 human beings, and he looks capable of dealing justly with 32,000 blocks of pine or gum-wood. That, possibly, is why he is Lieutenant-Governor of His Britannic Majesty's colony and dependency of Van Dieman's Land. A man with a heart would have been out of place in that chair.

❅   ❅   ❅

He touches a bell—twice. Mr. J. Fubster, Comptroller-General of Convicts, enters, bows deferentially, and is motioned to a chair.

"Good-morning, Mr. Comptroller!"

A soft "Good-morning, your Excellency" is breathed by Fubster. He is at liberty to begin now with business—and to seat himself.

"This day's business, your Excellency, is applications for Tickets for November last."

"Proceed, Mr. Comptroller!"

Standing up and clearing his throat, the Comptroller

began: "Memorial No. 666, Police No. 699, James Melrose, per *Malabar*, Middlesex Sessions, 30th June, 182–, life; Hobart Town, 5th August, 182–, seven years, same date, seven years; total term of transportation, life and fourteen years. Employed by Mrs. C. Wade, and recommended for ticket by her. Transported for burglary. His gaol report: 'In Newgate before', and his hulk report was 'orderly'. He stated this offence, breaking into a house. Colonial convictions are as follows:—August 5, 182–, by Supreme Court, stealing a pair of boots; plea, guilty; sentence, seven years' transportation to Macquarie Harbour. Same date and court, stealing soap; plea, guilty; sentence, seven years' transportation to Macquarie Harbour. March 27, 1827, exchanging his hat with prisoner who was about to abscond, 50 lashes. June 27, 182–, destroying his shirt, 25 lashes. October 28, 182–, not accomplishing his weekly task of work, 18 lashes. February 14, 1832, ordered 50 lashes by employer for disrespectful conduct and insolence to Miss Ann Wade, 50 lashes, and returned to service. November 20, 1832, drunk, admonished."

"Who signs?"

"Mr. Muster-Master Mason, your Excellency."

"What do you recommend?"

"I cannot recommend, sir."

"Quite right, Mr. Comptroller. There seems a hiatus in his record between 182–, and 1832. There must be some mistake there. It is impossible that a man of this desperate character should have committed no offences for several years!"

"That's what *I* think, your Excellency."

"Reprimand the record clerk——"

"The record clerk is a transport, sir."

"A transport! And to make such a serious omission! It must be intentional, Mr. Comptroller. Have him punished, sir—send him to the chain-gang."

"May I suggest, sir, that I should merely dock his allowances and severely caution him? He's a very useful writer, sir, on the whole."

"Oh, in that case, Mr. Comptroller, punish him as you suggest. And note, please, that this ticket is refused."

And so was Mr. James Melrose's chance of obtaining temporary freedom put back for at least six, and probably twelve months. On the hypothesis, as likely as not entirely erroneous, that the record clerk had made a serious mistake in transcribing, from the registers, on No. 699's report parchment the debits against his name, that perverse son of the System was doomed to a continued period of slavery. What to precisian Colonel Arthur, and what to disciplinarian Fubster, was it that the transport might be rendered desperate by the non-success of his mighty effort to win a "ticket" by good conduct? To the Men of the Régime it should have been easy enough to have read between the lines of the record. A man naturally of weak disposition, made worse by unspeakable surroundings and petty tyrannies—with impulses towards good even at Macquarie Harbour (witness that exchange of hats)—then coming under a master or mistress of more than average kindness of heart, whom he would, in the intervals of good conduct, brave by an occasional act of insolence or insubordination—that was this character obviously to men who understood the System.

Now, Colonel Arthur and Factotum Fubster professed to know the System. They knew, however, but the one side of it. The gap in No. 699's record was to them nothing but a convict-writer's error. That it could be accounted for by Melrose's abstinence from ill-doing—pooh! impossible! And so No. 699 was "put back".

*   *   *

"Next!"

"Memorial No. 667. Cole, Richard, Lancaster Assizes, 22nd April, 182–, life. Application recommended by Mr. J. England, J.A. Jackson, Esq., J. Simpson, Esq., and Mr. R. Court. Now employed in Freed Police, Campbell Town. Transported for stealing from the person; gaol report, 'twice convicted before'; hulk report, 'good'. Stated this offence, pocket-picking; denies having been convicted before. Colonial convictions: November 2, 182–, Supreme Court, aiding and abetting in assault on a woman, not guilty. January 11, 182–, Magistrate Fisher, neglect of duty for the last three days, 50 lashes, and 3rd class. February 8, 182–, absent from his gang, between 10 and 11 o'clock this day, 25 lashes. April 23, 182–, disobedience of orders and other improper conduct, 25 lashes. February 3, 182–, W. Abel, magistrate, assault, 25 lashes. March 10, 182–, same magistrate, threatening and abuse, six months' chain-gang and return to his master. June 18, 182–, chain-gang overseer, for being in state of intoxication at muster, sentenced him to 21 days' additional chain-gang. March 11, 182–, Abel, magistrate, neglect of duty, one month of irons at New Norfolk. March 31, 182–, in Public Works Gang, very riotous conduct, and assaulting watchman; transported to penal settlement for two years. June 16, 182–, by penitentiary superintendent, for reporting himself as sick, and not having anything the matter with him; reprimanded. December 26, 183–, by superior officer of Field Police, neglect of duty; fined 10s."

"Who signs?"

"Muster-Master Mason."

"And your recommendation is——?"

"I regret, your Excellency, that this man has been allowed to join the police. The circumstances attending the assault on the woman for which he was tried are still strongly in my recollection, as it occurred in my own neighbourhood."

"But he was found not guilty, did you not say?"

"Yes, sir, but——"

"Then, why say anything about the offence?" demanded the just Governor. He was always just was Arthur! A desire to be just was his strong point, he used to say.

"Apart from that altogether though, Mr. Comptroller," the Governor went on, as Fubster remained silent, "the applicant must be refused. The man seems a most improper subject for the police; but, being in it, the opportunity may be afforded him to prove that his is a reformed character."

"Yes, your Excellency. Shall I minute that observation?"

"Certainly. Now the next."

And, delaying just a minute to record the fact that Richard Cole, No. 473, per *Elphinstone*, would be allowed to derive further advantage from the moral associations of the Freed Police, the Comptroller-General passed to another of the current applications for tickets.

"Memorial No. 668, Police No. 1,701, Henfrey, Simon, tried at Nottingham, March 182–, life. Recommended by

Messrs. Hill, Gunning, and Butcher. Employed by Messrs.
Bignell and Hill. Transported for sheep-stealing. Gaol
report, 'not known before; good in gaol'. Hulk's report,
'orderly'. Stated his offence, sheep-stealing. Hath no
colonial offence recorded. Mason signs."

"No offence?" queried His Excellency. "Shall we give
him a ticket?"

"Well, sir, I think not. He has not served the regulated
period," rejoined the Comptroller-General.

"Refused, then!" said the Governor. And No. 1,701 was
"put back" also.

"Memorial No. 669, Police No. 2,693. Porter, John.
Tried at Stafford, 17th October, 182–. Seven years. Recommended by J. T. Gellibrand, Esq., who employs him. Transported for stealing from the person. Gaol report: 'An incorrigible youth; has been many times in prison, and connected with Wolverhampton thieves. Orderly in gaol'.
Stated his offence 'Stealing five shillings from a young
woman; twice for leaving my master'. Hath no colonial offences on record. The Muster-Master signs."

"What do you say, Mr. Comptroller?"

"This, your Excellency, is another case where applicant
has not served the regulated period."

"The transport is incorrigible, eh? Still, we must encourage him to hope, conditional on improvement. Refused
at present, but as he brought so bad a character, it is gratify-
ing to perceive that his conduct has been uniformly correct.
Grant him a ticket on the King's birthday. We must never
shut out hope altogether from the convicts, Mr. Comptroller. That has always been my policy, as you know. And I am
stating it at great length to Lord Goderich by the outgoing
mail. Are there many more applications?"

"Some fifty, your Excellency. The next has some peculiar
circumstances connected with it, sir. The applicant, of fair
conduct enough, obtained his master's frank to the cover of
the application, which was directed, of course, to the
Muster-Master, and then pasted a slip over the address.
Upon the slip there was a British address, and inside the
form he enclosed a letter for an English friend!"

"The rascal!" exclaimed His Excellency. "And how was
the fraud detected?"

"Well, sir, the ignorant fellow thought his master's signature would frank the letter out of the colony, as well as within it! That not being the case, the Post Office stopped the letter, sent it back to Captain Hepburn, the transport's master, and, of course, the thing was discovered."

"Then how does the application come before me? An application from such a man—why, 'tis scandalous!"

"So I remarked, your Excellency, but Captain Hepburn said he was prepared to overlook the wrong because of the man's ingenuity and the good tone of his letter. I have the letter here. Shall I read it, sir?"

His Excellency assented, and Mr. Fubster read this:—

St. Pauls Plains, Van Demans Land,
May 6th.

Dear George—This is now the first time that I have had the opportunity of writing to you since my arrival in this Forighn Land you desired me to write and Let you Know how I am doing. I must first tell you of my voyage across. There was Three Hundred of us poor fellows confined in one Deck 6 in a bed with very little to eat or Drink but I had better luck than the rest for I had a situation on board to serve out stores to the men so I Got on very well we had a very Good voyage of four Months we were all sent to a place called a tench and there we were signed off to Defferent masters I am cook at Mr. Hebron Esq Dear George you cannot forme any Idea of the Troble I have been I had to wear Heavy Irons on my Legs for 3 months because I should not run away this is an aweful country for you dont Know when you are safe for there are men prowling about who stile themselves Bushrangers who when they are Hungry come to our Huts and tye our Hands and then proseed to rob and plunder the House and if we offer any resistance they will Shoot you dead on the spot they rob the House and then make one of us carry the spoil into the bush. there was three at large last week who have been doing Horrible deeds among which they went into a publick House in the interior of this County not far from where there. Dear Friend I have that Bible still which your beloved parrent gave me and every time I look at it my heart Bleads to think how happy and comfortable I was then. Remember me to your kind and affectionate Wife & Family & Mrs Barton, and Tom tell him from me to be steady and industrous and not to be led away by the girls as they will shure to bring him ruin. Give my love to all the family ann I hope and trust they will forgive me for my ingratitude to them after the

Kindness they had shone to me Dear George would you be so Kind as to go to Mr. Greenwood for me and remember me Kindly to Him & Family and tell him were I am as he promised to do a little for me ask him to ask my uncle to send me an accordian as I think It might be of service to me here as there is none in the county, I have seen. Remember me to all my Friends that inquier after me Dear George write to me as soon as you can as I long to here from you how things are going on at home. I hope you will pardon me for Troubleing you with a letter But I Know you to be a Friend that I can Trust When you write to me Direct to Capt. Hepburn Esq. Rays Hill St Pauls Plains Van Demans Land

I have nothing more to say at Present May God Prosper you and your Family Adieu

    D.G. be shure and wite   A. S. Longden

    N.B. The master I am With is Capt. Hepburn, Esq. J.P. Brother-in-Law to Thos. Hosie Esq. Manager at Millers Wharf, London.

"Well!" exclaimed Arthur as Fubster concluded the reading. "And in face of that letter, the man's master recommends him for a ticket! Remove the employer from the list of eligibles, and send the man to the chain-gang."

"Yes, your Excellency, but—ah, may I suggest, sir, that the Captain has great—er—home influence?"

"H'm, ah! Perhaps the case, then, as regards the master will be met by a respectful letter pointing out that discipline will be subverted if he displays the like tolerance in the future. Why, he actually compounds a felony—obtaining a postal frank by false pretences is a felony, is it not?"

The Comptroller hesitates in his reply, and then begs to suggest that as the law is not quite explicit on the point, the question should be referred to the Crown-Solicitor. "'Tis an unusual offence, your Excellency—can scarcely have been anticipated by the Honourable the Council."

"Nevertheless, Mr. Comptroller, once done the deed will be repeated. Mr. Solicitor shall prepare a draft-clause making the offence felony."

"And the man, sir—the transport Longden?"

"I leave him to your jurisdiction, Comptroller. But, of course, ticket refused, and, I should think, the chain-gang."

And at a later period of the day Transport Longden is awarded, in his absence, twelve months' gang "for abusing his master's confidence".

*   *   *

The ingenious Longden having been thus helped forward to the next stage to perdition, Comptroller-General Fubster passed to other applications.

"A woman, your Excellency. Memorial No. 690. Ship No. 108, per *Fairlie*, Louisa Newnes; place of trial not known and transport refuses to state, but sentence, she says, 14 years——"

"Make a note, Mr. Comptroller, to ascertain how it is that the ship's indent was so imperfect. I must draw the Colonial Secretary's attention to the circumstance, and cause the Indent-clerk to be punished. What was the ship's captain about, to start with imperfect papers?"

"The ship started with papers complete, sir, but a male transport—the *Fairlie* was a double-classer,* sir—acting as surgeon's clerk, dropped all the papers overboard, with a 16-lb. shot attached."

"Mr. Comptroller! how is it I never heard of this before?" In his wrath, the Governor rose from his chair. "And why was not the Surgeon-Superintendent punished for employing a convict-writer contrary to Regulation in that case made and provided?"

"'Twas in Governor Sorell's time, sir! And he thought the least said soonest mended, particularly as the writer was, sir—dead, sir, when the ship arrived!"

"Dead? Oh, was that the yard-arm case?"

"Yes, your Excellency!"

"Ah, I recollect now. And was nothing done to the Surgeon?"

"Oh, yes, sir. We were short of doctors at the time, and so he was put on the permanent staff. It was Dr. Burleigh, sir!"

"Burleigh, was it? A good officer and a careful one now, whatever he may have been in the past. But proceed, Mr. Comptroller."

"She is recommended by Mr. J. Hutchinson and A. Turnbull, Esq. She says her gaol report was bad, and that she was capitally convicted at Newgate, receiving sentence of death, but commuted to two years in the penitentiary and fourteen

* "Double-classer": A ship conveying both male and female transports.

beyond seas. States offence as stealing silver teapot. Colonial report: Theft, committed for trial."

"You recommend?"

"Yes, your Excellency. The female is at present in the House of Correction under sentence. But the Surgeon wishes her to take the situation of nurse at the hospital, as she is skilful and kind-hearted."

"Under what sentence, did you say?"

The Comptroller re-scans the parchment and the application-form, but the information is not given in either document.

"Unstated, sir, I'm sorry to say!"

"Unstated, Mr. Comptroller! Is this a way to prepare a report for me? Her record says, 'Committed for trial'. How was she then disposed of?"

"She must have been sentenced, sir!" The Comptroller sees he is "in for it", and not enjoying the Colonel in one of his black moods, mentally resolves to make somebody suffer, "And the convict-writer must have omitted to enter the conviction."

"See that he's punished, Mr. Comptroller. And reprimand the Free Clerk in charge of the office!"

"Yes, your Excellency. We must make an example! So much depends on the records being accurately kept. What are your orders as to this woman, sir? The doctor wishes her services particularly."

"No, in this case I must refuse! Appointment to a nursing post would be an indulgence the woman does not merit. She herself says her home record was bad, and most likely her transportation-sentence was life, and that she is lying when she says it was for fourteen years only. No indulgence!"

Thus it was nearly always. A transport's statement against himself or herself was almost invariably accepted by the Authorities, but he or she was never believed when there was a possibility of the statement being in the transport's own favour.

Thus, too, was it generally in the matter of negligently-written-up records. It was a convict-writer who was punished; it was the Free Clerk, or the other official, who was really the offending person, who got off scot-free. Which was just; for a convict-writer was by virtue of the fact liable to punishment. The Régime did not recognise convict-writers, and, indeed, distinctly prohibited their employment; and, therefore, if they consented to be employed, they disobeyed "the Regulation in that case made and provided". The circumstance that they dare not refuse to be employed when so directed by an authority—say, the Governor or the Comptroller-General—went, of course, for nothing. If there was one thing more than another the System was partial to, it was the construction of dilemmas; and though the transport might object to being impaled on one horn, there was always the other at his convenience.

* * *

While we have been making this digression, Colonel Arthur has been refusing more and more applications, occasionally, it must be said, varying the process by an approval. One "Approved" to ten "Refused", that was about the average.

The list ended, the Governor condescended to consult the inferior (though still potent) official as to the terms of a despatch he was drafting to Viscount Goderich, Secretary of State for the Colonies.

"I chiefly desire, Mr. Comptroller, your opinion on this portion. It is with reference to the special and educated convicts, and their proposed treatment at Port Arthur. I am loth to abandon Macquarie Harbour as a Penal Settlement—we have derived great advantage from it—but the filling up of the bar is rendering navigation dangerous. So I have made up my mind to direct the abandonment of the Harbour, and to devote my attention to all the measures best calculated to render Tasman's Peninsula, which really seems to have been designed by Providence for a penitentiary, a perfect institution. Do you follow me, Mr. Comptroller?"

"Oh, most readily, sir. And if I may be permitted to say so, if anyone can devise a perfect penal establishment I am sure 'tis your Excellency!"

"Yes, Mr. Comptroller, I do not doubt my success, if I can depend upon the willing cooperation of able and experienced officers like yourself!"

"That, your Excellency, I need scarcely trouble to assure you of. The Staff are only too proud to have the opportunity of working under so brilliant and—er—h'm—philanthropic an administrator! You were saying about the specials, sir?"

"Oh, yes", and the pleased Governor, who, with all his strength of character, was never to be offended by the most fulsome of compliments, especially when they alluded to his philanthropy, went on to read what he had written.

"This is what I say to his Lordship in recommending the despatch to Port Arthur of this special class. 'The educated class are at present the link by which the free and the bond are so amalgamated as to make the distinction betwixt slavery and freedom less marked than it ought to be. It is desirable there should be no such mingling—a man should be either free or bond, and be treated as such.'"

"Very good, if I may say so, your Excellency. Most admirably put."

The Governor continued: "'I have long disapproved of the employment of convict clerks under any circumstances, and have taken every prudent means of limiting their numbers, for I am convinced that convict discipline cannot be considered perfect until every special is treated as an ordinary convict.'"

"That's true, your Excellency."

"'For if one receive indulgence irregularly, or be placed in any easy situation, enabling him to assume a respectable appearance, the System is broken in upon, and a single representation to his friends in England will be sufficient to deprive transportation of much of its terrors. Criminals do not, when writing to their friends, dwell upon the hardships they suffer, but rather delight in holding up the bright side of the picture.'"

"Quite accurate, your Excellency, quite!" Yet Longden's letter was before them!

"'As it appears specials dread transportation less than any other class, I have made arrangements for their deportation, upon arrival here, to Tasman's Peninsula, should such be the pleasure of His Majesty's Government, where they will be deprived even of the hope of eluding by artifice the miseries they have drawn upon themselves.' There, how will that do, Mr. Comptroller?"

"It must carry conviction to the Imperial Government, your Excellency, of the wisdom of your proposed step."

"Yes, I think it will. And the Right Honourable the

Secretary of State will not fail to appreciate an argument I propose to communicate unofficially, that the presence in the streets of this city of special convicts, who, for the most part, come from the upper order of society, is a direct inducement to the circulation of those revolutionary ideas which are so subversive of Law, Order and Society. How can the lower classes retain respect for the upper orders if members of the latter are seen walking public streets under the convict ban?"

"Very true, your Excellency, very true!"

"Then you agree, Mr. Comptroller, generally with my views?"

"Oh, yes! your Excellency, I can suggest no improvement."

"Then send the clerk who is your best penman to me in the morning. It is a most important despatch, as it quite alters our System, and I must have a clear copy for Downing Street made with the utmost care."

"Shall the clerk be 'free' or 'bond', sir?"

"Oh, your best."

"Then the ablest man I have, your Excellency, is Convict-writer Dallas".

"Well, let him be here at ten punctually tomorrow. And now," rising as he spoke, "this completes your business with me for the day?"

"Yes, sir, with the exception of one little matter—the executioner's oath."

"Ah! I was forgetting! Is the man in attendance? If so, produce him."

* * *

Convict Richard Johnson, successor to Dougherty in the onerous and well-paid post of hangman to His Majesty's Government in Vandemonia, had shown a tendency of late to partiality in the performance of his duties. After the last but two "dropping off", it was rumoured that one of the criminals who had, it was supposed, been hurried into the next world had been resuscitated within the time prescribed for the suspension of the body. The rumour as to this occurence had not reached the ears of the Authorities for three or four weeks after the ceremony; and owing to the lapse of that time, and to the admixture of quicklime with the bodies

which participated in the rites, it had been deemed inex-
pedient to attempt exhumation. The Authorities, though
content to let the matter—and the bodies—rest, thought it,
however, advisable to prevent a further instance of the like
partiality, and concluded that there was no better way of
securing their end than by imposing what had for some
years dropped into disuse—the executioner's oath.

Mr. Johnson, being so important a functionary, and the
occasion being so novel, it was thought well to impress him
by administering the oath in the overawing presence of the
Governor himself. The formula was to be the ancient
English one, and the incidents of the scene were framed after
the same pattern. Only, instead of the Testament being
tendered to the Executioner by the Sheriff, as was the old
English practice, the Comptroller-General, being the convict's nominal master and the man to whom Johnson was in
the last resort responsible, was to administer the oath.

Johnson was ushered in. He brought with him, pursuant
to instructions, a bag.

He saluted, and in obedience to a motion of Mr. Fubster's
hand, arranged the contents of the bag on a table. Two pairs
of handcuffs, a set of double leg-irons with bazils and
centre-link complete, and a new fifteen-foot rope, gathered
in a coil. A white cap and a black cap completed the number
of the dread insignia.

"You are Richard Johnson, per ship *Mangles?*" demanded
the Comptroller.

The executioner pulled his forelock.

"You are the public executioner of His Majesty's Colony
and Dependency of Van Dieman's Land?"

Johnson scraped his right foot and bent his head.

"Hitherto you have been unsworn, but it has been
thought necessary by his Excellency the Governor that you
should take an oath for the faithful, exact, true and impar-
tial performance of your duties. Are you willing to take that
obligation?"

"Yes, y'r Honour!"

The Comptroller-General lifted a Testament—there were
always copies available in every public office; oaths were
taken at every hour of the day—and, opening the book at
one of the Gospels, bade Johnson place his left hand on the

rope, and take the book in his right.

"Now, Johnson, follow me!" As the Comptroller read these words from a slip of blue paper, Johnson recited them after him:—

"I, Richard Johnson, Transport, acting under a ticket-of-leave as present executioner, do willingly undertake to well, faithfully, exactly and truly perform the duties appertaining to the office of the Common Executioner of His Majesty's Colony of Van Dieman's Land, and do now vow and make oath that I will carry out and fulfil such duties as the Law may direct upon the bodies and person of every felon committed to my charge without fear or favour, though the body and person be that of friend or kin, my father or my mother, my sister or my brother, my wife or my child, or other bone of my bone, or of other flesh of my flesh, So help me, God!"

Then he kissed the book.

The Comptroller turned to His Excellency. "Must the—ah—old command be given, your Excellency?"

The Governor motioning assent, the Comptroller, raising his right hand, and speaking with as much harshness as he could throw into his voice, cried—

"GET THEE HENCE, WRETCH!"

41. HENRY LAWSON

THE STAR OF AUSTRALASIA

We boast no more of our bloodless flag, that rose from a
    nation's slime;
Better a shred of a deep-dyed rag from the storms of the olden
    time.
From grander clouds in our "peaceful skies" than ever were
    there before
I tell you the Star of the South shall rise — in the lurid clouds
    of war.
It ever must be while blood is warm and the sons of men
    increase;
Forever the nations rose in storm, to rot in a deadly peace.
There comes a point that we will not yield, no matter if right
    or wrong,
And man will fight on the battle-field while passion and pride
    are strong —
So long as he will not kiss the rod, and his stubborn spirit
    sours,
And the scorn of Nature and curse of God are heavy on peace
    like ours.

There are boys out there by the western creeks, who hurry
    away from school
To climb the sides of the breezy peaks or dive in the shaded
    pool,
Who'll stick to their guns when the mountains quake to the
    tread of a mighty war,
And fight for Right or a Grand Mistake as men never fought
    before;
When the peaks are scarred and the sea-walls crack till the
    furthest hills vibrate,
And the world for a while goes rolling back in a storm of love
    and hate.

There are boys today in the city slum and the home of wealth
    and pride
Who'll have one home when the storm is come, and fight for it
    side by side,

Who'll hold the cliffs 'gainst the armoured hells that batter a
    coastal town,
Or grimly die in a hail of shells when the walls come crashing
    down.
And many a pink-white baby girl, the queen of her home
    today,
Shall see the wings of the tempest whirl the mist of our dawn
    away —
Shall live to shudder and stop her ears to the thud of the
    distant gun,
And know the sorrow that has no tears when a battle is lost
    and won —
As a mother or wife in the years to come, will kneel, wild-
    eyed and white,
And pray to God in her darkened home for the "men in the
    fort tonight".

But, oh! if the cavalry charge again as they did when the
    world was wide,
Twill be grand in the ranks of a thousand men in that glorious
    race to ride
And strike for all that is true and strong, for all that is grand
    and brave,
And all that ever shall be, so long as man has a soul to save,
He must lift the saddle, and close his "wings", and shut his
    angels out,
And steel his heart for the end of things, who'd ride with a
    stockman scout,
When the race is rode on the battle track, and the waning
    distance hums,
And the shelled sky shrieks or the rifles crack like stockwhip
    amongst the gums —
And the "straight" is reached and the field is "gapped" and
    the hoof-torn sward grows red
With the blood of those who are handicapped with iron and
    steel and lead;
And the gaps are filled, though unseen by eyes, with the spirit
    and with the shades
Of the world-wide rebel dead who'll rise and rush with the
    Bush Brigades.

All creeds and trades will have soldiers there — give every class
    its due —
And there'll be many a clerk to spare for the pride of the
    jackeroo.

They'll fight for honour and fight for love, and a few will
fight for gold,
For the devil below and for God above, as our fathers fought
of old;
And some half-blind with exultant tears, and some stiff-lipped,
stern-eyed,
For the pride of a thousand after-years and the old eternal
pride;
The soul of the world they will feel and see in the chase and
the grim retreat —
They'll know the glory of victory — and the grandeur of
defeat.

The South will wake to a mighty change ere a hundred years
are done
With arsenals west of the mountain range and every spur its
gun.
And many a rickety son of a gun, on the tides of the future
tossed,
Will tell how battles were really won that History says were
lost,
Will trace the field with his pipe, and shirk the facts that are
hard to explain,
As grey old mates of the diggings work the old ground over
again —
How "this was our centre, and this a redoubt, and that was a
scrub in the rear,
"And this was the point where the push held out, and the
enemy's lines was here."

They'll tell the tales of the nights before and the tales of the
ship and fort
Till the sons of Australia take to war as their fathers took to
sport,
Their breath come deep and their eyes grow bright at the tales
of our chivalry,
And every boy will want to fight, no matter what cause it
be —
When the children run to the doors and cry: "Oh, mother, the
troops are come!"
And every heart in the town leaps high at the first loud thud
of the drum.
They'll know, apart from its mystic charm, what music is at
last,

When, proud as a boy with a broken arm, the regiment
marches past.
And the variest wreck in the drink-fiend's clutch, no matter
how low or mean,
Will feel, when he hears the march, a touch of the man that he
might have been.

And fools, when the fiends of war are out and the city skies
aflame,
Will have something better to talk about than a sister or
brother's shame,
Will have something nobler to do by far than to jest at a
friend's expense,
Or to blacken a name in a public bar or over a backyard fence,
And this you learn from the libelled past, though its methods
were somewhat rude —
A nation's born where the shells fall fast, or its lease of life
renewed.
We in part atone for the ghoulish strife, for the crimes of the
peace we boast,
And the better part of a people's life in the storm comes
uppermost.

The self-same spirit that drives the man to the depths of drink
and crime
Will do the deeds in the heroes' van that live till the end of
time.
The living death in the lonely bush, the greed of the selfish
town,
And even the creed of the outlawed push is chivalry — upside
down.
'Twill be while ever our blood is hot, while ever the world
goes wrong,
The nations rise in a war, to rot in a peace that lasts too long.
And southern nation and southern state, aroused from their
dream of ease,
Must sign in the Book of Eternal Fate their stormy histories.

42. JOHN BERNARD O'HARA

AUSTRALIA'S CALL TO ARMS

Sons of ocean-girdled islands,
    Where the southern billows sigh,
Wake! arise! the dread Bellona
    Speeds her chariot through the sky;
Yea, the troubled star of danger
    On Britannia shineth down, —
Wake! arise! maintain her glory
    And renown, and renown!

In the hour of Britain's peril
    Shall we falter, while the fires
Still are glowing on our altars
    From the ashes of our sires?
Ho! brave hearts, for Britain's honour,
    For the lustre of her crown,
Wake! arise! maintain her glory
    And renown, and renown!

Ye are children of a nation,
    Ye are scions of the sires
That of old were in the vanguard
    Of the world's wide empires!
With the spirit of your fathers,
    With the fulness of their fame,
Wake! arise! maintain the honour
    Of her name, of her name!

Long to Britain may "the crimson
    Thread of kinship" bind our wings! —
Crimson thread that slowly slackens
    As the newer race upsprings:
Sons of heroes, men of courage
    That reverse could never tame,
Wake! arise! maintain the glory
    Of her name, of her name!

See! the star of ancient Britain,
    That hath never known decline,
By your valour lit up newly,
    With a glow of fiercer shine,
O'er the burning sands of Afric,
    With your loyalty aflame;
Once again maintain the glory
    Of her name, of her name!

43. HENRY LAWSON

FREEDOM ON THE WALLABY

Our fathers toiled for bitter bread
  While idlers thrived beside them;
But food to eat and clothes to wear
  Their native land denied them.
They left their native land in spite
  Of royalties' regalia,
And so they came, or if they stole
  Were sent out to Australia.

They struggled hard to make a home,
  Hard grubbing 'twas and clearing.
They weren't troubled much with toffs
  When they were pioneering;
And now that we have made the land
  A garden full of promise,
Old greed must crook his dirty hand
  And come to take it from us.

But Freedom's on the Wallaby,
  She'll knock the tyrants silly,
She's going to light another fire
  And boil another billy.
We'll make the tyrants feel the sting
  Of those that they would throttle;
They needn't say the fault is ours
  If blood should stain the wattle.

44. JOHN FARRELL

AUSTRALIA TO ENGLAND

JUNE 22, 1897

What of the years of Englishmen?
　　What have they brought of growth and grace
Since mud-built London by its fen
　　Became the Briton's breeding-place?
What of the Village, where our blood
　　Was brewed by sires, half man, half brute,
In vessels of wild womanhood,
　　From blood of Saxon, Celt and Jute?

What are its gifts, this Harvest Home
　　Of English tilth and English cost,
Where fell the hamlet won by Rome
　　And rose the city that she lost?
O! terrible and grand and strange
　　Beyond all phantasy that gleams
When Hope, asleep, sees radiant Change
　　Come to her through the halls of dreams!

A heaving sea of life, that beats
　　Like England's heart of pride today,
And up from roaring miles of streets
　　Flings on the roofs its human spray;
And fluttering miles of flags aflow,
　　And cannon's voice, and boom of bell,
And seas of fire tonight, as though
　　A hundred cities flamed and fell;

While, under many a fair festoon
　　And flowering crescent, set ablaze
With all the dyes that English June
　　Can lend to deck a day of days,
And past where mart and palace rise,
　　And shrine and temple lift their spears,
Below five million misted eyes
　　Goes a gray Queen of Sixty Years —

Go lords, and servants of the lords
    Of earth, with homage on their lips,
And kinsmen carrying English swords,
    And offering England battle-ships;
And tribute-payers, on whose hands
    Their English fetters scarce appear;
And gathered round from utmost lands
    Ambassadors of Love and Fear!

Dim signs of greeting waved afar,
    Far trumpets blown and flags unfurled,
And England's name an Avatar
    Of light and sound throughout the world —
Hailed Empress among nations, Queen
    Enthroned in solemn majesty,
On splendid proofs of what has been,
    And presages of what will be!

For this your sons, foreseeing not
    Or heeding not, the aftermath,
Because their strenuous hearts were hot
    Went first on many a cruel path,
And, trusting first and last to blows,
    Fed death with such as would gainsay
Their instant passing, or oppose
    With talk of Right strength's right of way!

For this their names are on the stone
    Of mountain spires, and carven trees
That stand in flickering wastes unknown
    Wait with their dying messages;
When fire blasts dance with desert drifts
    The English bones show white below,
And, not so white, when summer lifts
    The counterpane of Yukon's snow.

Condemned by blood to reach for grapes
    That hand in sight, however high,
Beyond the smoke of Asian capes,
    The nameless, dauntless, dead ones lie;
And where Sierran morning shines
    On summits rolling out like waves,
By many a brow of royal pines
    The noisiest find quiet graves.

By lust of flesh and lust of gold,
    And depth of loins and hairy breadth
Of breast, and hands to take and hold,
    And boastful scorn of pain and death,
And something more of manliness
    Than tamer men, and growing shame
Of shameful things, and something less
    Of final faith in sword and flame —

By many a battle fought for wrong,
    And many a battle fought for right,
So have you grown august and strong,
    Magnificent in all men's sight —
A voice for which the kings have ears,
    A face the craftiest statesmen scan;
A mind to mould the after years,
    And mint the destinies of man!

Red sins were yours: the avid greed
    Of pirate fathers, smocked as Grace,
Sent Judas missioners to read
    Christ's Word to many a feebler race —
False priests of Truth who made their tryst
    At Mammon's shrine, and reft or slew —
Some hands you taught to pray to Christ
    Have prayed His curse to rest on you!

Your way has been to pluck the blade
    Too readily, and train the guns.
We here, apart and unafraid
    Of envious foes, are but your sons:
We stretched a heedless hand to smutch
    Our spotless flag with Murder's blight —
For one less sacrilegious touch
    God's vengeance blasted Uzza white!

You vaunted most of forts and fleets,
    And courage proved in battle-feasts,
The courage of the beast that eats
    His torn and quivering fellow-beasts;
Your pride of deadliest armament —
    What is it but the self-same dint
Of joy with which the Caveman bent
    To shape a bloodier axe of flint?

But praise to you, and more than praise
    And thankfulness, for some things done;
And blessedness, and length of days
    As long as earth shall last, or sun!
You first among the peoples spoke
    Sharp words and angry questionings
Which burst the bonds and shed the yoke
    That made your men the slaves of Kings!

You set and showed the whole world's school
    The lesson it will surely read,
That each one ruled has right to rule —
    The alphabet of Freedom's creed
Which slowly wins it proselytes
    And makes uneasier many a throne;
You taught them all to prate of Rights
    In language growing like your own!

And now your holiest and best
    And wisest dream of such a tie
As, holding hearts from East to West,
    Shall strengthen while the years go by:
And of a time when every man
    For every fellow-man will do
His kindliest, working by the plan
    God set him. May the dream come true!

And greater dreams! O Englishmen,
    Be sure the safest time of all
For even the mightiest State is when
    Not even the least desires its fall!
Make England stand supreme for aye,
    Because supreme for peace and good,
Warned well by wrecks of yesterday
    That strongest feet may slip in blood!

45. HENRY LAWSON

SECOND CLASS WAIT HERE

On surburban railway stations — you may see them as you
    pass —
There are signboards on the platforms saying "Wait here second
    class";
And to me the whirr and thunder and the cluck of running
    gear
Seem to be for ever saying, saying "Second class wait here" —
"Wait here second class,
"Second class wait here."
Seem to be for every saying, saying "Second class wait here".

And the second class were waiting in the days of serf and
    prince,
And the second class are waiting — they've been waiting ever
    since.
There are gardens in the background, and the line is bare and
    drear,
Yet they wait beneath a signboard, sneering "Second class
    wait here".

I have waited oft in winter, in the morning dark and damp,
When the asphalt platform glistened underneath the lonely
    lamp.
Ghastly on the brick-faced cutting "Sellum's Soap" and
    "Blower's Beer";
Ghastly on enamelled signboards with their "Second class wait
    here".

And the others seemed like burglars, slouched and muffled to
    the throats,
Standing round apart and silent in their shoddy overcoats,
And the wind among the wires, and the poplars bleak and bare,
Seemed to be for ever snarling, snarling "Second class wait
    there".

Out beyond the further suburb, 'neath a chimney stack alone,
Lay the works of Grinder Brothers, with a platform of their
    own;
And I waited there and suffered, waited there for many a
    year,
Slaved beneath a phantom signboard, telling our class to wait
    here.

Ah! a man must feel revengeful for a boyhood such as mine.
God! I hate the very houses near the workshop by the line;
And the smell of railway stations, and the roar of running gear,
And the scornful-seeming signboards, saying "Second class
    wait here".

There's a train with Death for driver, which is ever going past,
And there are no class compartments, and we all must go at
    last
To the long white jasper platform with an Eden in the rear;
And there won't be any signboards, saying "Second class wait
    here".

46. VICTOR DALEY

A TREAT FOR THE LONDON POOR

From St. Paul's Cathedral the return journey will be by way of Cheapside, London Bridge, the Borough, St. George's Circus, Westminster Bridge and back to the Palace. The poorer classes on the south side of the water will thus have an opportunity of seeing their Sovereign and witnessing the day's spectacle.

— Melbourne *Argus*

They will troop in loyal thousands from the putrid purlieus where
Foul Disease and Crime and Famine have their pestilential lair;
They will crawl from foetid alley, they will creep from courts obscene,
When they hear the joyous tidings of the passing of their Queen.
She has reigned — aloft, sublime —
Sixty years — let joy-bells chime!
And these God forgotten wretches were her subjects all the time!

They are hungry; they are ragged; they are gaunt and hollow-eyed;
But their frowsy bosoms palpitate with fine old British pride;
And they'll belt their rags in tighter, and they'll hoarsely cry "Hooray!"
When their good Queen's circus passes on Sexagenary Day.
O the thunder of the drums,
And the cry of "here she comes!"
Will be better than a breakfast to the natives of the slums.

Sixty years their gracious Queen has reigned a-holding up the sky,
And a-bringing round the seasons, hot and cold, and wet and dry;
And in all that time she's never done a deed deserving gaol —
So let joy-bells ring out madly and Delirium prevail!
O her Poor will blessings pour
On their Queen whom they adore;
When she blinks with puffy eyes at them they'll hunger never more.

47. HENRY LAWSON

IN THE DAYS WHEN THE WORLD WAS WIDE

The world is narrow and ways are short, and our lives are dull
    and slow,
For little is new where the crowds resort, and less where the
    wanderers go;
Greater, or smaller, the same old things we see by the dull
    road-side —
And tired of all is the spirt that sings of the days when the
    world was wide.

When the North was hale in the march of Time, and the South
    and the West were new,
And the gorgeous East was a pantomime, as it seemed in our
    boyhood's view;
When Spain was first on the waves of change, and proud in the
    ranks of pride,
And all was wonderful, new and strange in the days when the
    world was wide.

Then a man could fight if his heart were bold, and win if his
    faith were true —
Were it love, or honour, or power, or gold, or all that our
    hearts pursue;
Could live to the world for the family name, or die for the
    family pride,
Could fly from sorrow, and wrong, and shame in the days when
    the world was wide.

They sailed away in ships that sailed ere science controlled the
    main,
When the strong, brave heart of a man prevailed as 'twill never
    prevail again;
They knew not whither, nor much they cared — let Fate or
    the winds decide —
The worst of the Great Unknown they dared in the days when
    the world was wide.

They raised new stars on the silent sea that filled their hearts
    with awe;
They came to many a strange countree and marvellous sights
    they saw.

The villagers gaped at the tales they told, and old eyes glistened
    with pride —
When barbarous cities were paved with gold in the days when
    the world was wide.

'Twas honest metal and honest wood — in the days of the
    Outward Bound —
When men were gallant and ships were good — roaming the
    wide world round.
The gods could envy a leader then when "Follow me, lads!"
    he cried —
They faced each other and fought like men in the days when
    the world was wide.

They tried to live as a freeman should — they were happier
    men than we,
In the glorious days of wine and blood, when Liberty crossed
    the sea;
'Twas a comrade true or a foreman then, and a trusty sword
    well tried —
They faced each other and fought like men in the days when
    the world was wide.

The good ship bound for the Southern seas when the beacon
    was Ballarat,
With a "Ship ahoy!" on the freshening breeze, "Where bound?"
    and "What ship's that?" —
The emigrant train to New Mexico — the rush to the Lachlan
    Side —
Ah! faint is the echo of Westward Ho! from the days when the
    world was wide.

South, East, and West in advance of Time — and, ay! in advance
    of Thought!
Those brave men rose to a height sublime — and is it for this
    they fought?
And is it for this damned life we praise the god-like spirit that
    died
At Eureka Stockade in the Roaring Days with the days when
    the world was wide?

We fight like women, and feel as much — the thoughts of our
    hearts we guard —
Where scarcely the scorn of a god could touch, the sneer of a
    sneak hits hard;
The treacherous tongue and cowardly pen, the weapons of curs,
    decide —
They faced each other and fought like men in the days when the
    the world was wide.

Think of it all — of the life that is! Study your friends and
    foes!
Study the past! And answer this: "Are these times better than
    those?"
The life-long quarrel, the paltry spite, the sting of your
    poisoned pride!
No matter who fell it were better to fight as they did when the
    world was wide.

Boast as you will of your mateship now — crippled and mean
    and sly —
The lines of suspicion on friendship's brow were traced since
    the days gone by.
There was room in the long, free lines of the van to fight for it
    side by side —
There was beating-room for the heart of a man in the days when
    the world was wide.

*   *   *

With its dull, brown days of a shilling-an-hour the dreary year
    drags round;
Is this the result of Old England's power? — the bourne of the
    Outward Bound?
Is this the sequel of Westward Ho! — of the days of Whate'er
    Betide?
The heart of the rebel makes answer "No! We'll fight till the
    world grows wide!"

The world shall yet be a wider world — for the tokens are mani-
    fest;
East and North shall the wrongs be hurled that followed us
    South and West.
The march of Freedom is North by the Dawn! Follow, whate'er betide!
Sons of the Exiles, march! March on! March till the world grows
    wide!

48. RODERIC QUINN

THE CIRCLING HEARTHS

My Countrymen, though we are young as yet
With little history, nought to show
Of lives enleagued against a foreign foe,
Torn flags and triumph, glory or regret:
Still some things make our kinship sweet,
Some deeds inglorious but of royal worth,
As when with tireless arms and toiling feet
We felled the tree and tilled the earth.

'T is no great way that we have travelled since
Our feet first shook the storied dust
Of England from them, when with love and trust
In one another, and large confidence
In God above, our ways were ta'en
'Neath alien skies — each keeping step in mind
And soul and purpose to one trumpet strain,
One urging music on the wind:

Yet tears of ours have wet the dust, have wooed
Some subtle green things from the ground —
Like violets — only violets never wound
Such tendrils round the heart: the solitude
Has seen young hearts with love entwine;
And many gentle friends gone down to death
Have mingled with the dust, and made divine
The very soil we tread beneath.

Thus we have learned to love our country, learned
To treasure every inch from foam
To foam; to title her with name of Home;
To light in her regard a flame that burned
No land in vain, that calls the eyes
Of men to glory heights and old renown;
That wild winds cannot quench, nor thunder-skies
Make dim, nor many waters drown.

Six hearths are circled round our shores, and round
The six hearths group a common race,
Though leagues divide, the one light on their face:
The same old songs and stories rise; the sound
Of kindred voices and the dear

Old English tongue make music; and men move
From hearth to hearth with little fear
Of aught, save open arms and love.

To keep these hearth-fires red, to keep the door
Of each house wide — this is our part:
Surely 't is noble! Surely heart to heart,
God's love upon us and one goal before,
Is something worth; something to win
Our hearts to effort; something it were good
To garner soon; and something 't would be sin
To cast aside in wanton mood.

My Countrymen, hats off! with heart and will
Thank God that you are free, and then
Arise and don your nationhood like men,
And manlike face the world for good or ill.
Peace be to you, and in the tide
Of years great plenty till Time's course be run:
Six Ploughmen in the same field side by side,
But, if need be, six Swords as one.

49. WILLIAM GAY

AUSTRALIAN FEDERATION

From all division let our land be free,
For God has made her one: complete she lies
Within the unbroken circle of the skies,
And round her indivisible the sea
Breaks on her single shore; while only we,
Her foster children, bound with sacred ties
Of one dear blood, one storied enterprise,
Are negligent of her integrity.
Her seamless garment, at great Mammon's nod,
With hands unfilial we have basely rent,
With pretty variance our souls are spent,
And ancient kinship under foot is trod;
O let us rise, united, penitent,
And be one people, — mighty, serving God!

50. BERNARD O'DOWD

YOUNG DEMOCRACY

Hark! Young Democracy from sleep
    Our careless sentries raps:
A backwash from the Future's deep
    Our Evil's foreland laps.

Unknown, these Titans of our Night
    Their New Creation make:
Unseen, they toil and love and fight
    That glamoured Man may wake.

Knights-errant of the human race,
    The Quixotes of today,
For man as man they claim a place,
    Prepare the tedious way.

They seek no dim-eyed mob's applause,
    Deem based the titled name,
And spurn, for glory of their Cause,
    The tawdry nymphs of Fame.

No masks of ignorance or sin
    Hide from them you or me
We're Man — no colour shames our skin,
    No race or caste have we.

The prognathous Neanderthal,
    To them, conceals the Bruce;
They see Dan Aesop in the thrall;
    From swagmen Christ deduce.

Tho' butt for lecher's ribaldry
    And scarred by woman's scorn,
In baby-burdened girl they see
    God-motherhood, forlorn.

With them, to racial siredom glides
    The savage we deprave;
That eunuch brilliant Narses hides:
    A Spartacus, that slave.

They Jesus find in manger waif;
    In horse-boys Shakespearehood:
And earthquake-Luthers nestling sage
    In German miner's brook.

The God that pulses everywhere
    They know fills Satan's veins;
No felon but they see Him there
    Behind His mirror's stains.

'T is theirs Earth's charnel rooms to clear,
    And ruthless sweep away
The Lares and Penates dear
    To man in his decay.

Their restless energy supplies
    Munitions that will wreck
The keeps whence feudal enemies
    Our free banditti check.

Their unrelenting wars they wage,
    These Furies of the Right,
Where myriad Falsehood's legions rage,
    Artilleried by Might;

Where Fashion's stupid iron clamps
    Young Innovation's head,
And Law the stalwart Present cramps
    In Past's Procrustes-bed;

Where Pride of learning, substance, blood,
    Or prowess in the strife,
Exacts from teeming lowlihood
    The lion's share of life;

Where Gluttony would to the brutes
    Degrade his loose-lipped gangs;
Where Tyranny his venom shoots
    From one or million fangs;

Where Cruelty, in Wisdom's mask,
    Piths fame from writhing beasts;
Where blest is racial Murder's task
    By Christ's apostate priests.

In Punic or in Persian fray
    With Love's and Conscience' foes,
Unadvertising Romans they,
    And Spartans free from pose.

Abused as mad or traitors by
    The trolls they would eject;
Cold-shouldered by wan Apathy;
    Of motives mean suspect;

Outcast from social gaieties;
    Denied life's lilied grace;
They mount their hidden Calvaries
    To save the human race.

The bowers of Art a few may know:
    A few wait highly placed:
Most bear the hods of common woe,
    And some you call disgraced.

But whether in the mob or school,
    In church or poverty,
They teach and love the Golden Rule
    Of Young Democracy: —

"That culture, joy and goodliness
    Be th' equal right of all:
That Greed no more shall those oppress
    Who by the wayside fall:

"That each shall share what all men sow:
    That colour, caste's a lie:
That man is God, however low —
    Is man, however high."

51. HENRY LAWSON

The Union Buries Its Dead

While out boating, one Sunday afternoon, on a billabong across the river, we saw a young man on horseback driving some horses along the bank. He said it was a fine day, and asked if the water was deep there. The joker of our party said it was deep enough to drown him, and he laughed and rode further up. We didn't take much notice of him.

Next day a funeral gathered at a corner pub and asked each other in to have a drink while waiting for the hearse. They passed away some of the time dancing jigs to a piano in the bar parlour. They passed away the rest of the time "sky-larking" and fighting.

The defunct was a young union laborer, about 25, who had been drowned the previous day, while trying to swim some horses across a billabong of the Darling.

He was almost a stranger in town, and the fact of his having been a union man accounted for the funeral. The police found some union papers in his swag, and called at the General Laborers' Union Office for information about him. That's how we knew. The secretary had very little information to give. The departed was a "Roman", and the majority of the town were otherwise—but unionism is stronger than creed. Drink, however, is stronger than unionism; and, when the hearse presently arrived, more than two-thirds of the funeral were unable to follow. They were too drunk.

The procession numbered 15, including the corpse—fourteen souls following the broken shell of a soul. Perhaps not one of the fourteen possessed a soul any more than the corpse did—but that doesn't matter.

Four or five of the funeral, who were boarders at the pub, borrowed a trap which the landlord used to carry passengers to and from the railway station. They were strangers to us on foot, and we to them. We were all strangers to the corpse.

A "horseman", who looked like a drover just returned

from a big trip, dropped into our dusty wake and followed us a few hundred yards, dragging his packhorse behind him, but a friend made wild and demonstrative signals from an hotel verandah—hooking at the air in front with his right hand and jobbing his left thumb over his shoulder in the direction of the bar—so the drover hauled off and didn't catch up to us any more. He was a stranger to the entire show.

We walked in twos. There were three twos. It was very hot and dusty; the heat rushed in fierce dazzling waves across every iron roof and light colored wall that was turned to the sun. One or two pubs closed respectfully 'til we got past. They closed their bar doors and the patrons went in and out through some side or back entrance for a few minutes. Bushmen seldom grumble at an inconvenience of this sort, when it is caused by a funeral. They have too much respect for the dead.

On the way to the cemetery we passed three shearers sitting on the shady side of a fence. One was drunk—very drunk. The other two covered their right ears with their hats, out of respect for the departed—whoever he might have been—and one of them kicked the drunk and muttered something to him.

He straightened himself up, stared before him and reached helplessly for his hat, which he shoved half off and then on again. Then he made a great effort to pull himself together—and succeeded. He stood up, braced his back against the fence, knocked off his hat, and remorsefully placed his foot on it to keep it off his head till the funeral passed.

A tall sentimental drover, who walked by my side, cynically quoted Byronic verses suitable to the occasion—to death—and asked with pathetic humor whether we thought the dead man's ticket would be recognised "over yonder". It was a G.L.U. ticket and the general opinion was that it would be recognised.

Presently my friend said:

"You remember, when we were in the boat yesterday, we saw a man driving some horses along the bank?"

"Yes."

He nodded at the hearse and said:

"Well, that's him."

I thought awhile.

"I didn't take any particular notice of him," I said. "He said something, didn't he?"

"Yes—said it was a fine day. You'd have taken more notice had you known that he was doomed to die in the hour, and that those were the last words he would say to any man on earth."

"To be sure," said a full voice from the rear. "If ye'd have known that ye'd have prolonged the conversation."

We plodded on across the railway line and along the hot, dusty road which ran to the cemetery—some of us talking about the accident, and lying about the narrow escapes we had had ourselves. Presently someone said:

"There's the devil."

I looked up and saw a priest standing in the shade of the tree by the cemetery gate. A Church of England parson would have done as well.

The hearse was drawn up and the tail-boards were opened. The funeral extinguished its right ear with its hat as three men lifted the coffin out and laid it over the grave. The priest—a pale, quiet young fellow—stood under the shade of a sapling which grew at the head of the grave. He took off his hat, dropped it carelessly on the ground and proceeded to business. I noticed that one or two heathens winced slightly when the holy water was sprinkled on the coffin. The drops quickly evaporated, and the little round black spots they left were soon dusted over; but the spots showed, by contrast, the cheapness and shabbiness of the cloth which covered the coffin. It seemed black before, now it looked a dusky grey.

Just here man's ignorance and vanity made a farce of the funeral. A big bull-necked publican—with heavy blotchy features, and a supremely ignorant expression—picked up the priest's straw hat and held it about two inches over the head of his reverence during the whole of the service. The father, be it remembered, was standing in the shade. A few shoved their hats on and off uneasily, struggling between their disgust for the living and their respect for the dead. The hat had a conical crown and a brim sloping down all round like a sunshade, and the publican held it with his great red claw spread over the crown.

To do the priest justice, perhaps, he didn't notice the incident. A stage priest or parson in the same position might have said, "Put the hat down, my friend; is not the soul or memory of our dear brother worth more than my complexion?" A wattlebard layman might have expressed himself in stronger language, none the less to the point. But my priest seemed unconscious of what was going on. Besides, the publican was a great and important pillar of the church. He couldn't, as an ignorant and conceited fool, lose such a good opportunity of asserting his faithfulness and importance to his creed. The grave looked very narrow under the coffin, and I drew a breath of relief when the box slid easily down. I saw a coffin get stuck once, at Rookwood, and it had to be yanked out with difficulty, and laid on the sods at the feet of the heart-broken relations, who howled dismally while the grave-diggers widened the hole. But they don't cut contracts so fine in the West. Our grave-digger was not altogether bowelless, and, out of respect for that human quality described as "feelin's", he scraped up some light and dusty soil and threw it down to deaden the fall of the clay lumps on the coffin. He also tried to steer the first few shovelsful gently down against the end of the grave with the back of the shovel turned outwards, but the hard dry Darling River clods rebounded and knocked all the same. It didn't matter much; nothing does; the fall of lumps of clay on a stranger's coffin doesn't sound any different from the fall of the same things on an ordinary wooden box, at least I didn't notice anything awsome or unusual in the sound; but, perhaps, one of us—the most sensitive—might have been impressed by being reminded of a burial of long ago, when the thump of every sod jolted his heart. That's nearly all about the funeral except that the priest did his work in an unusually callous and business-like way.

I left out the wattle—because it wasn't there. I also neglected to mention the heart-broken old mate with his grizzled head bowed and great pearly drops streaming down his rugged cheeks. He was absent—he was probably "Out Back". For similar reasons I omitted reference to the "suspicious" moisture in the eyes of a bearded bush ruffian named Bill. Bill failed to turn up, and the only moisture was that which was induced by the heat. I left out the "sad Australian sunset" because the sun was not going down at the time. The burial took place exactly at mid-day.

The dead bushman's name was Jim, apparently; but they found no portraits, nor locks of hair, nor any love letters, nor anything of that kind in his swag—not even a reference to his mother; only some papers relating to union matters. Most of us didn't know the name till we saw it on the coffin: we knew him as "that young feller that was drowned yesterday".

"So, his name's James Tyson," said my drover, acquaintance, looking at the plate.

"Why! Didn't you know that before?" I asked.

"No,—but I knew he was a union man."

It turned out, afterwards, that J.T. wasn't his real name—only "the name he went by".

Anyhow he was buried by it, and most of the "Great Australian Dailies" have mentioned in their brevity columns that a young man named James John Tyson was drowned in a billabong of the Darling River last Sunday.

We did hear, later on, what his real name was, but, if we do chance to read it among the missing friends in some agony column, we shall not be aware of it, and therefore not able to give any information to a "sorrowing sister" or "heart broken mother"—for we have already forgotten his name.

52. GEORGE ESSEX EVANS

A FEDERAL SONG

They lay the stone whose eyes may never see
    A Nation's turrets rise above the plain.
    They sow the seed who may not reap the grain;
        Futurity
    Will bless that toil which wrought thro' stress and strain,
        Her Unity.

It yet shall be. Build on, and heed not scorn;
    Build fair and strong a nation's towering height;
    In massy grandeur weld her scattered might
        By schism torn.
    After the darkness and the Dawn's gray light
        Cometh the Morn.

Build on! Build on! Hold with a nerve of steel,
    Above all meaner pride and jealous hate,
    That higher faith which mades a nation great.
        They rightly feel
    Who take for the broad basement of the State
        The Common-weal.

Build on! Build on! Deep-pulsing thro' the land,
    Thro' all this island-continent there stirs
    A throb, a voice, she feels, and knows is hers,
        From strand to strand
    A whisper stealing thro' the Dawn avers
        The hour at hand.

Build on! Build on! E'en as the restless blue
    Circles her sleeping mountains, silence-bound,
    Our hope, our faith, our love shall gird her round
        With fealty true,
    Whilst from the old-world wrecks which strew the ground,
        We build anew.

53. JAMES BRUNTON STEPHENS

FULFILMENT

AUSTRALIA FEDERATA, 1ST JANUARY, 1901

*Dedicated by special permission to Her Most Gracious Majesty
Queen Victoria*

We cried, "How long!" We sighed, "Not yet;"
And still with faces dawnward set
   "Prepare the way," said each to each,
     And yet again, "Prepare," we said;
   And toil, re-born of resolute speech,
     Made straight the path her feet should tread: —
Now triumph, faithful hands and steadfast wills,
For, lo! whose pomp the bannered Orient fills?
Whose feet are these upon the morning hills?

Farewell, Sweet Faith! thy silver ray
Now dies into the golden day.
   Farewell, Bright Dream, by minstrels sung!
     For She whom all our dreams foreran
   Has leaped to life, a Pallas sprung
     Consummate from the brain of man,
Whom now we hail in mortal guise and gait,
Thought clothed with flesh, partaker of our state,
Made corporal in us now corporate!

Ah, now we know the long delay
But served to assure a prouder day,
   For while we waited came the call
     To prove and make our title good —
   To face the fiery ordeal
     That tries the claim to Nationhood —
And now in pride of challenge we unroll,
For all the world to read, the record-scroll
Whose bloody script attests a Nation's soul.

O yet, our Dead, who at the call
Fared forth to fall as heroes fall,

Whose consecrated souls we failed
 To note beneath the common guise
Till all-revealing Death unveiled

  The splendour of your sacrifice,
Now, crowned with more than perishable bays,
Immortal in your country's love and praise,
Ye, too, have portion in this day of days!

And ye who sowed where now we reap,
Whose waiting eyes, now sealed in sleep,
 Beheld far off with prescient sight
  This triumph of rejoining lands —
 Yours, too, the day! for though its light
  Can pierce not to your folded hands,
These shining hours of advent but fulfil
The cherished purpose of your constant will,
Whose onward impulse liveth in us still.

Still lead thou vanward of our line,
Who, shaggy, massive, leonine,
 Could'st yet most finely phrase the event —
  For if a Pisgah view was all
 Vouchsafed to thine uncrowned intent,
  The echoes of thy herald-call
Not faintlier strive with our saluting guns,
And at thy words through all Australia's sons
The "crimson thread of kinship" redder runs.

But not the memory of the dead,
How loved so'er each sacred head,
 Today can change from glad to grave
  The chords that quire a Nation born —
 Twin offspring of the birth that gave,
  When yester-midnight chimed to morn,
Another age to the Redeemer's reign,
Another cycle to the widening gain
Of Good o'er Ill and Remedy o'er Pain.

Our sundering lines with love o'ergrown,
Our bounds the girdling seas along —
 Be this the burden of the psalm
  That every resonant hour repeats,
 Till day-fall dusk the fern and palm
  That forest our transfigured streets,
And night still vibrant with the note of praise
Thrill brother-hearts to song in woodland ways,
When gum-leaves whisper o'er the camp-fire's blaze.

    *   *   *

The Charter's read: the rites are o'er;
The trumpet's blare and cannon's roar
   Are silent, and the flags are furled;
      But so not ends the task to build
     Into the fabric of the world
      The substance of our hope fulfilled —
To work as those who greatly have divined
The lordship of a continent assigned
As God's own gift for service of mankind.

O People of the onward will,
Unit of Union greater still
   Than that today hath made you great,
     Your true Fulfilment waiteth there,
     Embraced within the larger fate
      Of Empire ye are born to share —
No vassal progeny of subject brood,
No satellite shed from Britain's plenitude,
But orbed with her in one wide sphere of good!

* * *

O Lady, in whose sovereign name
The crowning word of Union came
   That sheds upon thine honoured age
     The glory of a rising light,
    Across our record's earliest page,
      Its earliest word, thy name we write . . .
Symbol, Embodiment, and Guarantee
Of all that makes us and maintains us free,
Woman and Queen, God's grace abide with thee.

54. VICTOR DALEY

THE WORKER'S WORST FOE

The Fatman in his mansion fine
    Dwells royally at ease;
He drinks the most expensive wine;
    He eats the Gouda cheese.

The weeds he smokes are Havanese,
    The best that coin can buy,
And through their curling wreaths he sees
    Chateaux — *not* in the sky.

His workmanship in diamonds he
    Decks splendidly, of course —
Those gems should blood-red rubies be,
    To signify their source.

His horses are of noble blood,
    All full of pride and fire;
He owns indeed as fine a stud
    As Fatman could desire.

Such horses! Biped trudging by —
    Scant dinner in your can —
Just pause and watch them prancing high,
    And ponder, Working-Man!

Ill-clothed your children are; your wife,
    What clothes should *she* require? —
The Fatman's womenkind through life
    Go clad in *silk* attire.

The Fatman's daughters and his sons
    Right daintily are fed;
Your wan-faced wife and little ones
    Thank God when they have bread.

He lives for many years, and dies
    In smell of sanctity;
For he is strong, and he is wise,
    And hard of grasp is he.

You live as long as you can slave,
    And like a dog you die.
"You'll go to Heav'n if you behave!"
    Bah! Fatman owns the sky.

He runs the creeds of all the world,
    And, smiling in his pew,
Hears lurid maledictions hurled
    At wickedness — that's *you*.

And is he, then, your fellest foe,
    This Fatman full of glee,
Who sweats your blood and brain? Ah, no!
    There is a worse than he.

In your own ranks the traitor lurks,
    All smug, and slick, and prim;
Blame not the Fatman, or his works,
    For your distress. Blame *him*.

He bows beneath the Fatman's yoke,
    And never feels it gall.
He doesn't drink, he doesn't smoke,
    He slaves and saves — that's all.

He sneers at your aspirings grand,
    And quietly says he: —
"I have a steady billet, and
    That's good enough for me."

And if he's "sacked" with notice curt
    He doesn't storm or rage,
But worm-like crawls through kindred dirt
    To take the lowest wage.

The Fatman is a man of might,
    And open foe is he:
But this fish-blooded parasite
    Is your worst enemy.

The City or
the Bush?

EDITOR'S NOTE

The "debate" begun by Lawson and Paterson in the *Bulletin* in 1892 may have been deliberately staged, but it did point to an underlying tension in Australian society, a tension frequently reflected in the literature of the nineties: the city versus the bush. Neither writer sought to deny the importance of the bush as a source of inspiration in local writing. It was a question of how it was described, a matter of the writer's relationship to his material. For Paterson, country life had a freedom and an excitment unknown in the towns. In "An Answer to Various Bards" (*Bulletin*, 10 October 1892) he castigated those whose "dreadful, dismal stories of the Overlander's camp" painted a picture fit to "fill one's soul with gloom". Paterson's Clancy (55), "gone to Queensland droving", had "pleasures that the townsfolk never know". Lawson's replies to this argument (62 and 64) are not a defence of the city so much as a recognition of the fact that one's view of the bush depends on one's perspective. The sundowner, humping his bluey, will see things differently from the squatter mounted on his thoroughbred. This distinction suggests a political dimension to the debate too. Lawson's depictions of the miseries of bush life were frequently couched in terms which suggested that those who most suffered were the victims of an oppressive social order. This was anathema to the conservative Paterson. He held that those who preach revolution are "agitators", too lazy themselves to put in a solid day's work. Lawson's rejoinder was that this is the view of a "city bushman" who has never known what it is to slave for an absentee landlord or to be up to his ears in debt in the drought season.

Though popular feeling at the time (and today?) seems to have been on the side of the bush, Lawson was right in insisting that Australians would never know their country until writers depicted it as it actually is, rather than as they hoped or wished it to be. He was the first to admit that the city had many shortcomings, and that the bush had a grandness and opportunities for achievement unknown to urban people. But country life could all too easily be as harsh and debilitating as life in any city slum. Certainly Victor Daley found the country rather dull: it may have been "calm and sane, and wholesome", but it lacked the excitement, and the sense of a literary community, to be found in Sydney (59).

55.   A. B. PATERSON

CLANCY OF THE OVERFLOW

I had written him a letter which I had, for want of better
Knowledge, sent to where I met him down the Lachlan,
    years ago,
He was shearing when I knew him, so I sent the letter to him,
Just "on spec", addressed as follows, "Clancy, of
    The Overflow".

And an answer came directed in a writing unexpected,
(And I think the same was written with a thumb-nail dipped
    in tar)
'Twas his shearing mate who wrote it, and *verbatim* I will
    quote it:
"Clancy's gone to Queensland droving, and we don't know
    where he are."

* * *

In my wild erratic fancy visions come to me of Clancy
Gone a-droving "down the Cooper" where the Western drovers
    go;
As the stock are slowing stringing, Clancy rides behind them
    singing,
For the drover's life has pleasures that the townsfolk never
    know.

And the bush hath friends to meet him, and their kindly voices
    greet him
In the murmur of the breezes and the river on its bars,
And he sees the vision splendid of the sunlit plains extended,
And at night the wond'rous glory of the everlasting stars.

* * *

I am sitting in my dingy little office, where a stingy
Ray of sunlight struggles feebly down between the houses
    tall,
And the foetid air and gritty of the dusty, dirty city
Through the open window floating, spreads its foulness over
    all.

And in place of lowing cattle, I can hear the fiendish rattle
Of the tramways and the 'buses making hurry down the
    street,
And the language uninviting of the gutter children fighting,
Comes fitfully and faintly through the ceaseless tramp of
    feet.

And the hurrying people daunt me, and their pallid faces
    haunt me
As they shoulder one another in their rush and nervous haste,
With their eager eyes and greedy, and their stunted forms and
    weedy,
For townsfolk have no time to grow, they have no time to
    waste.

And I somehow rather fancy that I'd like to change with
    Clancy,
Like to take a turn at droving where the seasons come and go,
While he faced the round eternal of the cash-book and the
    journal —
But I doubt he'd suit the office, Clancy, of "The Overflow".

56. HARRY MORANT

THE AUSTRAL "LIGHT"

We were standing by the fireside at the pub one wintry night
Drinking grog and "pitching fairies" while the lengthening
   hours took flight,
And a stranger there was present, one who seemed quite city-
   bred —
There was little showed about him to denote him "mulga-fed".

For he wore a four-inch collar, tucked-up pants, and boots of
   tan —
You might take him for a new-chum, or a Sydney city man —
But in spite of cuff or collar, Lord ! he gave himself away
When he cut and rubbed a pipeful and had filled his coloured
   clay.

For he never asked for matches — although in that boozing
   band
There was more than one man standing with a matchbox
   in his hand;
And I knew him for a bushman 'spite his tailor-made attire
As I saw him stoop and fossick for a fire-stick from the fire.

And that mode of weed-ignition to my memory brought
   back
Long nights when nags were hobbled on a far North-western
   track;
Recalled campfires in the timber, when the stars shone big
   and bright,
And we learned the matchless virtues of a glowing gidgee light.

And I thought of piney sand-ridges — and somehow I could
   swear
That this tailor-made young johnny had at one time been
   "out there".
And as he blew the white ash from the tapering, glowing coal,
Faith! my heart went out towards him for a kindred country
   soul.

57. A. B. PATERSON

THE MAN FROM IRONBARK

It was the man from Ironbark who struck the Sydney town,
He wandered over street and park, he wandered up and down.
He loitered here, he loitered there, till he was like to drop,
Until at last in sheer despair he sought a barber's shop.
"'Ere! shave my beard and whiskers off, I'll be a man of mark,
"I'll go and do the Sydney toff up home in Ironbark."

The barber man was small and flash, as barbers mostly are,
He wore a strike-your-fancy sash, he smoked a huge cigar;
He was a humorist of note and keen at repartee,
He laid the odds and kept a "tote", whatever that may be,
And when he saw our friend arrive, he whispered "Here's a lark!
"Just watch me catch him all alive, this man from Ironbark."

There were some gilded youths that sat along the barber's wall.
Their eyes were dull, their heads were flat, they had no brains
    at all;
To them the barber passed the wink, his dexter eyelid shut,
"I'll make this bloomin' yokel think his bloomin' throat is
    cut."
And as he soaped and rubbed it in he made a rude remark:
"I s'pose the flats is pretty green up there in Ironbark."

A grunt was all reply he got; he shaved the bushman's chin,
Then made the water boiling hot and dipped the razor in.
He raised his hand, his brow grew black, he paused awhile to
    gloat,
Then slashed the red-hot razor-back across his victim's throat;
Upon the newly-shaven skin it made a livid mark —
No doubt it fairly took him in — the man from Ironbark.

He fetched a wild up-country yell might wake the dead to
    hear,
And though his throat, he knew full well, was cut from ear to
    ear,
He struggled gamely to his feet, and faced the murd'rous foe:
"You've done for me! you dog, I'm beat! one hit before I go!
"I only wish I had a knife, you blessed murdering shark!
"But you'll remember all your life, the man from Ironbark."

He lifted up his hairy paw, with one tremendous clout
He landed on the barber's jaw, and knocked the barber out.
He set to work with nail and tooth, he made the place a wreck;
He grabbed the nearest gilded youth, and tried to break his
    neck.
And all the while his throat he held to save his vital spark,
And "Murder! Bloody Murder!" yelled the man from Ironbark.

A peeler man who heard the din came in to see the show;
He tried to run the bushman in, but he refused to go.
And when at last the barber spoke, and said "'Twas all in fun —
"'Twas just a little harmless joke, a trifle overdone."
"A joke!" he cried, "By George, that's fine; a lively sort of
    lark;
"I'd like to catch that murdering swine some night in Ironbark."

And now while round the shearing floor the list'ning shearers
    gape,
He tells the story o'er and o'er and brags of his escape.
"Them barber chaps what keeps a tote, By George, I've had
    enough,
"One tried to cut my bloomin' throat, but thank the Lord it's
    tough."
And whether he's believed or no, there's one thing to remark,
That flowing beards are all the go way up in Ironbark.

58. BARCROFT BOAKE

AN EASTER RHYME

Easter Monday in the city —
    Rattle, rattle, rumble, rush!
Tom and Jerry, Nell and Kitty,
    All the down-the-harbour "push" —
Little thought have they, or pity,
    For a wanderer from the bush.

Shuffle, feet, a merry measure!
    Hurry, Jack, and find your Jill!
Let her — if it give her pleasure —
    Flaunt her furbelow and frill!
Kiss her while you have the leisure;
    For tomorrow brings the mill.

Go ye down the harbour winding
    'Mid the eucalypts and fern,
Respite from your troubles finding;
    Kiss her till her pale cheeks burn;
For tomorrow will the grinding
    Millstones of the city turn.

Stunted figures, sallow faces,
    Sad girls striving to be gay
In their cheap sateens and laces . . .
    Ah! how different 'tis today
Where they're going to the races
    Yonder — up Monaro way!

Light mist flecks the Murrumbidgee's
    Bosom with a silver stain:
On the trembling wire bridge is
    Perched a single long-legged crane;
While the yellow, slaty ridges
    Sweep up proudly from the plain.

Somebody is after horses —
    Donald, Charlie, or young Mac —
Suddenly his arm he tosses;
    Presently you'll hear the crack,
As the symbol of the cross is
    Made on Possum's steaming back.

Stirling first! the Masher follows —
    Ly-ee-moon and old Trump Card;
Helter-skelter through the shallows
    Of the willow-shaded ford:
Up the lane and past the gallows,
    Driven panting to the yard.

In the homestead, what a clatter!
    Habits black and habits blue.
Full a dozen red lips patter:
    'Who is going to ride with who?"
Mixing sandwiches and chatter;
    Gloves to button, hair to do.

Horses stamp and stirrups jingle,
    "Dash the filly! won't she wait?"
Voices, bass and treble, mingle.
    "*Look* sharp, May, or we'll be late!"
How the pulses leap and tingle
    As you lift her featherweight!

At the thought the heart beats quicker
    Than an old Bohemian's should —
Beating like my battered ticker
    (Pawned this time, I fear, for good).
Bah! I'll go and have a liquor
    With the genial Jimmy Wood.

59. VICTOR DALEY

IN ARCADY

The brown hills brood around me, crowned with gums of
    sombre sheen;
They look like drowsy giants all in smoking-caps of green.
There's not a voice familiar, or a face that's known to me:
The Lord He knows, but I suppose that this is Arcady.

I sit on the verandah at the closing of the day
And compare myself to Ovid in my modest little way —
To Ovid in his exile, dreaming evermore of Rome,
And in vain beseeching Caesar to forgive and take him home.

He dwelt amongst barbarians, and sang his mournful song
Beside the frozen Ister and the Euxine shore along;
But I, midst kindly Irish, dwell upon an upland plain —
And still I long for Sydney and its narrow streets again.

The wheat is cut and garnered, and the ploughing has begun,
The ruddy soil lies naked to the kisses of the sun;
There's harrowing, and burning-off, and other sights to see,
And great potato-digging in the fields of Arcady.

The farmers use, to break the ground, a fine four-furrow
    plough.
Their ancestors would smile if they could see the Irish now —
For they wrought hard with wooden shares their frugal crops
    to raise,
When Cecht, the Plough, they worshipped in the old Dedanaan
    days.

In spite of new machines the world is full of wonder sweet;
There's still as much of magic in the springing of the wheat
As when around the fields at night, the ancient legends tell,
The Naked Maid in darkness walked and wove a magic spell.

A homely-looking folk they are, these people of my kin;
Their hands are hard as horse-shoes, but their hearts come
    through the skin;
They are all right well-connected in this land of Arcady;
And if your name's not Hogan here it must be Hegarty.

And Nature, God preserve her well, is kindly Irish too;
The winds croon Irish melodies the swaying gum-trees through;
And ev'ry little hill about, with green cap cocked and curled,
Says "Come upon the top of me and look around the world!"

The stream goes singing on its way, and well I know the tune —
'Tis "Slantha" in the morning, and at night "Eileen Aroon";
The magpie warbling in the woods with rich, clear purple note,
Pretends that he's a blackbird with a Cork brogue in his throat.

They love the land they live in, all these folk that I esteem —
But the land they left behind them is an everlasting dream.
Old Michael Cleary said to me — his age is seventy-seven —
"There's no place like Australia, barrin' Ireland and Heaven."

There's rest and peace in plenty here, and eggs and milk to
    spare;
The scenery is calm and sane, and wholesome is the air;
The folk are kind, the cows behave like cousins unto me . . .
But, please the Lord, on Monday morn, I'm leaving Arcady.

60. WILL OGILVIE

IN TOWN

Where the smoke-clouds scarcely drift
    And the breezes seem to sleep,
Where the sunbeams never lift
    Half the gloom of alleys deep,
Comrades! must we languish ever,
    Beat our hearts against the bars
While the vine-trees kiss the river
    And the ranges greet the stars?
There are stormy tints and tender
    In the pictures that we pass —
But it's O, for day-dawn's splendour
    And the dewdrops in the grass!

Though the old life fades behind us,
    Though the new life leaps before,
Old-time spells are strong to bind us
    Yearning for our yokes of yore;
In the whirl of toil and duty,
    In the pride of pomp and power,
We can find no grander beauty
    Than the red West's bridal dower;
There is music in the rattle
    Of the horse-hoofs down the street —
But it's O, for ringing cattle
    And the thunder of their feet!

Wanton Pleasure laughs beside us
    Where the life-streams ebb and flow,
Folly's cap and bells deride us,
    Nodding close to Want and Woe;
Lordly pageants round us glisten,
    At our feet Life's joys are cast,
But we have no heart to listen
    With the Bush-wind whispering past;
Silver nights of love may hold us
    Till we half forget the stars —
But it's O, for foam-white shoulders
    And the clink of snaffle-bars!

61. EDWARD DYSON

IN TOWN

Out of work and out of money — out of friends that means,
    you bet —
Out of firewood, togs and tucker, out of everything but debt —
And I loathe the barren pavements, and the crowds a fellow
    meets,
And the maddening repetition of the suffocating streets.

With their stinks my soul is tainted, and the tang is on my
    tongue
Of that sour and smoky suburb and the push we're thrown among
And I sicken at the corners polished free of paint and mirk
By the shoulders of the men who're always hanging round for
    work.

Home — good Lord! a three-roomed hovel 'twixt a puddle and a
    drain,
In harmonious connection on the left with Liver Lane,
Where a crippled man is dying, and a horde of children fight,
And a woman in the horrors howls remorsefully at night.

It has stables close behind it, and an ash-heap for a lawn,
And is furnished with the tickets of the things we have in pawn;
And all day the place is haunted by a melancholy crowd
Who beg everything or borrow, and to steal are not too proud.

Through the day come wary women, too, with famine-haunted
    eyes,
Hawking things that are not wanted — things that no one ever
    buys.
And I hate the prying neighbours, in their animal content,
And the devillish persistence of the man who wants the rent.

I, who cared for none, and faltered at no work a man might do,
Felt a fierce delight possess me when the trucks went surging
    through,
When the flood raced in the sluices, or the giant gums swung
    round
'Fore my axe, and flung their mighty limbs all mangled on the
    ground —

I who hewed and built and burrowed, and who asked no man to
    give
When a strong arm was excuse enough for venturing to live —
I am creeping by the gutters, with a simper and a smirk,
To the Fates in spats and toppers for the privilege of *work*.

Far away the hills are all aflame; the blossom golden fair
Streams up the gladdened ranges, and its scent is everywhere,
And the kiddies of the settlers on the creek are red and sweet,
Whilst my youngsters have the sallowness and savour of the
    street.

To escape these endless vaults of brick, and pitch a tent out
    back,
If I get a chance I'll graft until my very sinews crack,
Meanwhile may all the angels up in Paradise look down
On a man of sin who died not, but was damned and sent to
    town.

62. HENRY LAWSON

UP THE COUNTRY

I am back from up the country — very sorry that I went —
Seeking for the Southern poets' land whereon to pitch my tent;
I have lost a lot of idols, which were broken on the track,
Burnt a lot of fancy verses, and I'm glad that I am back.
Further out may be the pleasant scenes of which our poets
    boast,
But I think the country's rather more inviting round the coast.
Anyway, I'll stay at present at a boarding-house in town,
Drinking beer and lemon-squashes, taking baths and cooling
    down.

"Sunny plains!" Great Scott! — those burning wastes of barren
    soil and sand
With their everlasting fences stretching out across the land!
Desolation where the crow is! Desert where the eagle flies,
Paddocks where the luny bullock starts and stares with reddened
    eyes;
Where, in clouds of dust enveloped, roasted bullock-drivers
    creep
Slowly past the sun-dried shepherd dragged behind his crawling
    sheep.
Stunted peak of granite gleaming, glaring like a molten mass
Turned, from some infernal furnace, on a plain devoid of grass.

Miles and miles of thirsty gutters — strings of muddy water-
    holes
In the place of "shining rivers", walled by cliffs and forest boles.
Barren ridges, gullies, ridges! where the ever-madding flies —
Fiercer than the plagues of Egypt — swarm about your blighted
    eyes!
Bush! where there is no horizon! where the buried bushman
    sees
Nothing — Nothing! but the sameness of the ragged, stunted
    trees!
Lonely hut where drought's eternal, suffocating atmosphere
Where the God-forgotten hatter dreams of city life and beer.

Treacherous tracks that trap the stranger, endless roads that
    gleam and glare,
Dark and evil-looking gullies, hiding secrets here and there!

Dull dumb flats and stony rises, where the toiling bullocks
bake,
And the sinister "goanna", and the lizard, and the snake.
Land of day and night — no morning freshness, and no
afternoon,
When the great white sun in rising bringeth summer heat in
June.
Dismal country for the exile, when the shades begin to fall
From the sad heart-breaking sunset, to the new-chum worst of
all.

Dreary land in rainy weather, with the endless clouds that drift
O'er the bushman like a blanket that the Lord will never lift —
Dismal land when it is raining — growl of floods and, oh! the
woosh
Of the rain and wind together on the dark bed of the bush —
Ghastly fires in lonely humpies where the granite rocks are piled
In the rain-swept wildernesses that are wildest of the wild.

Land where gaunt and haggard women live alone and work like
men,
Till their husbands, gone a-droving, will return to them again:
Homes of men! if home had ever such a God-forgotten place
Where the wild selector's children fly before a stranger's face.
Home of tragedy applauded by the dingoes' dismal yell,
Heaven of the shanty-keeper — fitting fiend for such a hell —
And the wallaroos and wombats and, of course, the curlew's
call —
And the lone sundowner tramping ever onward through it all!

I am back from up the country, up the country where I went
Seeking for the Southern poets' land whereon to pitch my tent;
I have shattered many idols out along the dusty track,
Burnt a lot of fancy verses — and I'm glad that I am back —
I believe the Southern poets' dream will not be realised
Till the plains are irrigated and the land is humanised.
I intend to stay at present, as I said before, in town
Drinking beer and lemon-squashes, taking baths and cooling
down.

63. A. B. PATERSON

IN DEFENCE OF THE BUSH

So you're back from up the country, Mister Townsman, where
    you went,
And you're cursing all the business in a bitter discontent;
Well, we grieve to disappoint you, and it makes us sad to hear
That it wasn't cool and shady — and there wasn't plenty beer,
And the loony bullock snorted when you first came into view;
Well, you know it's not so often that he sees a swell like you;
And the roads were hot and dusty, and the plains were burnt
    and brown,
And no doubt you're better suited drinking lemon-squash in
    town.

Yet perchance, if you should journey down the very track you
    went
In a month or two at furthest you would wonder what it meant,
Where the sunbaked earth was gasping like a creature in its pain
You would find the grasses waving like a field of summer grain,
And the miles of thirsty gutters blocked with sand and choked
    with mud,
You would find them mighty rivers with a turbid, sweeping
    flood;
For the rain and drought and sunshine make no changes in the
    street,
In the sullen line of buildings and the ceaseless tramp of feet;
But the bush hath moods and changes, as the seasons rise and
    fall,
And the men who know the bush-land — they are loyal through
    it all.

*   *   *

But you found the bush was dismal and a land of no delight,
Did you chance to hear a chorus in the shearers' huts at night?
Did they 'rise up, William Riley" by the camp-fire's cheery
    blaze?
Did they rise him as we rose him in the good old droving days?
And the women of the homesteads and the men you chanced to
    meet —
Were their faces sour and saddened like the "faces in the street",
And the "shy selector children" — were they better now or
    worse

Than the little city urchins who would greet you with a curse?
Is not such a life much better than the squalid street and square
Where the fallen women flaunt it in the fierce electric glare,
Where the semptress plies her sewing till her eyes are sore and
  red
In a filthy, dirty attic toiling on for daily bread?
Did you hear no sweeter voices in the music of the bush
Than the roar of trams and 'buses, and the war-whoop of "the
  push"?
Did the magpies rouse your slumbers with their carol sweet and
  strange?
Did you hear the silver chiming of the bell-birds on the range?
But, perchance, the wild birds' music by your senses was
  despised,
For you say you'll stay in townships till the bush is civilised.
Would you make it a tea-garden and on Sundays have a band
Where the "blokes" might taken their "donahs", with a "public"
  close at hand?
You had better stick to Sydney and make merry with the
  "push",
For the bush will never suit you, and you'll never suit the bush.

64. HENRY LAWSON

THE CITY BUSHMAN

It was pleasant up the country, City Bushman, where you went,
For you sought the greener patches and you travelled like a
    gent,
And you curse the trams and buses and the turmoil and the push,
Though you know the squalid city needn't keep you from the
    bush;
But we lately heard you singing of the "plains where shade is
    not".
And you mentioned it was dusty — "all was dry and all was hot".

True, the bush "hath moods and changes" — and the bushman
    hath 'em too,
For he's not a poet's dummy — he's a man, the same as you;
But his back is growing rounder — slaving for the absentee —
And his toiling wife is thinner than a country wife should be,
For we noticed that the faces of the folks we chanced to meet
Should have made a greater contrast to the faces in the street;
And, in short, we think the bushman's being driven to the wall,
And it's doubtful if his spirit will be "loyal thro' it all".

Though the bush has been romantic and it's nice to sing about,
There's a lot of patriotism that the land could do without —
Sort of *British Workman* nonsense that shall perish in the scorn
Of the drover who is driven and the shearer who is shorn —
Of the struggling western farmers who have little time for rest,
And are ruined on selections in the sheep-infested West —
Droving songs are very pretty, but they merit little thanks
From the people of a country in possession of the Banks.

And the "rise and fall of seasons" suits the rise and fall of
    rhyme,
But we know that western seasons do not run on schedule time;
For the drought will go on drying while there's anything to dry,
Then it rains until you'd fancy it would bleach the sunny sky —
Then it pelters out of reason, for the downpour day and night
Nearly sweeps the population to the Great Australian Bight,
It is up in Northern Queensland that the seasons do their best,
But it's doubtful if you ever saw a season in the West,
There are years without an autumn or a winter or a spring,
There are broiling Junes — and summers when it rains like
    anything.

In the bush my ears were opened to the singing of the bird,
But the "carol of the magpie" was a thing I never heard.
Once the beggar roused my slumbers in a shanty. it is true,
But I only heard him asking, "Who the blanky blank are you?"
And the bell-bird in the ranges — but his "silver chime" is harsh
When it's heard beside the solo of the curlew in the marsh.

Yes, I heard the shearers singing "William Riley", out of tune,
Saw 'em fighting round a shanty on a Sunday afternoon,
But the bushman isn't always "trapping brumbies in the night",
Nor is he forever riding when "the morn is fresh and bright",
And he isn't always singing in the humpies on the run —
And the camp-fire's "cheery blazes" are a trifle overdone;
We have grumbled with the bushmen round the fire on rainy
  days,
When the smoke would blind a bullock and there wasn't any
  blaze —
Save the blazes of our language, for we cursed the fire in turn
Till the atmosphere was·heated and the wood began to burn.
Then we had to wring our blueys which were rotting in the
  swags,
And we saw the sugar leaking through the bottoms of the bags,
And we couldn't raise a "chorus", for the toothache and the
  cramp,
While we spent the hours of darkness draining puddles round
  the camp.

Would you like to change with Clancy — go a-droving? tell us
  true,
For we rather think that Clancy would be glad to change with
  you
And be something in the city; but 'twould give your muse a
  shock
To be losing time and money through the foot-rot in the flock,
And you wouldn't mind the beauties underneath the starry dome
If you had a wife and children and a lot of bills at home.

Did you ever guard the cattle when the night was inky-black,
And it rained, and icy water trickled gently down your back
Till your saddle-weary backbone fell a-aching to the roots
And you almost felt the croaking of the bull-frog in your boots —
Sit and shiver in the saddle, curse the restless stock and cough
Till a squatter's irate dummy cantered up to warn you off?
Did you fight the drought and pleuro when the "seasons" were
  asleep —
Felling sheoaks all the morning for a flock of starving sheep;
Drinking mud instead of water — climbing trees and lopping
  boughs
For the broken-hearted bullocks and the dry and dusty cows?

Do you think the bush was better in the "good old droving
    days",
When the squatter ruled supremely as the king of western ways,
When you got a slip of paper for the little you could earn,
But were forced to take provisions from the station in return —
When you couldn't keep a chicken at your humpy on the run,
For the squatter wouldn't let you — and your work was never
    done;
When you had to leave the missus in a lonely hut forlorn
While you "rose up Willy Riley" — in the days ere you were
    born?

Ah! we read about the drovers and the shearers and the like
Till we wonder why such happy and romantic fellows "strike".
Don't you fancy that the poets better give the bush a rest
Ere they raise a just rebellion in the over-written West?
Where the simple-minded bushman gets a meal and bed and rum
Just by riding round reporting phantom flocks that never come;
Where the scalper — never troubled by the "war-whoop of the
    push" —
Has a quiet little billet — breeding rabbits in the bush;
Where the idle shanty-keeper never fails to make a draw,
And the dummy gets his tucker through provisions in the law;
Where the labour-agitator — when the shearers rise in might —
Makes his money sacrificing all his substance for The Right;
Where the squatter makes his fortune, and "the seasons rise and
    fall",
And the poor and honest bushman has to suffer for it all;
Where the drovers and the shearers and the bushmen and the
    rest
Never reach the Eldorado of the poets of the West.

And you think the bush is purer and that life is better there,
But it doesn't seem to pay you like the "squalid street and
    square".
Pray inform us, City Bushman, where you read, in prose or
    verse,
Of the awful "city urchin who would greet you with a curse",
There are golden hearts in gutters, though their owners lack the
    fat,
And we'll back a teamster's offspring to outswear a city brat.
Do you think we're never jolly where the trams and buses rage?
Did you hear the gods in chorus when "Ri-tooral" held the
    stage?
Did you catch a ring of sorrow in the city urchin's voice
When he yelled for "Billy Elton", when he thumped the floor
    for "Royce"?
Do the bushmen, down on pleasure, miss the everlasting stars
When they drink and flirt and so on in the glow of private
    bars?

You've a down on "trams and buses", or the "roar" of 'em you
    said,
And the "filthy, dirty attic", where you never toiled for bread.
(And about that self-same attic — Lord! wherever have you
    been?
For the struggling needlewoman mostly keep her attic clean.)
But you'll find it very jolly with the cuff-and-collar push,
And the city seems to suit you, while you rave about the bush.

             *   *   *

You'll admit that Up-the-Country, more especially in drought,
Isn't quite the Eldorado that the poets rave about,
Yet at times we long to gallop where the reckless bushman
    rides
In the wake of startled brumbies that are flying for their hides;
Long to feel the saddle tremble once again between our knees
And to hear the stockwhips rattle just like rifles in the trees!
Long to feel the bridle-leather tugging strongly in the hand
And to feel once more a little like a native of the land.
And the ring of bitter feeling in the jingling of our rhymes
Isn't suited to the country nor the spirit of the times.
Let us go together droving, and returning, if we live,
Try to understand each other while we reckon up the div.

Up the Country

EDITOR'S NOTE

Stories and verses of up-country life are the most familiar examples of Australian writing from the 1890s. The selection stories of "Steele Rudd", the ballads of Lawson, Paterson, and Ogilvie, "Squeaker's Mate" from *Bush Studies*, *My Brilliant Career*, "The Drover's Wife", *Such is Life*, "How M'Dougall Topped the Score": these works are among the best known and most admired in the whole range of our writing. In making my selection for the final part of this anthology I have tried to include many of those pieces which give the literary achievement of the nineties its main flavour.

And that flavour is not a celebration of up-country life but a recurrent sense of hardship, betrayal, and alienation from the full potential of humanity. Barbara Baynton's story (80) is a bitterly ironic tale of how Squeaker deserts his lady "mate" once she is injured and no longer useful. Lawson's drover's wife (83) leads a life of impoverishment and loneliness, with only the dog to help her kill the snake. Little Mary O'Halloran in *Such is Life* (87) dies from exposure just before the search party finds her. Paterson and Lawson are united here (66 and 67) in their lament for the passing of a golden age. Miles Franklin, in an extract from her first novel published when she was only twenty-one, writes of how "the iron ungodly hand of class distinction has settled surely down upon Australian Society—Australia's Democracy is only a tradition of the past". It is this concept of an unfulfilled potential which I see as the principal theme of our writing from the 1890s. When the traditional Australian values of mateship, hard work, and good humour are dramatized against the hardships of the land and the betrayals of friends and family, they seem very frail values indeed.

65. "STEELE RUDD"

Starting the Selection

It's twenty years ago now since we settled on the Creek.
Twenty years! I remember well the day we came from
Stanthorpe, on Jerome's dray—eight of us, and all the
things—beds, tubs, a bucket, the two cedar chairs with the
pine bottoms and backs that Dad put in them, some pint-
pots and old Crib. It was a scorching hot day, too—talk
about thirst! At every creek we came to we drank till it stopped running.

Dad didn't travel up with us: he had gone some months
before, to put up the house and dig the waterhole. It was a
slabbed house, with shingled roof, and space enough for
two rooms; but the partition wasn't up. The floor was earth;
but Dad had a mixture of sand and fresh cow-dung, with
which he used to keep it level. About once every month he
would put it on; and everyone had to keep outside that day
till it was dry. There were no locks on the doors: pegs were
put in to keep them fast at night; and the slabs were not very
close together, for we could easily see through them
anybody coming on horseback. Joe and I used to play at
counting the stars through the cracks in the roof.

The day after we arrived Dad took Mother and us out to
see the paddock and the flat on the other side of the gully
that he was going to clear for cultivation. There was no fence
round the paddock, but he pointed out on a tree the sur-
veyor's marks, showing the boundary of our ground. It must
have been fine land, the way Dad talked about it! There was
very valuable timber on it, too, so he said; and he showed us
a place, among some rocks on a ridge, where he was sure
gold would be found, but we weren't to say anything about
it. Joe and I went back that evening and turned over every
stone on the ridge, but we didn't find any gold.

No mistake, it was a real wilderness—nothing but trees,
"goannas", dead timber, and bears; and the nearest

house—Dwyer's—was three miles away. I often wonder
how the women stood it the first few years; and I can
remember how Mother, when she was alone, used to sit on a
log, where the lane is now, and cry for hours. Lonely! It *was*
lonely.

Dad soon talked about clearing a couple of acres and putting in corn—all of us did, in fact—till the work commenced. It was a delightful topic before we started; but in
two weeks the clusters of fires that illumined the whooping
bush in the night, and the crash upon crash of the big trees
as they fell, had lost all their poetry.

We toiled and toiled clearing those four acres, where the
haystacks are now standing, till every tree and sapling that
grew there was down. We thought then the worst was over;
but how little we knew of clearing land! Dad was never tired
of calculating and telling us how much the crop would fetch
if the ground could only be got ready in time to put it in; so
we laboured the harder.

With our combined male and female forces and the aid of
a sapling lever we rolled the thundering big logs together in
the face of Hell's own fires; and when there were no logs to
roll it was tramp, tramp, the day through, gathering armfuls
of sticks, while the clothes clung to our back with a muddy
perspiration. Sometimes Dan and Dave would sit in the
shade beside the billy of water and gaze at the small patch
that had taken so long to do; then they would turn hopelessly to what was before them and ask Dad (who would never
take a spell) what was the use of thinking of ever getting such
a place cleared? And when Dave wanted to know why Dad
didn't take up a place on the plain, where there were no
trees to grub and plenty of water, Dad would cough as if
something was sticking in his throat, and then curse terribly
about the squatters and political jobbery. He would soon
cool down, though, and get hopeful again.

"Look at the Dwyers," he'd say; "from ten acres of wheat
they got £70 last year, besides feed for the fowls; they've got
corn in now, and there's only the two."

It wasn't only burning off! Whenever there came a short
drought the waterhole was sure to run dry; then it was take
turns to carry water from the springs—about two miles. We
had no draught horse, and if we had there was neither

watercask, trolly, nor dray; so we humped it—and talk about a drag! By the time you returned, if you hadn't drained the bucket, in spite of the big drink you'd take before leaving the springs, more than half would certainly be spilt through the vessel bumping against your leg every time you stumbled in the long grass. Somehow, none of us liked carrying water. We would sooner keep the fires going all day without dinner than do a trip to the springs.

One hot, thirsty day it was Joe's turn with the bucket, and he managed to get back without spilling very much. We were all pleased because there was enough left after the tea had been made to give each a drink. Dinner was nearly over; Dan had finished, and was taking it easy on the sofa, when Joe said:

"I say, Dad what's a nater-dog like?" Dad told him: "Yellow, sharp ears and bushy tail."

"Those muster bin some then thet I seen—I don't know 'bout the bushy tail—all th' hair had comed off." "Where'd y' see them, Joe?" we asked. "Down 'n th' springs floating about—dead".

Then everyone seemed to think hard and look at the tea. *I* didn't want any more. Dan jumped off the sofa and went outside; and Dad looked after Mother.

At last the four acres—excepting the biggest of the iron-bark trees and about fifty stumps—were pretty well cleared; and then came a problem that couldn't be worked-out on a draught-board. I have already said that we hadn't any draught horses; indeed, the only thing on the selection like a horse was an old "tuppy" mare that Dad used to straddle. The date of her foaling went further back than Dad's, I believe; and she was shaped something like an alderman. We found her one day in about eighteen inches of mud, with both eyes picked out by the crows, and her hide bearing evidence that a feathery tribe had made a roost of her carcase. Plainly, there was no chance of breaking up the ground with her help. We had no plough, either; how then was the corn to be put in? That was the question.

Dan and Dave sat outside in the corner of the chimney, both scratching the ground with a chip and not saying anything. Dad and Mother sat inside talking it over. Sometimes Dad would get up and walk round the room shaking his head; then he would kick old Crib for lying under the table. At last Mother struck something which brightened him up, and he called Dave.

"Catch Topsy and——" He paused because he remembered the old mare was dead.

"Run over and ask Mister Dwyer to lend me three hoes."

Dave went; Dwyer lent the hoes; and the problem was solved. That was how *we* started.

66. A. B. PATERSON

THE MAN FROM SNOWY RIVER

There was movement at the station, for the word had passed
    around
That the colt from old Regret had got away,
And had joined the wild bush horses — he was worth a
    thousand pound,
So all the cracks had gathered to the fray.
All the tried and noted riders from the stations near and far
Had mustered at the homestead overnight,
For the bushmen love hard riding where the wild bush horses
    are,
And the stock-horse snuffs the battle with delight.

There was Harrison, who made his pile when Pardon won the
    cup,
The old man with his hair as white as snow;
But few could ride beside him when his blood was fairly up —
He would go wherever horse and man could go.
And Clancy of the Overflow came down to lend a hand,
No better horseman ever held the reins;
For never horse could throw him while the saddle-girths would
    stand,
He learnt to ride while droving on the plains.

And one was there, a stripling on a small and weedy beast,
He was something like a racehorse undersized,
With a touch of Timor pony — three parts thorough-bred at
    least —
And such as are by mountain horsemen prized.
He was hard and tough and wiry — just the sort that won't say
    die —
There was courage in his quick impatient tread;
And he bore the badge of gameness in his bright and fiery eye,
And the proud and lofty carriage of his head.

But still so slight and weedy, one would doubt his power to
    stay,
And the old man said, "That horse will never do
"For a long and tiring gallop — lad, you'd better stop away,
"Those hills are far too rough for such as you."
So he waited sad and wistful — only Clancy stood his friend —
"I think we ought to let him come," he said;
"I warrant he'll be with us when he's wanted at the end,
"For both his horse and he are mountain bred."

"He hails from Snowy River, up by Kosciusko's side,
"Where the hills are twice as steep and twice as rough,
"Where a horse's hoofs strike firelight from the flint stones every
     stride,
"The man that holds his own is good enough.
"And the Snowy River riders on the mountains make their
     home,
"Where the river runs those giant hills between;
"I have seen full many horsemen since I first commenced to
     roam,
"But nowhere yet such horsemen have I seen."

So he went — they found the horses by the big mimosa
     clump —
They raced away towards the mountain's brow,
And the old man gave his orders, "Boys, go at them from the
     jump,
"No use to try for fancy riding now.
"And Clancy, you must wheel them, try and wheel them to
     the right.
"Ride boldly, lad, and never fear the spills,
"For never yet was rider that could keep the mob in sight,
"If once they gain the shelter of those hills."

So Clancy rode to wheel them — he was racing on the wing
Where the best and boldest riders take their place,
And he raced his stock-horse past them, and he made the
     ranges ring
With the stockwhip, as he met them face to face.
Then they halted for a moment, while he swung the dreaded
     lash,
But they saw their well-loved mountain full in view,
And they charged beneath the stockwhip with a sharp and
     sudden dash,
And off into the mountain scrub they flew.

Then fast the horsemen followed, where the gorges deep and
     black
Resounded to the thunder of their tread,
And the stock-whip woke the echoes, and they fiercely
     answered back
From cliffs and crags that beetled overhead.
And upward, ever upward, the wild horses held their way,
Where mountain ash and kurrajong grew wide;
And the old man muttered fiercely, "We may bid the
     mob good day,
"*No* man can hold them down the other side."

When they reached the mountain's summit, even Clancy took
     a pull,

It well might make the boldest hold their breath,
The wild hop scrub grew thickly, and the hidden ground was
    full
Of wombat holes, and any slip was death.
But the man from Snowy River let the pony have his head,
And he swung his stockwhip round and gave a cheer,
And he raced him down the mountain like a torrent down its
    bed,
While the others stood and watched in very fear.

He sent the flint stones flying, but the pony kept his feet,
He cleared the fallen timber in his stride,
And the man from Snowy River never shifted in his seat —
It was grand to see that mountain horseman ride.
Through the stringy barks and saplings, on the rough and
    broken ground,
Down the hillside at a racing pace he went;
And he never drew the bridle till he landed safe and sound,
At the bottom of that terrible descent.

He was right among the horses as they climbed the further hill,
And the watchers on the mountain standing mute,
Saw him ply the stockwhip fiercely, he was right among them
    still,
As he raced across the clearing in pursuit.
Then they lost him for a moment, where two mountain
    gullies met
In the ranges , but a final glimpse reveals
On a dim and distant hillside the wild horses racing yet,
With the man from Snowy River at their heels.

And he ran them single-handed till their sides were white with
    foam.
He followed like a bloodhound on their track,
Till they halted cowed and beaten, then he turned their heads
    for home,
And alone and unassisted brought them back.
But his hardy mountain pony he could scarcely raise a trot,
He was blood from hip to shoulder from the spur;
But his pluck was still undaunted, and his courage fiery hot,
For never yet was mountain horse a cur.

And down by Kosciusko, where the pine-clad ridges raise
Their torn and rugged battlements on high,
Where the air is clear as crystal, and the white stars fairly
    blaze
At midnight in the cold and frosty sky,
And where around the Overflow the reedbeds sweep and sway
To the breezes, and the rolling plains are wide,
The man from Snowy River is a household word today,
And the stockmen tell the story of his ride.

THE ROARING DAYS

The night too quickly passes
    And we are growing old,
So let us fill our glasses
    And toast the Days of Gold;
When finds of wondrous treasure
    Set all the South ablaze,
And you and I were faithful mates
    All through the roaring days!

Then stately ships came sailing
    From every harbour's mouth,
And sought the land of promise
    That beaconed in the South;
Then southward streamed their streamers
    And swelled their canvas full
To speed the wildest dreamers
    E'er borne in vessel's hull.

Their shining Eldorado,
    Beneath the southern skies,
Was day and night forever
    Before their eager eyes.
The brooding bush, awakened,
    Was stirred in wild unrest,
And all the year a human stream
    Went pouring to the West.

The rough bush roads re-echoed
    The bar-room's noisy din,
When troops of stalwart horsemen
    Dismounted at the inn.
And oft the hearty greetings
    And hearty clasp of hands
Would tell of sudden meetings
    Of friends from other lands;
When, puzzled long, the new-chum
    Would recognize at last,
Behind a bronzed and bearded skin,
    A comrade of the past.

And when the cheery camp-fire
    Explored the bush with gleams,
The camping-grounds were crowded
    With caravans of teams;
Then home the jests were driven,
    And good old songs were sung,
And choruses were given
    The strength of heart and lung.
Oh, they were lion-hearted
    Who gave our country birth!
Oh, they were of the stoutest sons
    From all the lands on earth!

Oft when the camps were dreaming,
    And fires began to pale,
Through rugged ranges gleaming
    Would come the Royal Mail.
Behind six foaming horses,
    And lit by flashing lamps,
Old "Cobb and Co.'s". in Royal State,
    Went dashing past the camps.

Oh, who would paint a goldfield,
    And limn the picture right,
As we have often seen it
    In early morning's light;
The yellow mounds of mullock
    With spots of red and white,
The scattered quartz that glistened
    Like diamonds in light;
The azure line of ridges,
    The bush of darkest green,
The little homes of calico
    That dotted all the scene.

I hear the fall of timber
    From distant flats and fells,
The pealing of the anvils
    As clear as little bells,
The rattle of the cradle,
    The clack of windlass-boles
The flutter of the crimson flags
    Above the golden holes.

*   *   *

Ah, then our hearts were bolder,
    And if Dame Fortune frowned,
Our swags we'd lightly shoulder
    And tramp to other ground.
But golden days are vanished,
    And altered is the scene;
The diggings are deserted,
    The camping-grounds are green;
The flaunting flag of progress
    Is in the West unfurled,
The mighty bush with iron rails
    Is tethered to the world.

68. MILES FRANKLIN

Disjointed Sketches and Grumbles (from My Brilliant Career)

It was my duty to "rare the poddies". This is the most
godless occupation in which it has been my lot to engage. I
did a great amount of thinking while feeding them—for, by
the way, I am afflicted with the power of thought, which is a
heavy curse. The less a person thinks and inquires regarding
the why and the wherefore and the justice of things, when
dragging along through life, the happier it is for him, and
doubly, trebly so, for her.

Poor little calves! Slaves to the greed of man! Bereft of the
mothers with which Nature has provided them, and compel-
led to exist on milk from the separator, often thick, sour,
and icy cold.

Besides the milking I did, before I went to school every
morning, for which I had to prepare myself and the younger
children, and to which we had to walk two miles, I had to
feed thirty calves and wash the breakfast dishes. On returning from school in the afternoon, often in a state of exhaus-
tion from walking in the blazing sun, I had the same duties
over again, and in addition boots to clean and home lessons
to prepare for the morrow. I had to relinquish my piano
practice for want of time.

Ah! those short, short nights of rest and long, long days
of toil! It seems to me that dairying means slavery in the
hands of poor people who cannot afford hired labour. I am
not writing of dairy-farming, the genteel and artistic profession as eulogised in leading articles of agricultural newspapers and as taught in agricultural colleges. I am depicting
practical dairying as I have lived it, and seen it lived, by
dozens of families around me.

It takes a great deal of work to produce even one pound
of butter fit for market. At the time I mention it was 3d. and
4d. per lb., so it was much work and small pay. It was slaving

and delving from morning till night—Sundays, week-days, and holidays, all alike were work-days to us.

Hard graft is a great leveller. Household drudgery, wood-cutting, milking, and gardening soon roughen the hands and dim the outside polish. When the body is wearied with much toil the desire to cultivate the mind, or the cultivation it has already received, is gradually wiped out. Thus it was with my parents. They had dropped from swelldom to peasantism. They were among and of the peasantry. None of their former acquaintances came within their circle now, for the iron ungodly hand of class distinction has settled surely down upon Australian Society—Australia's Democracy is only a tradition of the past.

I say nought against the lower life. The peasantry are the bulwarks of every nation. The life of a peasant is to a peasant who is a peasant with a peasant's soul, when times are good and when seasons smile, a grand life. It is honest, clean, and wholesome. But the life of a peasant to me is purgatory. Those around me worked from morning till night and then enjoyed their well-earned sleep. They had but two states of existence—work and sleep.

There was a third part in me which cried out to be fed. I longed for the arts. Music was a passion with me. I borrowed every book in the neighbourhood and stole hours from rest to read them. This told upon me and made my physical burdens harder for me than for other children of my years around me. That third was the strongest part of me. In it I lived a dream-life with writers, artists, and musicians. Hope, sweet, cruel, delusive Hope, whispered in my ear that life was long with much by-and-bye, and in that by-and-bye my dream-life would be real. So on I went with that gleaming lake in the distance beckoning me to come and sail on its silver waters, and Inexperience, conceited, blind Inexperience, failing to show the impassable pit between it and me.

To return to the dairying.

Old and young alike we earned out scant livelihood by the heavy sweat of our brows. Still, we *did* gain an honest living. We were not ashamed to look day in the face, and fought our way against all odds with the stubborn independence of our British ancestors. But when '94 went out without rain, and '95, hot, dry, pitiless '95, succeeded it, there came a time when it was impossible to make a living.

The scorching furnace-breath winds shrivelled every blade of grass, dust and the moan of starving stock filled the air—vegetables became a thing of the past. The calves I had reared died one by one, and the cows followed in their footsteps.

I had left school then, and my mother and father and I spent the days in lifting our cows. When our strength proved inadequate, the help of neighbours had to be called in, and father would give his services in return. Only a few of our more well-to-do neighbours had been able to send their stock away, or had any better place to which to transfer them. The majority of them were in as tight a plight as ourselves. This cow-lifting became quite a trade, the whole day being spent in it and in discussing the bad prospect ahead if the drought continued.

Many an extra line of care furrowed the brows of the disheartened bushmen then. Not only was their living taken from them by the drought, but there is nothing more heartrending than to have poor beasts, especially dairy cows, so familiar, valued, and loved, pleading for food day after day in their piteous dumb way when one has it not to give.

We shore ourselves of all but the bare necessaries of life, but even they for a family of ten are considerable, and it was a might tussle to get both ends within cover of meeting. We felt the full force of the heavy hand of poverty—the most stinging kind of poverty too, that which still holds up its head and keeps an outside appearance. Far more grinding is this than the poverty inherited from generations which is not ashamed of itself, and has not as an accompaniment the wounded pride and humiliation which attacked us.

Some there are who argue that poverty does not mean unhappiness. Let those try what it is to be destitute of even one companionable friend, what it means to be forced to exist in an alien sphere of society, what it is like to be unable to afford a stamp to write to a friend; let them long as passionately as I have longed for reading and music, and be unable to procure it because of poverty; let poverty force them into doing work against which every fibre of their being revolts, as it has forced me, and then see if their lives will be happy.

My school life had been dull and uneventful. The one incident of any note had been the day that the teacher, better known as old Harris, "stood up" to the inspector. The latter was a precise, collar-and-cuffs sort of little man. He gave one the impression of having all his ideas on the subjects he thought worthy of attention carefully culled and packed in his brain-pan, and neatly labelled, so that he might without fluster pounce upon any of them at a moment's warning. He was gentlemanly and respectable, and discharged his duties punctiliously in a manner reflecting credit on himself and his position, but, comparing the mind of a philanthropist to the Murrumbidgee in breadth, his, in comparison, might be likened to the flow of a bucket of water in a dray-rut.

On the day in question—a precious hot one it was—he had finished examining us in most subjects, and was looking at our copy-books. He looked up from them, ahemed! and fastidiously straightened his waistcoat.

"Mr. Harris!"

"Yes, sir."

"Comparisons are odious, but, unfortunately, I am forced to draw one now."

"Yes, sir."

"This writing is much inferior to that of town scholars. It is very shaky and irregular. Also, I notice that the children seem stupid and dull. I don't like putting it so plainly, but, in fact, ah, they seem to be possessed with the proverbial stupidity of country people. How do you account for this?"

Poor old Harris! In spite of his drunken habits and inability to properly discharge his duties, he had a warm heart and much fellowshiply humanity in him. He understood and loved his pupils, and would not have aspersions cast upon them. Besides, the "nip" he had taken to brace himself to meet the inspector had been two or three, and they robbed him of the discretion which otherwise might have kept him silent.

"Si-r-r-r, I can and will account for it. Look you at every one of those children. Every one, right down to this little tot," indicating a little girl of five, "has to milk and work hard before and after school, besides walk on an average two miles to and from school in this infernal heat. Most of the elder boys and girls milk on an average fourteen cows morning and evening. You try that treatment for a week or two, my fine gentleman, and then see if your fist doesn't ache and shake so that you can't write at all. See if you won't look a trifle dozy. Stupidity of country people be hanged! If you had to work from morning till night in the heat and dust, and get precious little for it too, I bet you wouldn't have much time to scrape your finger-nails, read science notes, and look smart." Here he took off his coat and shaped up to his superior.

The inspector drew back in consternation.

"Mr. Harris, you forget yourself!"

At this juncture they went outside together. What happened there we never knew. That is all we heard of the matter except the numerous garbled accounts which were carried home that afternoon.

A DROUGHT IDYLL

"Sybylla, what are you doing? Where is your mother?"

"I'm ironing. Mother's down at the fowl-house seeing after some chickens. What do you want?"

It was my father who addressed me. Time, 2 o'clock p.m. Thermometer hung in the shade of the verandah registering $105\frac{1}{2}°$.

"I see Blackshaw coming across the flat. Call your mother. You bring the leg-ropes—I've got the dog-leg. Come at once; we'll give the cows another lift. Poor devils! might as well knock 'em on the head at once, but there might be rain next moon. This drought can't last for ever."

I called mother, got the leg-ropes, and set off, pulling my sun-bonnet closely over my face to protect my eyes from the dust which was driving from the west in blinding clouds. The dog-leg to which father had referred was three poles about eight or ten feet long, strapped together so they could be stood up. It was an arrangement father had devised to facilitate our labour in lifting the cows. A fourth and longer pole was placed across the fork formed by the three, and to one end of this were tied a couple of leg-ropes, after being placed round the beast, one beneath the flank and one around the girth. On the other end of this pole we would put our weight while one man would lift with the tail and another with the horns. New chum cows would sulk, and we would have great work with them; but those used to the performance would help themselves, and up they'd go as nice as a daisy. The only art needed was to draw the pole back quickly before the cows could move, or the leg-ropes would pull them over again.

On this afternoon we had six cows to lift. We struggled manfully, and got five on their feet, and then proceeded to where the last one was lying, back downwards, on a shadeless stony spot on the side of a hill. The men slewed her round by the tail, while mother and I fixed the dog-leg and adjusted the ropes. We got the cow up, but the poor beast was so weak and knocked about that she immediately fell down again. We resolved to let her have a few minutes' spell before making another attempt at lifting. There was not a blade of grass to be seen, and the ground was too dusty to sit on. We were too overdone to make more than one-worded utterances, so waited silently the blazing sun, closing our eyes against the dust.

Weariness! Weariness!

A few light wind-smitten clouds made wan streaks across the white sky, haggard with the fierce relentless glare of the afternoon sun. Weariness was written across my mother's delicate careworn features, and found expression in my father's knitted brows and dusty face. Blackshaw was weary, and said so, as he wiped the dust, made mud with perspiration, off his cheeks. I was weary—my limbs ached with the heat and work. The poor beast stretched at our feet was weary. All nature was weary, and seemed to sing a dirge to that effect in the furnace-breath wind which roared among the trees on the low ranges at our back and smote the parched and thirsty ground. All were weary, all but the sun. He seemed to glory in his power, relentless and untiring, as he swung boldly in the sky, triumphantly leering down upon his helpless victims.

Weariness! Weariness!

This was life—my life—my career, my brilliant career! I was fifteen—fifteen! A few fleeting hours and I would be old as those around me. I looked at them as they stood there , weary, and turning down the other side of the hill of life.

When young, no doubt they had hoped for, and dreamed of, better things—had even known them. But here they were. This had been their life; this was their career. It was, and in all probability would be, mine too. My life—my career—my brilliant career!

Weariness! Weariness!

The summer sun danced on. Summer is fiendish, and life is a curse, I said in my heart. What a great dull hard rock the world was! On it were a few barren narrow ledges, and on these, by exerting ourselves so that the force wears off our finger-nails, it allows us to hang for a year or two, and then hurls us off into outer darkness and oblivion, perhaps to endure worse torture than this.

The poor beast moaned. The lifting had strained her, and there were patches of hide worn off her the size of breakfast-plates, sore and most harrowing to look upon.

It takes great suffering to wring a moan from the patience of a cow. I turned my head away, and with the impatience and onesided reasoning common to fifteen, asked God what He meant by this. It is well enough to heap suffering on human beings, seeing it is supposed to be merely a probation for a better world, but animals—poor, innocent animals—why are they tortured so?

"Come now, we'll lift her once more," said my father. At it we went again; it is surprising what weight there is in the poorest cow. With great struggling we got her to her feet once more, and were careful this time to hold her till she got steady on her legs. Father and mother at the tail and Blackshaw and I at the horns, we marched her home and gave her a bran mash. Then we turned to our work in the house while the men sat and smoked and spat on the verandah, discussing the drought for an hour, at the end of which time they went to help some one else with their stock. I made up the fire and we continued our ironing, which had been interrupted some hours before. It was hot unpleasant work on such a day. We were forced to keep the doors and windows closed on account of the wind and dust. We were hot and tired, and our feet ached so that we could scarcely stand on them.

Weariness! Weariness!

Summer is fiendish and life is a curse, I said in my heart.

Day after day the drought continued. Now and again there would be a few days of the raging wind before mentioned, which carried the dry grass off the paddocks and piled it against the fences, darkened the air with dust, and seemed to promise rain, but ever it dispersed whence it came, taking with it the few clouds it had gathered up; and for weeks and weeks at a stretch, from horizon to horizon, was never a speck to mar the cruel dazzling brilliance of the metal sky.

Weariness! Weariness!

I said the one thing many times, but ah! it was a weary thing which took much repetition that familiarity might wear away a little of its bitterness.

69. WILL OGILVIE

NORTHWARD TO THE SHEDS

There's a whisper from the regions out beyond the Barwon
   banks;
There's a gathering of the legions and a forming of the ranks;
There's a murmur coming nearer with the signs that never
   fail,
And it's time for every shearer to be out upon the trail.
They must leave their girls behind them and their empty
   glasses, too,
For there's plenty left to mind them when they cross the dry
   Bacroo;
There'll be kissing, there'll be sorrow such as only sweethearts
   know,
But before the noon tomorrow they'll be singing as they go —

For the Western creeks are calling,
   And the idle days are done,
With the snowy fleeces falling
   And the Queensland sheds begun!

There is shortening of the bridle, there is tightening of the
   girth,
There is fondling of the idol that they love the best on earth;
Northward from the Lachlan River and the sun-dried
   Castlereagh,
Outward to the Never-Never ride the ringers on their way.
From the green bends of the Murray they have run their
   horses in,
For there's haste and there is hurry when the Queensland
   sheds begin;
On the Bogan they are bridling, they are saddling on the
   Bland,
There is plunging and there's sidling — for the colts don't
   understand

That the Western creeks are calling,
   And the idle days are done,
With the snowy fleeces falling
   And the Queensland sheds begun!

They will camp below the station, they'll be cutting peg and
    pole,
Rearing tents for occupation till the calling of the roll;
And it's time the nags were driven, and it's time to strap the
    pack,
For there's never licence given to the laggards on the track.
Hark the music of the battle! it is time to bare our swords:
Do you hear the rush and rattle as they tramp along the
    boards?
They are past the pen-doors picking light-wooled weaners one
    by one;
I can hear the shear-blades clicking, and I know the fight's
    begun!

70.   A. B. PATERSON

THE GEEBUNG POLO CLUB

It was somewhere up the country, in a land of rock and scrub,
That they formed an institution called the Geebung Polo Club.
They were long and wiry natives from the rugged mountain
  side,
And the horse was never saddled that the Geebungs couldn't
  ride;
But their style of playing polo was irregular and rash —
They had mighty little science, but a mighty lot of dash:
And they played on mountain ponies that were muscular and
  strong,
Though their coats were quite unpolished, and their manes and
  tails were long.
And they used to train those ponies wheeling cattle in the
  scrub:
They were demons, were the members of the Geebung Polo
  Club.

It was somewhere down the country, in a city's smoke and
  steam,
That a polo club existed, called "The Cuff and Collar Team".
As a social institution 'twas a marvellous success,
For the members were distinguished by exclusiveness and
  dress.
They had natty little ponies that were nice, and smooth, and
  sleek,
For their cultivated owners only rode 'em once a week.
So they started up the country in pursuit of sport and fame,
For they meant to show the Geebungs how they ought to play
  the game;
And they took their valets with them — just to give their boots
  a rub
Ere they started operations on the Geebung Polo Club.

Now my readers can imagine how the contest ebbed and
  flowed,
When the Geebung boys got going it was time to clear the
  road;
And the game was so terrific that ere half the time was gone
A spectator's leg was broken — just from merely looking on.
For they waddied one another till the plain was strewn with
  dead,

While the score was kept so even that they neither got ahead.
And the Cuff and Collar Captain, when he tumbled off to die,
Was the last surviving player — so the game was called a tie.

Then the Captain of the Geebungs raised him slowly from the
    ground,
Though his wounds were mostly mortal, yet he fiercely gazed
    around;
There was no one to oppose him — all the rest were in a
    trance,
So he scrambled on his pony for his last expiring chance,
For he meant to make an effort to get victory to his side;
So he stuck at goal — and missed it — then he tumbled off and
    died.

By the old Campaspe River, where the breezes shake the grass,
There's a row of little gravestones that the stockmen never pass,
For they bear a crude inscription saying, "Stranger, drop a tear,
"For the Cuff and Collar players and the Geebung boys lie
    here."
And on misty moonlit evenings, while the dingoes howl around,
You can see their shadows flitting down that phantom polo
    ground;
You can hear the loud collisions as the flying players meet,
And the rattle of the mallets, and the rush of ponies' feet,
Till the terrified spectator rides like blazes to the pub —
He's been haunted by the spectres of the Geebung Polo Club.

71. "STEELE RUDD"

The Night We Watched for Wallabies

It had been a bleak July day, and as night came on a bitter westerly howled through the trees. Cold! wasn't it cold! The pigs in the sty, hungry and half-fed (we wanted for ourselves the few pumpkins that had survived the drought) fought savagely with each other for shelter, and squealed all the time like—well, like pigs. The cows and calves left the place to seek shelter away in the mountains; while the draught horses, their hair standing up like barbed-wire, leaned sadly over the fence and gazed at the green lucerne. Joe went about shivering in an old coat of Dad's with only one sleeve to it—a calf had fancied the other one day that Dad hung it on a post as a mark to go by while ploughing.

"My! it'll be a stinger tonight," Dad remarked to Mrs. Brown—who sat, cold-looking, on the sofa—as he staggered inside with an immense log for the fire. A log! Nearer a whole tree! But wood was nothing in Dad's eyes.

Mrs. Brown had been at our place five or six days. Old Brown called occasionally to see her, so we knew they couldn't have quarrelled. Sometimes she did a little housework, but more often she didn't. We talked it over together, but couldn't make it out. Joe asked Mother, but she had no idea—so she said. We were full up, as Dave put it, of Mrs. Brown, and wished her out of the place. She had taken to ordering us about, as though she had something to do with us.

After supper we sat round the fire—as near to it as we could without burning ourselves—Mrs. Brown and all, and listened to the wind whistling outside. Ah, it was pleasant beside the fire listening to the wind! When Dad had warmed himself back and front he turned to us and said:

"Now, boys, we must go directly and light some fires and keep those wallabies back."

That was a shock to us, and we looked at him to see if he

were really in earnest. He was, and as serious as a judge.

"*Tonight!*" Dave answered, surprisedly—"why tonight any more than last night or the night before? Thought you had decided to let them rip?"

"Yes, but we might as well keep them off a bit longer."

"But there's no wheat there for them to get now. So what's the good of watching them? There's no sense in *that*."

Dad was immovable.

"Anyway"—whined Joe—"*I'm* not going—not a night like this—not when I ain't got boots."

That vexed Dad. "Hold your tongue, sir!" he said—"you'll do as you're told."

But Dave hadn't finished. "I've been following that harrow since sunrise this morning," he said, "and now you want me to go chasing wallabies about in the dark, a night like this, and for nothing else but to keep them from eating the ground. It's always the way here, the more one does the more he's wanted to do," and he commenced to cry. Mrs. Brown had something to say. *She* agreed with Dad and thought we ought to go, as the wheat might spring up again.

"Pshah!" Dave blurted out between his sobs, while we thought of telling her to shut her mouth.

Slowly and reluctantly we left that roaring fireside to accompany Dad that bitter night. It *was* a night!—dark as pitch, silent, forlorn and forbidding, and colder than the busiest morgue. And just to keep wallabies from eating nothing! They *had* eaten all the wheat—every blade of it—and the grass as well. What they would start on next —ourselves or the cart-harness—wasn't quite clear.

We stumbled along in the dark one behind the other, with our hands stuffed into our trousers. Dad was in the lead, and poor Joe, bare-shinned and bootless, in the rear. Now and again he tramped on a Bathurst-burr, and, in sitting down to extract the prickle, would receive a cluster of them elsewhere. When he escaped the burr it was only to knock his shin against a log or leave a toe-nail or two clinging to a stone. Joe howled, but the wind howled louder, and blew and blew.

Dave, in pausing to wait on Joe, would mutter:

"To *hell* with everything! Whatever he wants bringing us

out a night like this, I'm *damned* if *I* know!"

Dad couldn't see very well in the dark, and on this night couldn't see at all, so he walked up against one of the old draught horses that had fallen asleep gazing at the lucerne. And what a fright they both got! The old horse took it worse than Dad—who only tumbled down—for he plunged as though the devil had grabbed him, and fell over the fence, twisting every leg he had in the wires. How the brute struggled! We stood and listened to him. After kicking panels of the fence down and smashing every wire in it, he got loose and made off, taking most of it with him.

"That's one wallaby on the wheat, anyway," Dave muttered, and we giggled. *We* understood Dave; but Dad didn't open his mouth.

We lost no time lighting the fires. Then we walked through the "wheat" and wallabies! May Satan reprove me if I exaggerate their number by one solitary pair of ears—from the row and scatter they made there was a *million*.

Dad told Joe, at last, he could go to sleep if he liked, at the fire. Joe went to sleep—*how*, I don't know. Then Dad sat beside him, and for long intervals would stare silently into the darkness. Sometimes a string of the vermin would hop past close to the fire, and another time a curlew would come near and screech its ghostly wail, but he never noticed them. Yet he seemed to be listening.

We mooched around from fire to fire, hour after hour, and when we wearied of heaving fire-sticks at the enemy we sat on our heels and cursed the wind, and the winter, and the night-birds alternately. It was a lonely, wretched occupation.

Now and again Dad would leave his fire to ask us if we could hear a noise. We couldn't, except that of wallabies and mopokes. Then he would go back and listen again. He was restless, and, somehow, his heart wasn't in the wallabies at all. Dave couldn't make him out.

The night wore on. By-and-by there was a sharp rattle of wires, then a rustling noise, and Sal appeared in the glare of the fire. *"Dad!"* she said. That was all. Without a word, Dad bounced up and went back to the house along with her.

"Something's up!" Dave said, and, half-anxious, half-afraid, we gazed into the fire and thought and thought. Then we stared, nervously, into the night, and listened for Dad's return, but heard only the wind and the mopoke.

At dawn he appeared again, with a broad smile on his face, and told us that mother had got another baby—a fine little chap. *Then* we knew why Mrs. Brown had been staying at our place.

72. HENRY LAWSON

THE SLIPRAILS AND THE SPUR

The colours of the setting sun
    Withdrew across the Western land —
He raised the sliprails, one by one,
    And shot them home with trembling hand;
Her brown hands clung — her face grew pale —
    Ah! quivering chin and eyes that brim! —
One quick, fierce kiss across the rail,
    And, "Good-bye, Mary!" "Good-bye, Jim!"
        Oh! he rides hard to race the pain
            Who rides from love, who rides from home;
        But he rides slowly home again,
            Whose heart has learnt to love and roam.

A hand upon the horse's mane,
    And one foot in the stirrup set,
And, stooping back to kiss again,
    With "Good-bye, Mary! don't you fret!
"When I come back" — he laughed for her —
    "We do not know how soon 'twill be:
"I'll whistle as I round the spur —
    "You let the sliprails down for me."

She gasped for sudden loss of hope,
    As, with a backward wave to her,
He cantered down the grassy slope
    And swiftly round the dark'ning spur.
Black-pencilled panels standing high,
    And darkness fading into stars,
And blurring fast against the sky,
    A faint white form beside the bars.

And often at the set of sun,
    In winter bleak and summer brown,
She'd steal across the little run,
    And shyly let the sliprails down.
And listen there when darkness shut
    The nearer spur in silence deep;
And when they called her from the hut
    Steal home and cry herself to sleep.

* * *

A great white gate where sliprails were,
　A brick house 'neath the mountain brow,
The "mad girl" buried by the spur
　So long ago, forgotten now.
　　And he rides hard to dull the pain
　　　Who rides from one that loves him best:
　　And he rides slowly back again,
　　　Whose restless heart must rove for rest.

73. HENRY LAWSON

THE TEAMS

A cloud of dust on the long white road,
    And the teams go creeping on
Inch by inch with the weary load;
And by the power of the green-hide goad
    The distant goal is won.

With eyes half-shut to the blinding dust,
    And necks to the yokes bent low,
The beasts are pulling as bullocks must;
And the shining tires might almost rust
    While the spokes are turning slow.

With face half-hid 'neath a broad-brimmed hat
    That shades from the heat's white waves,
And shouldered whip with its green-hide plait,
The driver plods with a gait like that
    Of his weary, patient slaves.

He wipes his brow, for the day is hot,
    And spits to the left with spite.
He shouts at "Bally", and flicks at "Scot",
And raises dust from the back of "Spot",
    And spits to the dusty right.

He'll sometimes pause as a thing of form
    In front of a settler's door,
And ask for a drink, and remark "It's warm",
Or say "There's signs of a thunder-storm";
    But he seldom utters more.

But the rains are heavy on roads like these;
    And, fronting his lonely home,
For weeks together the settler sees
The teams bogged down to the axletrees,
    Or ploughing the sodden loam.

And then when the roads are at their worst,
    The bushman's children hear
The cruel blows of the whips reversed
While bullocks pull as their hearts would burst,
    And bellow with pain and fear.

And thus with little of joy or rest
    Are the long, long journeys done;
And thus — 'tis a cruel war at the best —
Is distance fought in the mighty West,
    And the lonely battles won.

74. HENRY LAWSON

The Shanty-Keeper's Wife

There were about a dozen of us jammed into the coach,
on the box seat and hanging on to the roof and tailboard as
best we could. We were shearers, bagmen, agents, a squatter,
a cockatoo, the usual joker—and one or two professional
spielers, perhaps. We were tired and stiff and nearly
frozen—too cold to talk and too irritable to risk the inevitable argument which an interchange of ideas would have
led up to. We had been looking forward for hours, it
seemed, to the pub where we were to change horses. For the
last hour or two all that our united efforts had been able to
get out of the driver was a grunt to the effect that it was
"'bout a couple o' miles". Then he said, or grunted,
"'Tain't fur now," a couple of times, and refused to commit
himself any further; he seemed grumpy about having committed himself that far.

He was one of those men who take everything in dead
earnest; who regard any expression of ideas outside their
own sphere of life as trivial, or, indeed, if addressed directly
to them, as offensive; who, in fact, are darkly suspicious of
anything in the shape of a joke or laugh on the part of an
outsider in their own particular dust-hole. He seemed to be
always thinking, and thinking a lot; when his hands were not
both engaged, he would tilt his hat forward and scratch the
base of his skull with his little finger, and let his jaw hang.
But his intellectual powers were mostly concentrated on a
doubtful swingle-tree, a misfitting collar, or that there bay
or piebald (on the off or near side) with the sore shoulder.

Casual letters or papers, to be delivered on the road, were
matters which troubled him vaguely, but constantly—like
the abstract ideas of his passengers.

The joker of our party was a humourist of the dry order,
and had been slyly taking rises out of the driver for the last
two or three stages. But the driver only brooded. He wasn't

the one to tell you straight if you offended him, or if he fancied you offended him, and thus gain your respect, or prevent a misunderstanding which would result in life-long enmity. He might meet you in after years when you had forgotten all about your trespass—if indeed you had ever been conscious of it—and "stoush" you unexpectedly on the ear.

Also you might regard him as your friend, on occasion, and yet he would stand by and hear a perfect stranger tell you the most outrageous lies, to your hurt, and know that the stranger was telling lies, and never put you up to it. It would never enter his head to do so. It wouldn't be any affair of his—only an abstract question.

It grew darker and colder. The rain came as if the frozen south were spitting at your face and neck and hands, and our feet grew as big as camel's, and went dead, and we might as well have stamped the footboards with wooden legs for all the feeling we got into ours. But they were more comfortable that way, for the toes didn't curl up and pain so much, nor did our corns stick out so hard against the leather, and shoot.

We looked out eagerly for some clearing, or fence, or light—some sign of the shanty where we were to change horses—but there was nothing save blackness all round. The long, straight, cleared road was no longer relieved by the ghostly patch of light, far ahead, where the bordering tree-walls came together in perspective and framed the ether. We were down in the bed of the bush.

We pictured a haven of rest with a suspended lamp burning in the frosty air outside and a big log fire in a cosy parlour off the bar, and a long table set for supper. But this is a land of contradictions; wayside shanties turn up unexpectedly and in the most unreasonable places, and are, as likely as not, prepared for a banquet when you are not hungry and can't wait, and as cold and dark as a bushman's grave when you are and can.

Suddenly the driver said: "We're there now." He said this as if he had driven us to the scaffold to be hanged, and was fiercely glad that he'd got us there safely at last. We looked but saw nothing; then a light appeared ahead and seemed to come towards us; and presently we saw that it was a lantern

held up by a man in a slouch hat, with a dark bushy beard,
and a three-bushel bag around his shoulders. He held up his
other hand, and said something to the driver in a tone that
might have been used by the leader of a search party who
had just found the body. The driver stopped and then went
on slowly.

"What's up?" we asked. "What's the trouble?"

"Oh, it's all right," said the driver.

"The publican's wife is sick," somebody said, "and he
wants us to come quietly."

The usual little slab and bark shanty was suggested in the
gloom, with a big bark stable looming in the background.
We climbed down like so many cripples. As soon as we
began to feel our legs and be sure we had the right ones and
the proper allowance of feet, we helped, as quietly as possible, to take the horses out and round to the stable.

"Is she very bad?" we asked the publican, showing as
much concern as we could.

"Yes," he said, in a subdued voice of a rough man who
had spent several anxious, sleepless nights by the sick bed of
a dear one. "But, God willing, I think we'll pull her
through."

Thus encouraged we said, sympathetically: "We're very
sorry to trouble you, but I suppose we could manage to get a
drink and a bit to eat?"

"Well," he said, "there's nothing to eat in the house, and
I've only got rum and milk. You can have that if you like."

One of the pilgrims broke out here.

"Well of all the pubs," he began, "that I've ever—"

"Hush-sh-sh!" said the publican.

The pilgrim scowled and retired to the rear. You can't express your feelings freely when there's a woman dying close
handy.

"Well, you says rum and milk?" asked the joker, in a low
voice.

"Wait here," said the publican, and disappeared into the
little front passage.

Presently a light showed through a window, with a
scratched and fly-bitten B and A on two panes, and a
mutilated R on the third, which was broken. A door opened,
and we sneaked into the bar. It was like having drinks after

hours where the police are strict and independent.

When we came out the driver was scratching his head and looking at the harness on the verandah floor.

"You fellows'll have ter put in the time for an hour or so. The horses is out back somewheres," and he indicated the interior of Australia with a side jerk of his head, "and the boy ain't back with 'em yet."

"But dash it all," said the Pilgrim, "me and my mate——"

"Hush!" said the publican.

"How long are the horses likely to be?" we asked the driver.

"Dunno," he grunted. "Might be three or four hours. It's all accordin'"

"Now, look here," said the Pilgrim, "me and my mate wanter catch the train."

"Hush-sh-sh!" from the publican in a fierce whisper.

"Well, boss," said the joker, "can you let us have beds, then? I don't want to freeze here all night, anyway."

"Yes," said the landlord, "I can do that, but some of you will have to sleep double and some of you'll have to take it out of the sofas, and one or two'll have to make a shakedown on the floor. There's plenty of bags in the stable, and you've got rugs and coats with you. Fix it up amongst yourselves."

"But look here!" interrupted the Pilgrim, desperately, "we can't afford to wait! We're only 'battlers', me and my mate, pickin' up crumbs by the wayside. We're got to catch the——"

"Hush!" said the publican, savagely. "You fool, didn't I tell you my missus was bad? I won't have any noise."

"But look here," protested the Pilgrim, "we must catch the train at Dead Camel——"

"You'll catch my boot presently," said the publican, with a savage oath, "and go further than Dead Camel. I won't have my missus disturbed for you or any other man! Just you shut up or get out, and take your blooming mate with you."

We lost patience with the Pilgrim and sternly took him aside.

"Now, for God's sake, hold your jaw," we said. "Haven't you got any consideration at all? Can't you see the man's wife is ill—dying perhaps—and he nearly worried off his head?"

The Pilgrim and his mate were scraggy little bipeds of the city push variety, so they were suppressed.

"Well," yawned the joker, "I'm not going to roost on a stump all night. I'm going to turn in."

"It'll be eighteenpence each," hinted the landlord. "You can settle now if you like to save time."

We took the hint, and had another drink. I don't know how we "fixed it up amongst ourselves", but we got settled down somehow. There was a lot of mysterious whispering and scuffling round by the light of a couple of dirty greasy bits of candle. Fortunately we dared not speak loud enough to have a row, though most of us were by this time in the humour to pick a quarrel with a long-lost brother.

The Joker got the best bed, as good-humoured, good-natured chaps generally do, without seeming to try for it. The growler of the party got the floor and chaff bags, as selfish men mostly do—without seeming to try for it either. I took it out of one of the "sofas", or rather that sofa took it out of me. It was short and narrow and down by the head, with a leaning to one corner on the outside, and had more nails and bits of gin-case than original sofa in it.

I had been asleep for three seconds, it seemed; when somebody shook me by the shoulder and said:

"Take yer seats."

When I got out, the driver was on the box, and the others were getting rum and milk inside themselves (and in bottles) before taking their seats.

It was colder and darker than before, and the South Pole seemed nearer, and pretty soon, but for the rum, we should have been in a worse fix than before.

There was a spell of grumbling. Presently someone said:

"I don't believe them horses was lost at all. I was round behind the stable before I went to bed, and seen horses there; and if they wasn't them same horses there, I'll eat 'em raw!"

"Would yer?" said the driver, in a disinterested tone.

"I would," said the passenger. Then, with a sudden ferocity, "and you too!"

The driver said nothing. It was an abstract question which

didn't interest him.

We saw that we were on delicate ground, and changed the subject for awhile. Then someone else said:

"I wonder where his missus was? I didn't see any signs of her about, or any other woman about the place, and we was pretty well all over it."

"Must have kept her in the stable," suggested the Joker.

"No, she wasn't, for Scotty and that chap on the roof was there after bags."

"She might have been in the loft," reflected the Joker.

"There was no loft," put in a voice from the top of the coach.

"I say, Mister—Mister man," said the Joker suddenly to the driver, "Was his mussus sick at all?"

"I dunno," replied the driver. "She might have been. He said so, anyway. I ain't got no call to call a man a liar."

"See here," said the cannibalistic individual to the driver, in the tone of a man who has made up his mind for a row, "has that shanty-keeper got a wife at all?"

"I believe he has."

"And is she living with him?"

"No, she ain't—if yer wanter know."

"Then where is she?"

"I dunno. How am I to know? She left him three or four years ago. She was in Sydney last time I heard of her. It ain't no affair of mine, anyways."

"And is there any woman about the place at all, driver?" inquired a professional wanderer reflectively.

"No—not that I knows on. There useter be a old black gin come pottering round sometimes, but I ain't seen her lately."

"And excuse me, driver, but is there anyone round there at all?" enquired the professional wanderer, with the air of a conscientious writer, collecting material for an Australian novel from life, with an eye to detail.

"Naw," said the driver—and recollecting that he was expected to be civil and obliging to his employers' patrons, he added in surly apology, "Only the boss and the stableman, that I knows of." Then repenting of the apology, he asserted his manhood again, and asked, in a tone calculated to risk a breach of the peace, "Any more questions, gentlemen—

while the shop's open?"

There was a long pause.

"Driver," asked the Pilgrim appealingly, "was them horses lost at all?"

"I dunno," said the driver. "He said they was. He's got the looking after them. It was nothing to do with me."

*   *   *

"Twelve drinks at sixpence a drink"—said the Joker, as if calculating to himself—"that's six bob, and, say on an average, four shouts—that's one pound four. Twelve beds at eighteenpence a bed—that's eighteen shillings; and say ten bob in various drinks and the stuff we brought with us, that's two pound twelve. That publican didn't do so bad out of us in two hours."

We wondered how much the driver got out of it, but thought it best not to ask him.

*   *   *

We didn't say much for the rest of the journey. There was the usual man who thought as much and knew all about it from the first, but he wasn't appreciated. We suppressed him. One or two wanted to go back and "stoush" that landlord, and the driver stopped the coach cheerfully at their request; but they said they'd come across him again and allowed themselves to be persuaded out of it. It made us feel bad to think how we had allowed ourselves to be delayed, and robbed, and had sneaked round on tiptoe, and how we had set on the inoffensive Pilgrim and his mate, and all on account of a sick wife who didn't exist.

The coach arrived at Dead Camel in an atmosphere of mutual suspicion and distrust, and we spread ourselves over the train and departed.

75. ALBERT DORRINGTON

A Bush Tanqueray

The coach creaked round a path hewn out of the grey sandstone, leading to the road that ran white and bare over the summit of a hill. The driver pulled up. Away down in the smoke-laden hollow a number of men gathered and sent up a faint cheer. Then a shirt of many colours, supported by yellow moleskin trousers, rose solemnly from the box-seat and made some parabolic gestures in return. The driver touched his leader tenderly on the flank, and the coach wound through lichen-covered boulders into a dingy mulga background. Simultaneously the crowd below adjourned to the public-house. A mottle-faced old whaler peeped in at the door to remark, for the fifth time, that "water was bad, and the road too stinkin' for anything". No one noticed him until, pressed by a great thirst, he hazarded another cast of the die:

"Anybody want to 'ear a song—a real blanky song without funny business? Ever 'eared 'When Molly marries the Ringer'? I'd sing 'Billy the Bound'ry', only I'm gone in the 'igh notes through sleepin' in the wet without a bluey."

A derisive, withering reply sent him hobbling to the kerb to examine further the grey ridges that bounded an everlasting plain, and the question of his life—the road. Conversation in the bar turned upon Benjamin Stokes, the man who had just left by coach for Sydney. Everybody admitted that Ben was too reserved and sullen. In the first place, his life had been spent beyond the enlightening influence of his fellow-townsmen, in long night-watches with stamping herds and vicious colts. "And the result," said Tackler, the school-master, "is a product as rough as Nature, his god. Gentlemen," continued Tackler, seizing a gin-and-peppermint, "the man Stokes is a heathen idolater."

And Mottle-face went lamely over the hill, his tattered clothes flapping weirdly through a vista of white dust.

Ben's trip was to last a month, and each week of his absence was duly notched off on the post outside the pub. When the notches grew to ten, and he did not return, the circumstance was referred to in the *Deep Creek Dabbler*.

Ben had never seen a train before; his ideas of city life had been drawn from the rough word-pictures of bushmen. The cause of his prolonged absence was explained in the first page of his new pocket-book—

Stoping two Teath, one ginny. Millysent Lee—cab—Mattrymonal agenc, 3£ 2s. 6d.

One afternoon the coach dropped them at the door of a hut near the creek. The driver shook hands with Ben, winked at Ben's wife, and flogged his horses over the wooden bridge to the township. They stood watching the coach till attention was claimed by a tabby cat which brought out several blind kittens for inspection. Her sinful pride led to painful consequences, for a few minutes later the anxious mother mewed piteously near the tank, while Benjamin did strange things with her blind offspring in a bucket of water.

Millicent threw herself wearily on a biscuit-box and slowly took out her hat-pins. The room was stuffy and dark; the tiny window and the little tin mirror filled her with profound astonishment. In a corner was a narrow bed that met the requirements of a long single man, and its presence plainly indicated that the whole wedlock business was unpremeditated. A sporting print on the wall depicted "Jimmy the Biff" going sweet and fresh after ten hard rounds with "Mick the Nipper" from Bendigo.

Through a large hole in the wall near the fire-place Ben apologised for the speckled condition of the nuptial chamber—due, he explained, to the goats and fowls. By-and-by he might nail up the hole with a bag; it was getting too big. Some night an enterprising cow would squeeze through and breathe over a married couple—he'd nail it up now. He rushed away, and there were sounds of a man chopping wood.

The next day was Sunday. Ben took out a concertina from the hollow log where it had lain for weeks; and, tucking it under his arm, stole down to the creek bend, where the belt of coolabahs would hide his musical proceedings from Mill. He began to wonder if she were really fond of music. Anyhow, he would practise a bit before submitting anything to her judgment. She had lived all her life in swell boarding-houses where the aristocracy sat down to the piano and gave it what for. He reckoned that Mill would be very hard to please; still, a concertina was as good as a piano, and if he could only get hold of a few rattling tunes he'd spring 'em on her suddenly—he'd go marching up the track swinging his instrument over his head and filling the bush with an imitation of cathedral bells. His mother used to say he had a grand forehead for music. He looked back over his shoulder to see if Mill were watching him from the door. A screw of smoke trailed from the tiny chimney, winding like a scarf across the roof of the bush.

How different the country seemed since he had returned! The blazed eucalypt that had always reminded him of a crucified man looked quite cheerful; the cattle were in better condition; the very atmosphere held some hidden witchery that set him aglow as if he had drunk wine from the billy instead of tea.

He sat on a boulder hugging his concertina. The coming of this grey-eyed town-girl would change his life. There were times when he used to sit alone clasping his knees and smoking until he felt sick and giddy. People said he was sulkier than a calf. Yet there were hundreds of lads who lived as he had lived, with the unresponsive bush for a mistress and slavering red-eyed cattle for comrades.

The first few notes from his concertina seemed to wake the morning stillness; a couple of inquisitive magpies chortled back melodiously as if defying the big sun-tanned stripling to out-clamour them.

He rose suddenly and pitched a stone in their direction. "Go way, yer blooming cadgers! yous sneak about when yous ain't wanted. Gerrout!"

"*Ha, ha, ha! ho, ho, ho!*"

A kingfisher sailed over the hut roof and settled on the lower branch of a gum.

"Ho, ho, ho!"

The savage, insulting laughter cracked discordantly along the hollow.

For a moment the hot blood swam in Ben's cheeks; the same bird had shed laughter a thousand times over his hut, but never till now had he felt how closely the cackle resembled the fierce mockery from a human throat.

When he returned Mill was clearing out the garnered litter of his bachelor days—leaky, rust-eaten billies, old boots and bridle straps, fearsome pictures of groggy pugilists and bush racehorses. He whistled softly, with his body half in the doorway, wondering whether he had better take off his hat before entering.

After breakfast Millicent hinted weakly about going to church. "Right, Mill!" said Ben, dropping the saw he was greasing, "we'll go now, though I've never been before. Put on your grey dress and the hat with the big black feather."

He followed her inside.

When they started Ben walked ahead swinging his arms so that the shortness of his sleeves might not attract Mill's attention. For the first time in his life he took an interest in the long shadow that stretched about six fathoms ahead. In the middle of it was a hideous kink where the saddle had pressed his coat-tail outwards. The ridiculous shape of it hurt Ben beyond words.

Mill panted after him—he was sublimely unconscious that his terrific pace distressed her. She caught his hand: he slackened instantly and blushed a peony red.

The track swung over a boulder-strewn hillock where the scattered cairns of pick-torn stone recalled a one-time mining camp. They rested awhile: Ben propped himself against a blue-gum.

"Yer git a good breeze here on hot nights, Mill. Grand place fer a breeze."

She did not answer; her fingers were shut over his, her parted lips drank the mountain air.

The rocks filtered great drops of mouth-cooling water into their outstretched hands: the sun stalked valiantly across the naked East over treeless gullies and rolling downs. Through the still scrub they caught the moving gleams of tawny light radiated from leaf to leaf into the deeps of ebon shadows. He touched her hand unconsciously, and the wanton blood leaped to her throat and temples. She looked at him, and he seemed to her a part of the big, secret bush. The light of morning was in his eyes, a fierce young light that she had not seen in the eyes of men who lurked under gasaliers and crouched over desks. He was staring absently at the red cattle wallowing in the reed-choked lagoon. He turned suddenly; his long arm went out towards the tin-roofed box in the hollow.

"It ain't a flash place I've brought yer to, Mill. Yer might have done better."

Mill tugged at her cheap gloves and laughed softly. "Yer right, Ben, it ain't flash; but, Lord! we'll pull through."

"Course we will." He glanced at her stealthily, and noted the handful of half-dead violets tucked cunningly under the brim of her straw hat. There wasn't a woman in the township who could fix violets over her little ear in the same way. He moistened his lips.

"We oughter be happy here, Mill," he said, "seein' it's me an' you."

"Yes, Ben," she acquiesced.

"They're alright people in Pyers when you know 'em," went on Ben; "an' they're bound to take to you—bein' friendly with me, yer see."

She rose and took his arm. "O' course, Ben."

He stretched himself on his disengaged side and breathed lustily. The world seemed so young and glorious—it made his eyes water. His voice trembled a little as he said, "Yer wouldn't believe what a place this is fer a breeze."

They moved onwards.

He chose a seat directly under the pulpit. "Keep yer 'head agin the mahogany, Mill; they'll be dyin' to see yer face when they come in; don't let 'em!"

The church at this time was empty; but it filled—filled to overflowing. "Don't forgit the mahogany, Mill," whispered Ben behind his hand.

Their pew remained as sacred as a Hindu cow. The coach-driver pointed them out from a crowded porch, and his audience appeared spasmodically grateful for the information concerning Mrs. Ben. The driver admitted regretfully that his friend, Sam Hopkins, knew her pretty well, thanks—"wished I knew her as well". Still, it wasn't for him to take away the character of a respectable married woman. Heard that she could cook as good a feed as anybody in Pyers, and if—— The organ took it up, and sent out a moaning "Adeste Fideles".

The minister thundered at his stoic congregation, and charged the air with strange, charitable precepts. At the end he waved a calm benediction over his respectable flock: "Go in peace, and sin no more!"

The men leered at Ben and Mill as they passed out; young girls gathered up skirts and scattered; obese wives and mothers cannoned in circling, agitated groups.

"Thank God the roof didn't fall on us this blessed day! The idea!"

Ben lifted his head and eyed the hostile gathering; some of them had known him for years—since the time when he used to drive about Pyers in a billy-goat tandem. A shout of mocking laughter followed them to the gate. Ben clinched his mouth; an unknown shame spread to his neck and face: something gripped his arm, and a word hummed in his ear that an ordinary woman never uses at any period of her life.

So they tramped along, voiceless and sullen, through paddocks where flowers nodded to a caressing wind, while the sun warmed perfumes from the moist Spring earth. Mill's right hand bruised her breast savagely; the other held his sleeve.

She glanced furtively at him across the room—his head down, his chin resting in the heel of his palm.

"Did I ever say I was a good girl, Ben? I ain't, Gawd 'elp me!"

She thrust herself beside him, shaking and trembling. Then Benjamin Stokes listened, almost for the first time in his life, to the commonest story in the world—a betrayal, a little shame, a gradual hardening, a world-defiance.

"The old woman at the boardin'-house said she'd clear me out unless I was obligin' and civil to the gentlemen. So there was presents for Mill, and gloves planted in my bed ... It all helped to take my head away from the damned 'ard

scrubbin'. I ain't old—nineteen ain't very old, is it? Gimme
a chance, Ben—gimme a chance!"

Something simmered in the fireplace; plates clattered; a
shadowy girl moved about him all the afternoon in a dull,
half-frightened way. He stumbled outside to the wood-
heap, and the soft-eyed collie hung at his heels for a word.

The sun dropped to the edge of the plains, drenching the
far-off hills with yellow mist. A rush of cool air brought the
clang of bells; he raised a rough and haggard face and spoke
a word to the night—a word he used when punching cattle
through an overflow. The dog fawned joyously ... "Away,
you beast!"—and a savage kick sent it howling down the
track.

A candle flickered in the little bedroom, throwing a shape
across the chintz curtain. "That bell again!" He walked a
short distance from the house. How everyone knew! How
everyone guessed the truth! What had happened at the
church today would happen again with sickening regularity.
He might force the men to respect him with his fists; but
that cackling brood in the porch! He struck a match and
groped in to the room to fling a word of hate at this
Magdalen—and fell into a chair, silenced. The face was so
pretty, so weak—prey for every libertine. The minister had
said something about a woman who wiped the feet of Christ
with her long meshes of hair; nobody believed it, of course;
if they did, why was Mill treated as she had been? He sat
through the long night, heavy-browed and brooding, until a
grey light from the east whitened the window-pane.

"Mill!" She smiled sleepily at the word.

"Mill!" The sound of his voice made her crouch on the
rough pallet; she stared at the white haggard face in the
half-light.

"Don't be frightened, Mill!—don't be frightened; I shan't
hit yer. I've been thinkin'; and we ain't goin' to church
again to let 'em worry us. I'll build another place over at
Red Point on the hundred-acre patch; if they come there to
carry on I'll be about to receive 'em."

Her face was hidden from him, but her hand crept into
his big palm.

A few hours later Ben led a bay horse to the front and hopped into the saddle. She came to the door, her white arms splashed with milk and flour.

"It's a long way to the Point, ain't it, Ben?"

"Yeh!"

She stole nearer—obviously to examine the horse. He threw himself forward and kissed her on the lips.

76. W. T. GOODGE

DRIFTING DOWN THE DARLING

It was in the early eighties,
    When a man could see some fun,
In the eighties when the praties
    Stood at twenty pounds a ton,
And a working-man's resources
Wouldn't run to feeding horses,
That we started down the Darling with McGindy!
Now McGindy was a wonder,
    Though we'd often thought him daft,
And he worked away like thunder
    Till he made a sort of raft,
And a decent craft we thought her
When we launched her on the water,
And we drifted down the Darling to Menindie!

Drifting down the Darling on McGindy's rickety raft!
When the snags were all before us and the breeze was
    right abaft,
She was lumpy, rough, and ugly, and a cranky kind o'
    craft,
When we drifted down the Darling to Menindie!

And McGindy'd been a sailor,
    And of course he rigged the raft,
He'd been mate aboard a whaler,
    And he understood the graft.
Well you should have heard the cheering
And the borak and the jeering
When he started down the Darling with McGindy!
It was awful work to steer her,
    For she *wouldn't* come to port,
And whene'er a snag came near her
    You can bet the raft was caught;
But the laughter and the singing!
It was splendid, it was ringing,
When we drifted down the Darling to Menindie!

Drifting down the Darling, etc.!

Thompson came from Ena-Weena
    Where the wool he'd had to class,
And he played the concertina
    Pretty nearly up to Cass.
I was Mozart on the whistle,
And we made the welkin bristle
When we started down the Darling with McGindy!
Old McGindy, as a singer,
    Was the dandy of the West,
He was recognized the ringer,
    And the absolutely best;
And he'd simply made you shiver
If you'd heard him on the river
When we drifted down the Darling to Menindie!

Drifting down the Darling, etc.!

77. LOUISA LAWSON

THE LONELY CROSSING

A man on foot came down to the river,
    A silent man, on the road alone,
And dropped his swag with a chill-born shiver,
    And sat to rest on a wind-worn stone.

He slid then down to the long grass, bending
    His arms above as the resting do,
And watched a snow-white chariot trending
    Its wind-made way o'er the wedgewood blue.

In it sat one of the fairest ladies
    That mind could mould, in a crown of white,
But close beside came a fiend from Hades
    In a chariot black as the heart of night.

The man, he sighed as the fiend would clasp her,
    Then smiled as the wind by a wise decree
Her white steeds turned to the streets of Jaspar,
    And Satan drove to a sin-black sea.

The wattles waved, and their sweet reflection
    In crystal fathoms responses made;
The sunlight silted each soft inflection
    And fretted with silver the short'ning shade.

A restless fish made the thin reeds shiver,
    A waking wind made the willows moan.
But the resting man by the noon-bright river
    Lay dreaming on, in the long grass prone.

        * * *

The bell-bird called to its tardy lover,
    The grebe clouds all to the west had sped,
But the river of death had a soul crossed over,
    The man with the swag on the bank was dead.

78. WILL OGILVIE

ABANDONED SELECTIONS

On the crimson breast of the sunset
  The Gray Selections lie,
And their lonely, grief-stained faces
  Are turned to a pitiless sky;
They are wrinkled and seamed with drought-fire
  And wound at the throat with weeds,
They sob in the aching loneness
  But never a passer heeds.

I pity you, Gray Selections,
  As I pass you by in the light,
And I turn again with the shadows
  To take your hand in the night;
In homesteads and yards deserted
  'T is little the world can see,
But the wail of your endless sorrow
  Throbs under the moon to me.

I come to you, Gray Selections,
  When the crickets gather and croon,
An hour at the back of the sunset,
  An hour in advance of the moon:
How eager they are to whisper
  Their tale, as they hear me pass!
Twenty at once in the oak trees;
  Ten at a time in the grass.

The night-winds are chanting above you
  A dirge in the cedar trees
Whose green boughs groan at your shoulder,
  Whose dead leaves drift to your knees;
You cry, and the curlews answer;
  You call, and the wild-dogs hear;
Through gaps in the old log-fences
  They creep when the night is near.

I stand by your fenceless gardens
    And weep for the splintered staves;
I watch by your empty ingles
    And mourn by your white-railed graves;
I see from your crumbled doorways
    The whispering white forms pass,
And shiver to hear dead horses
    Crop-cropping the long gray grass.

Where paddocks are dumb and fallow
    And wild weeds waste to the stars
I can hear the voice of the driver,
    The thresh of the swingle-bars;
I can hear the hum of the stripper
    That follows the golden lanes,
The snort of the tiring horses.
    The clink of the bucking chains.

It is night; but I see the smoke-wreaths
    Float over the dancing haze;
I can hear the jackass laughing
    When South winds rustle the maize;
I can catch the axes' ringing,
    And out on the range's crown
I can hear the red fires roaring
    And the great trees thundering down.

I pity you, Gray Selections,
    Your hearths as cold as a stone.
The days you must pass unaided
    The nights you must brave alone;
But most when the wailing curlews
    Call over the drear lagoon,
And out of the ring-barked timber
    Comes blazing the red, red moon.

They fought for you, Gray Selections,
    The battle of long dry years,
Through seedtimes of sweat and sorrow
    To harvests of hunger and tears;
You turned from the lips that wooed you,
    And Justice, awake on her throne,
For sake of those brave hearts broken,
    Is watching you break your own!

79. A. B. PATERSON

SALTBUSH BILL

Now this is the law of the Overland that all in the West obey,
A man must cover with travelling sheep a six-mile stage a day;
But this is the law which the drovers make, right easily
  understood,
They travel their stage where the grass is bad, but they camp
  where the grass is good;
They camp, and they ravage the squatter's grass till never a
  blade remains,
Then they drift away as the white clouds drift on the edge of
  the saltbush plains,
From camp to camp and from run to run they battle it hand
  to hand,
For a blade of grass and the right to pass on the track of the
  Overland.

For this is the law of the Great Stock Routes, 'tis written in
  white and black —
The man that goes with a travelling mob must keep to a half-
  mile track;
And the drovers keep to a half-mile track on the runs where
  the grass is dead,
But they spread their sheep on a well-grassed run till they go
  with a two-mile spread.
So the squatters hurry the drovers on from dawn till the fall
  of night,
And the squatters' dogs and the drovers' dogs get mixed in a
  deadly fight;
Yet the squatters' men, though they hunt the mob, are willing
  the peace to keep,
For the drovers learn how to use their hands when they go
  with the travelling sheep;
But this is the tale of a Jackaroo that came from a foreign
  strand,
And the fight that he fought with Saltbush Bill, the King of
  the Overland.

Now Saltbush Bill was a drover tough, as ever the country
  knew,
He had fought his way on the Great Stock Routes from the
  sea to the Big Barcoo;

He could tell when he came to a friendly run that gave him a
chance to spread,
And he knew where the hungry owners were that hurried his
sheep ahead;
He was drifting down in the Eighty drought with a mob that
could scarcely creep,
(When the kangaroos by the thousands starve, it is rough on
the travelling sheep),
And he camped one night at the crossing-place on the edge of
the Wilga run,
"We must manage a feed for them here," he said, "or the half
of the mob are done!"
So he spread them out when they left the camp wherever they
liked to go,
Till he grew aware of a Jackaroo with a station-hand in tow,
And they set to work on the straggling sheep, and with many a
stockwhip crack
They forced them in where the grass was dead in the space of
the half-mile track;
So William prayed that the hand of fate might suddenly strike
him blue
But he'd get some grass for his starving sheep in the teeth of
that Jackaroo.
So he turned, and he cursed the Jackaroo, he cursed him alive
or dead,
From the soles of his great unwieldy feet to the crown of his
ugly head,
With an extra curse on the moke he rode and the cur at his
heels that ran,
Till the Jackaroo from his horse got down and he went for the
drover-man;
With the station-hand for his picker-up, though the sheep ran
loose the while,
They battled it out on the saltbush plain in the regular prize-
ring style.

Now the new chum fought for his honour's sake and the pride
of the English race,
But the drover fought for his daily bread with a smile on his
bearded face;
So he shifted ground and he sparred for wind and he made it a
lengthy mill,
And from time to time as his scouts came in they whispered to
Saltbush Bill —
"We have spread the sheep with a two-mile spread, and the
grass it is something grand,
"You must stick to him, Bill, for another round for the pride
of the Overland."

The new chum made it a rushing fight, though never a blow
    got home,
Till the sun rode high in the cloudless sky and glared on the
    brick-red loam,
Till the sheep drew in to the shelter-trees and settled them
    down to rest,
Then the drover said he would fight no more and he gave his
    opponent best.
So the new chum rode to the homestead straight and he told
    them a story grand
Of the desperate fight that he fought that day with the King of
    the Overland.
And the tale went home to the Public Schools of the pluck of
    the English swell,
How the drover fought for his very life, but blood in the end
    must tell.
But the travelling sheep and the Wilga sheep were boxed on
    the Old Man Plain.
'Twas a full week's work ere they drafted out and hunted
    them off again,
With a week's good grass in their wretched hides, with a curse
    and a stockwhip crack,
They hunted them off on the road once more to starve on the
    half-mile track.
And Saltbush Bill, on the Overland, will many a time recite
How the best day's work that ever he did was the day that he
    lost the fight.

80. BARBARA BAYNTON

Squeaker's Mate

The woman carried the bag with the axe and maul and wedges; the man had the billy and clean tucker bags; the cross-cut saw linked them. She was taller than the man, and the equability of her body contrasting with his indolent slouch, accentuated the difference. "Squeaker's mate" the men called her, and these agreed that she was the best long-haired mate that ever stepped in petticoats. The selectors' wives pretended to challenge her right to womanly garments, but if she knew what they said, it neither turned nor troubled Squeaker's mate.

Nine prospective posts and maybe sixteen rails—she calculated this yellow gum would yield. "Come on," she encouraged the man; "let's tackle it."

From the bag she took the axe, and ring barked a preparatory circle, while he looked for a shady spot for the billy and tucker bags.

"Come on." She was waiting with the greased saw. He came. The saw rasped through a few inches, then he stopped and looked at the sun.

"It's nigh tucker time," he said, and when she dissented, he exclaimed, with sudden energy, "There's another bee! Wait, you go on with the axe, an' I'll track 'im."

As they came, they had already followed one and located the nest. She could not see the bee he spoke of, though her grey eyes were as keen as a Black's. However she knew the man, and her tolerance was of the mysteries.

She drew out the saw, spat on her hands, and with the axe began weakening the inclining side of the tree.

Long and steadily and in secret the worm had been busy in the heart. Suddenly the axe blade sank softly, the tree's wounded edges closed on it like a vice. There was a "settling" quiver on its top branches, which the woman heard and understood. The man, encouraged by the sounds of the axe, had returned with an armful of sticks for the billy. He shouted gleefully, "It's fallin', look out."

But she waited to free the axe.

With a shivering groan the tree fell, and as she sprang aside, a thick worm-eaten branch snapped at a joint and silently she went down under it.

"I tole yer t' look out," he reminded her, as with a crowbar, and grunting earnestly, he forced it up. "Now get out quick."

She tried moving her arms and the upper part of her body. Do this; do that, he directed, but she made no movement after the first.

He was impatient, because for once he had actually to use his strength. His share of a heavy lift usually consisted of a make-believe grunt, delivered at a critical moment. Yet he hardly cared to let it again fall on her, though he told her he would, if she "didn't shift".

Near him lay a piece broken short; with his foot he drew it nearer, then gradually worked it into a position, till it acted as a stay to the lever.

He laid her on her back when he drew her out, and waited expecting some acknowledgement of his exertions, but she was silent, and as she did not notice that the axe, she had tried to save, lay with the fallen trunk across it, he told her. She cared almost tenderly for all their possessions and treated them as friends. But the half-buried broken axe did not affect her. He wondered a little, for only last week she had patiently chipped out the old broken head, and put in a new handle.

"Feel bad?" he inquired at length.

"Pipe" she replied with slack lips.

Both pipes lay in the fork of a near tree. He took his, shook out the ashes, filled it, picked up a coal and puffed till it was alight—then he filled hers. Taking a small firestick he handed her the pipe. The hand she raised shook and closed in an uncertain hold, but she managed by a great effort to get it to her mouth. He lost patience with the swaying hand that tried to take the light.

"Quick," he said "quick, that damn dog's at the tucker."

He thrust it into her hand that dropped helplessly across her chest. The lighted stick falling between her bare arm and the dress, slowly roasted the flesh and smouldered the clothes.

He rescued their dinner, pelted his dog out of sight—hers was lying near her head, put on the billy, then came back to her.

The pipe had fallen from her lips; there was blood on the stem.

"Did yer jam yer tongue?" he asked.

She always ignored trifles he knew, therefore he passed her silence.

He told her that her dress was on fire. She took no heed. He put it out, and looked at the burnt arm, then with intentness at her.

Her eyes were turned unblinkingly to the heavens, her lips were grimly apart, and a strange greyness was upon her face, and the sweat-beads were mixing.

"Like a drink er tea? Asleep?"

He broke a green branch from the fallen tree and swished from his face the multitudes of flies that had descended with it.

In a heavy way he wondered why did she sweat, when she was not working? Why did she not keep the flies out of her mouth and eyes? She'd have bungy eyes, if she didn't. If she was asleep, why did she not close them?

But asleep or awake, as the billy began to boil, he left her, made the tea, and ate his dinner. His dog had disappeared, and as it did not come to his whistle, he threw the pieces to hers, that would not leave her head to reach them.

He whistled tunelessly his one air, beating his own time with a stick on the toe of his blucher, then looked overhead at the sun and calculated that she must have been lying like that for "close up an hour". He noticed that the axe handle was broken in two places, and speculated a little as to whether she would again pick out the back-broken handle or burn it out in his method, which was less trouble, if it did spoil the temper of the blade. He examined the worm-dust in the stump and limbs of the newly-fallen tree; mounted it and looked round the plain. The sheep were straggling in a manner that meant walking work to round them, and he supposed he would have to yard them tonight, if she didn't liven up. He looked down at unenlivened her. This changed his "chune" to a call for his hiding dog.

"Come on, ole feller," he commanded her dog. "Fetch 'em back." He whistled further instructions, slapping his thigh and pointing to the sheep.

But a brace of wrinkles either side the brute's closed mouth demonstrated determined disobedience. The dog would go if she told him, and by and bye she would.

He lighted his pipe and killed half an hour smoking. With the frugality that hard graft begets, his mate limited both his and her own tobacco, so he must not smoke all afternoon. There was no work to shirk, so time began to drag. Then a goanna crawling up a tree attracted him. He gathered various missiles and tried vainly to hit the seemingly grinning reptile. He came back and sneaked a fill of her tobacco, and while he was smoking, the white tilt of a cart caught his eye. He jumped up. "There's Red Bob goin' t'our place fur th' 'oney," he said, "I'll go an' weigh it an' get the gonz" (money).

He ran for the cart, and kept looking back as if fearing she would follow and thwart him.

Red Bob the dealer was, in a business way, greatly concerned, when he found that Squeaker's mate was "avin' a sleep out there 'cos a tree fell on her". She was the best honey strainer and boiler that he dealt with. She was straight and square too. There was no water in her honey whether boiled or merely strained, and in every kerosene tin the weight of honey was to an ounce as she said. Besides he was suspicious and diffident of paying the indecently eager Squeaker before he saw the woman. So reluctantly Squeaker led to where she lay. With many fierce oaths Red Bob sent her lawful protector for help, and compassionately poured a little from his flask down her throat, then swished away the flies from her till help came.

Together these men stripped a sheet of bark, and laying her with pathetic tenderness upon it, carried her to her hut. Squeaker followed in the rear with the billy and tucker.

Red Bob took his horse from the cart, and went to town for the doctor. Late that night at the back of the old hut (there were two) he and others who had heard that she was hurt, squatted with unlighted pipes in their mouths, waiting to hear the doctor's verdict. After he had given it and gone, they discussed in whispers, and with a look seen only on bush faces, the hard luck of that woman who alone had hard-grafted with the best of them for every acre and hoof on that selection. Squeaker would go through it in no time. Why she had allowed it to be taken up in his name, when the money had been her own, was also for them among the mysteries.

Him they called "a nole woman", not because he was hanging round the honey tins, but after man's fashion to eliminate all virtue. They beckoned him, and explaining his mate's injury, cautioned him to keep from her the knowledge that she would be for ever a cripple.

"Jus' th' same, now then fur 'im," pointing to Red Bob, "t' pay me, I'll 'ev t' go t' town."

They told him in whispers what they thought of him, and with a cowardly look towards where she lay, but without a word of parting, like shadows these men made for their homes.

Next day the women came. Squeaker's mate was not a favourite with them—a woman with no leisure for yarning was not likely to be. After the first day they left her severely alone, their plea to their husbands, her uncompromising independence. It is in the ordering of things that by degrees most husbands accept their wives' views of other women.

The flour bespattering Squeaker's now neglected clothes spoke eloquently of his clumsy efforts at damper making. The women gave him many a feed, agreeing that it must be miserable for him.

If it were miserable and lonely for his mate, she did not complain; for her the long, long days would give place to longer nights—those nights with the pregnant bush silence suddenly cleft by a bush voice. However, she was not fanciful, and being a bush scholar knew 'twas a dingo, when a long whine came from the scrub on the skirts of which lay the axe under the worm-eaten tree. That quivering wail from the billabong lying murkily mystic towards the East was only the cry of the fearing curlew.

Always her dog—wakeful and watchful as she—patiently waiting for her to be up and about again. That would be soon, she told her complaining mate.

"Yer won't. Yer back's broke," said Squeaker laconically.

"That's wot's wrong er yer; injoory t' th' spine. Doctor says that means back's broke, and yer won't never walk no more. No good not t' tell yer, cos I can't be doin' everythin.'

A wild look grew on her face, and she tried to sit up.

"Erh," said he, "see! yer carnt, yer jes' ther same as a snake w'en ees back's broke, on'y yer don't bite yerself like a snake does w'en 'e carnt crawl. Yer did bite yer tongue w'en yer fell."

She gasped, and he could hear her heart beating when she let her head fall back a few moments; though she wiped her wet forehead with the back of her hand, and still said that was the doctor's mistake. But day after day she tested her strength, and whatever the result, was silent, though white witnesses, halo-wise, gradually circled her brow and temples.

"'Tisn't as if yer was agoin' t' get better t'morrer, the doctor says yer won't never work no more, an' I can't be cookin' an' workin' an' doin' everythin'!"

He muttered something about "sellin' out", but she firmly refused to think of such a monstrous proposal.

He went into town one Saturday afternoon soon after, and did not return till Monday.

Her supplies, a billy of tea and scraps of salt beef and damper (her dog got the beef), gave out the first day, though that was as nothing to her compared with the bleat of the penned sheep, for it was summer and droughty, and her dog could not unpen them.

Of them and her dog only she spoke when he returned. He d—d him, and d—d her, and told her to "double up yer ole broke back an' bite yerself". He threw things about, made a long-range feint of kicking her threatening dog, then sat outside in the shade of the old hut, nursing his head till he slept.

She, for many reasons, had when necessary made these trips into town, walking both ways, leading a pack horse for supplies. She never failed to indulge him in a half pint—a pipe was her luxury.

The sheep waited till next day, so did she.

For a few days he worked a little in her sight; not much—he never did. It was she who always lifted the heavy end of the log, and carried the tools; he—the billy and tucker.

She wearily watched him idling his time; reminded him that the wire lying near the fence would rust, one could run the wire through easily, and when she got up in a day or so, she would help strain and fasten it. At first he pretended he had done it, later said he wasn't goin' t' go wirin' or nothin' else by 'imself if every other man on the place did.

She spoke of many other things that could be done by one, reserving the great till she was well. Sometimes he whistled while she spoke, often swore, generally went out, and when this was inconvenient, dull as he was, he found the "Go and bite yerself like a snake", would instantly silence her.

At last the work worry ceased to exercise her, and for night to bring him home was a rare thing.

Her dog rounded and yarded the sheep when the sun went down and there was no sign of him, and together they kept watch on their movements till dawn. She was mindful not to speak of this care to him, knowing he would have left if for them to do constantly, and she noticed that what little interest he seemed to share went to the sheep. Why, was soon demonstrated.

Through the cracks her ever watchful eyes one day saw the dust rise out of the plain. Nearer it came till she saw him and a man on horseback rounding and driving the sheep into the yard, and later both left in charge of a little mob. Their "Baa-baas" to her were cries for help; many had been pets. So he was selling her sheep to the town butchers.

In the middle of the next week he came from town with a fresh horse, new saddle and bridle. He wore a flash red shirt, and round his neck a silk handkerchief. On the next occasion she smelt scent, and though he did not try to display the dandy meerschaum, she saw it, and heard the squeak of the new boots, not bluchers. However he was kinder to her this time, offering a fill of his cut tobacco; he had long ceased to keep her supplied. Several of the men who sometimes in passing took a look in, would have made up her loss had they known, but no word of complaint passed her lips.

She looked at Squeaker as he filled his pipe from his pouch, but he would not meet her eyes, and seemingly dreading something, slipped out.

She heard him hammering in the old hut at the back,

which served for tools and other things which sunlight and rain did not hurt. Quite briskly he went in and out. She could see him through the cracks carrying a narrow strip of bark, and understood, he was making a bunk. When it was finished he had a smoke, then came to her and fidgeted about; he said this hut was too cold, and that she would never get well in it. She did not feel cold, but, submitting to his mood, allowed him to make a fire that would roast a sheep. He took off his hat, and fanning himself, said he was roastin', wasn't she? She was.

He offered to carry her into the other; he would put a new roof on it in a day or two, and it would be better than this one, and she would be up in no time. He stood to say this where she could not see him.

His eagerness had tripped him.

There were months to run before all the Government conditions of residence, etc., in connection with the selection, would be fulfilled, still she thought perhaps he was trying to sell out, and she would not go.

He was away four days that time, and when he returned slept in the new bunk.

She compromised. Would he put a bunk there for himself, keep out of town, and not sell the place? He promised instantly with additions.

"Try could yer crawl yerself?" he coaxed, looking at her bulk.

Her nostrils quivered with her suppressed breathing, and her lips tightened, but she did not attempt to move.

It was evident some great purpose actuated him. After attempts to carry and drag her, he rolled her on the sheet of bark that had brought her home, and laboriously drew her round.

She asked for a drink, he placed her billy and tin pint besides the bunk, and left her gasping and dazed to her sympathetic dog.

She saw him run up and yard his horse, and though she called him, he would not answer nor come.

When he rode swiftly towards the town, her dog leaped on the bunk, and joined a refrain to her lamentation, but the cat took to the bush.

He came back at dusk next day in a spring cart—not alone—he had another mate. She saw her though he came a roundabout way, trying to keep in front of the new hut.

There were noises of moving many things from the cart to the hut. Finally he came to a crack near where she lay, and whispered the promise of many good things to her if she kept quiet, and that he would set her hut afire if she didn't. She was quiet, he need not have feared, for that time she was past it, she was stunned.

The released horse came stumbling round to the old hut, and thrust its head in the door in a domesticated fashion. Her dog promptly resented this straggler mistaking their hut for a stable. And the dog's angry dissent, together with the shod clatter of the rapidly disappearing intruder, seemed to have a disturbing effect on the pair in the new hut. The settling sounds suddenly ceased, and the cripple heard the stranger close the door, despite Squeaker's assurances that the woman in the old hut could not move from her bunk to save her life, and that her dog would not leave her.

Food, more and better, was placed near her—but, dumb and motionless, she lay with her face turned to the wall, and her dog growled menacingly at the stranger. The new woman was uneasy, and told Squeaker what people might say and do if she died.

He scared at the "do", went into the bush and waited.

She went to the door, not the crack, the face was turned that way, and said she had come to cook and take care of her.

The disabled woman, turning her head slowly, looked steadily at her. She was not much to look at. Her red hair hung in an uncurled bang over her forehead, the lower part of her face had robbed the upper, and her figure evinced imminent motherhood, though it is doubtful if the barren woman, noting this, knew by calculation the paternity was not Squeaker's. She was not learned in these matters, though she understood all about an ewe and lamb.

One circumstance was apparent—ah! bitterest of all bitterness to women—she was younger.

The thick hair that fell from the brow of the woman on the bunk was white now.

Bread and butter the woman brought. The cripple looked at it, at her dog, at the woman. Bread and butter for a dog! but the stranger did not understand till she saw it offered to the dog. The bread and butter was not for the dog. She brought meat.

All next day the man kept hidden. The cripple saw his dog, and knew he was about.

But there was an end of this pretence when at dusk he came back with a show of haste, and a finger of his right hand bound and ostentatiously prominent. His entrance caused great excitement to his new mate. The old mate, who knew this snake-bite trick from its inception, maybe, realised how useless were the terrified stranger's efforts to rouse the snoring man after an empty pint bottle had been flung on the outside heap.

However, what the sick woman thought was not definite, for she kept silent always. Neither was it clear how much she ate, and how much she gave to her dog, though the new mate said to Squeaker one day that she believed that the dog would not take a bite more than its share.

The cripple's silence told on the stranger, especially when alone. She would rather have abuse. Eagerly she counted the days past and to pass. Then back to the town. She told no word of that hope to Squeaker, he had no place in her plans for the future. So if he spoke of what they would do by-and-bye when his time would be up, and he able to sell out, she listened in uninterested silence.

She did tell him she was afraid of "her", and after the first day would not go within reach, but every morning made a billy of tea, which with bread and beef Squeaker carried to her.

The rubbish heap was adorned, for the first time, with jam and fish tins from the table in the new hut. It seemed to be understood that neither woman nor dog in the old hut required them.

Squeaker's dog sniffed and barked joyfully around them till his licking efforts to bottom a salmon tin sent him careering in a muzzled frenzy, that caused the younger woman's thick lips to part grinningly till he came too close.

The remaining sheep were regularly yarded. His old mate heard him whistle as he did it. Squeaker began to work about a little burning off. So that now, added to the other bush voices, was the call from some untimely falling giant. There is no sound so human as that from the riven souls of these tree people, or the trembling sighs of their upright neighbours whose hands in time will meet over the victim's fallen body.

There was no bunk on the side of the hut to which her eyes turned, but her dog filled that space, and the flash that passed between this back-broken woman and her dog might have been the spirit of these slain tree folk, it was so wondrous ghostly. Still, at times, the practical in her would be dominant, for in a mind so free of fancies, backed by bodily strength, hope died slowly, and forgetful of self she would almost call to Squeaker her fears that certain bees' nests were in danger.

He went into town one day and returned, as he had promised, long before sundown, and next day a clothes line bridged the space between two trees near the back of the old hut; and—an equally rare occurrence—Squeaker placed across his shoulders the yoke that his old mate had fashioned for herself, with two kerosene tins attached, and brought them filled with water from the distant creek; but both only partly filled the tub, a new purchase. With utter disregard of the heat and Squeaker's sweating brow, his new mate said, even after another trip, two more now for the blue water. Under her commands he brought them, though sullenly, perhaps contrasting the old mate's methods with the new.

His old mate had periodically carried their washing to the creek, and his mole-skins had been as white as snow without aid of blue.

Towards noon, on the clothes line many strange garments fluttered, suggestive of a taunt to the barren woman. When the sun went down she could have seen the assiduous Squeaker lower the new prop-sticks and considerably stoop to gather the pegs his inconsiderate new mate had dropped. However, after one load of water next morning, on hearing her estimate that three more would put her own things through, Squeaker struck. Nothing he could urge would induce the stranger to trudge to the creek, where thirst-slaked snakes lay waiting for someone to bite. She sulked and pretended to pack up, till a bright idea struck Squeaker. He fastened a cask on a sledge and harnessing the new horse, hitched him to it, and, under the approving eyes of his new mate, led off to the creek, though, when she went inside, he bestrode the spiritless brute.

He had various mishaps, any one of which would have served as an excuse to his old mate, but even babes soon know on whom to impose. With an energy new to him he persevered and filled the cask, but the old horse repudiated such a burden even under Squeaker's unmerciful welts. Almost half was sorrowfully baled out, and under a rain of whacks the horse shifted it a few paces, but the cask tilted and the thirsty earth got its contents. All Squeaker's adjectives over his wasted labour were as unavailing as the cure for spilt milk.

It took skill and patience to rig the cask again. He partly filled it, and just as success seemed probable, the rusty wire fastening the cask to the sledge snapped with the strain, and springing free coiled affectionately round the terrified horse's hocks. Despite the sledge (the cask had been soon disposed of) that old town horse's pace then was his record. Hours after, on the plain that met the horizon, loomed two specks: the distance between them might be gauged, for the larger was Squeaker.

Anticipating a plentiful supply and lacking in bush caution the new mate used the half bucket of water to boil the salt mutton. Towards noon she laid this joint and bread on the rough table, then watched anxiously in the wrong direction for Squeaker.

She had drained the new tea-pot earlier, but she placed the spout to her thirsty mouth again.

She continued looking for him for hours.

Had he sneaked off to town, thinking she had not used that water, or not caring whether or no. She did not trust him; another had left her. Besides she judged Squeaker by his treatment of the woman who was lying in there with wide-open eyes. Anyhow no use to cry with only that silent woman to hear her.

Had she drunk all hers?

She tried to see at long range through the cracks, but the hanging bed clothes hid the billy. She went to the door, and avoiding the bunk looked at the billy.

It was half full.

Instinctively she knew that the eyes of the woman were

upon her. She turned away, and hoped and waited for thirsty minutes that seemed hours.

Desperation drove her back to the door, dared she? No, she couldn't.

Getting a long forked propstick, she tried to reach it from the door, but the dog sprang at the stick. She dropped it and ran.

A scraggy growth fringed the edge of the plain. There was the creek. How far? she wondered. Oh, very far, she knew, and besides there were only a few holes where water was, and the snakes; for Squeaker, with a desire to shine in her eyes, was continually telling her of snakes—vicious and many—that daily he did battle with.

She recalled the evening he came from hiding in the scrub with a string round one finger, and said a snake had bitten him. He had drunk the pint of brandy she had brought for her sickness, and then slept till morning. True, although next day he had to dig for the string round the blue swollen finger, he was not worse than the many she had seen at the "Shearer's Rest" suffering a recovery. There was no brandy to cure her if she were bitten.

She cried a little in self pity, then withdrew her eyes, that were getting red, from the outlying creek, and went again to the door. She of the bunk lay with closed eyes.

Was she asleep? The stranger's heart leapt, yet she was hardly in earnest as she tip-toed billy-wards. The dog, crouching with head between two paws, eyed her steadily, but showed no opposition. She made dumb show. "I want to be friends with you, and won't hurt her." Abruptly she looked at her, then at the dog. He was motionless and emotionless. Beside if that dog—certainly watching her—wanted to bite her (her dry mouth opened), it could get her any time.

She rated this dog's intelligence almost human, from many of its actions in omission and commission in connection with this woman.

She regretted the pole, no dog would stand that.

Two more steps.

Now just one more; then, by bending and stretching her arm, she would reach it. Could she now? She tried to encourage herself by remembering how close on the first day she had been to the woman, and how delicious a few mouthfuls would be—swallowing dry mouthfuls.

She measured the space between where she had first stood and the billy. Could she get anything to draw it to her. No, the dog would not stand that, and besides the handle would rattle, and she might hear and open her eyes.

The thought of those sunken eyes suddenly opening made her heart bound. Oh! she must breathe—deep, loud breaths. Her throat clicked noisily. Looking back fearfully, she went swiftly out.

She did not look for Squeaker this time, she had given him up.

While she waited for her breath to steady, to her relief and surprise the dog came out. She made a rush to the new hut, but he passed seemingly oblivious of her, and bounding across the plain began rounding the sheep. Then he must know Squeaker had gone to town.

Stay! Her heart beat violently; was it because she on the bunk slept and did not want him?

She waited till her heart quieted, and again crept to the door.

The head of the woman on the bunk had fallen towards the wall as in deep sleep; it was turned from the billy, to which she must creep so softly.

Slower, from caution and deadly earnestness, she entered.

She was not so advanced as before, and felt fairly secure, for the woman's eyes were still turned to the wall, and so tightly closed, she could not possibly see where she was.

She would bend right down, and try and reach it from where she was.

She bent.

It was so swift and sudden, that she had not time to scream when those bony fingers had gripped the hand that she prematurely reached for the billy. She was frozen with horror for a moment, then her screams were piercing. Panting with victory, the prostrate one held her with a hold that the other did not attempt to free herself from.

Down, down she drew her.

Her lips had drawn back from her teeth, and her breath almost scorched the face that she held so close for the starting eyes to gloat over. Her exultation was so great, that she could only gloat and gasp, and hold with a tension that had stopped the victim's circulation.

As a wounded, robbed tigress might hold and look, she held and looked.

Neither heard the swift steps of the man, and if the tigress saw him enter, she was not daunted. "Take me from her," she repeated it again, nothing else. "Take me from her."

He hastily fastened the door and said something that the shrieks drowned, then picked up the pole. It fell with a thud across the arms which the tightening sinews had turned into steel. Once, twice, thrice. Then the one that got the fullest force bent; that side of the victim was free.

The pole had snapped. Another blow with a broken end freed the other side.

Still shrieking "Take me from her, take me from her," she beat on the closed door till Squeaker opened it.

Then he had to face and reckon with his old mate's maddened dog, that the closed door had baffled.

The dog suffered the shrieking woman to pass, but though Squeaker, in bitten agony, broke the stick across the dog, he was forced to give the savage brute best.

"Call 'im orf, Mary, 'e's eatin' me" he implored. "Oh corl 'im orf."

But with stony face the woman lay motionless.

"Sool 'im on t' 'er. He indicated his new mate who, as though all the plain led to the desired town, still ran in unreasoning terror.

"It's orl 'er doin'," he pleaded, springing on the bunk beside his old mate. But when, to rouse her sympathy, he would have laid his hand on her, the dog's teeth fastened in it and pulled him back.

81. BARCROFT BOAKE

FROM THE FAR WEST

'Tis a song of the Never Never land —
Set to the tune of a scorching gale
    On the sandhills red,
    When the grasses dead
Loudly rustle, and bow the head
To the breath of its dusty hail:

Where the cattle trample a dusty pad
Across the never-ending plain,
    And come and go
    With muttering low
In the time when the rivers cease to flow,
And the Drought King holds his reign;

When the fiercest piker who ever turned
With lowered head in defiance proud,
    Grown gaunt and weak,
    Release doth seek
In vain from the depths of the slimy creek —
His sepulchre and his shroud;

His requiem sung by an insect host,
Born of the pestilential air,
    That seethe and swarm
    In hideous form
Where the stagnant waters lie thick and warm,
And Fever lurks in his lair:

Where a placid, thirst-provoking lake
Clear in the flashing sunlight lies —
    But the stockman knows
    No water flows
Where the shifting mirage comes and goes
Like a spectral paradise;

And crouched in the saltbush' sickly shade,
Murmurs to Heaven a piteous prayer:
    "O God ! must I
      Prepare to die?"
And, gazing up at the brazen sky,
Reads his death-warrant there.

Gaunt, slinking dingoes snap and snarl,
Watching his slowly-ebbing breath;
    Crows are flying,
    Hoarsely crying
Burial service o'er the dying —
Foul harbingers of Death.

Full many a man has perished there,
Whose bones gleam white from the waste of sand —
    Who left no name
    On the scroll of Fame,
Yet died in his tracks, as well became
A son of that desert land.

82. BARCROFT BOAKE

ON THE BOUNDARY

I love the ancient boundary-fence —
    That mouldering chock-and-log:
When I go ride the boundary
    I let the old horse jog,
And take his pleasure in and out
    Where sandalwood grows dense,
And tender pines clasp hands across
    The log that tops the fence.

'Tis pleasant on the boundary-fence
    These sultry summer days;
A mile away, outside the scrub,
    The plain is all ablaze.
The sheep are panting on the camps —
    The heat is so intense;
But here the shade is cool and sweet
    Along the boundary-fence.

I love to loaf along the fence:
    So does my collie dog:
He often finds a spotted cat
    Hid in a hollow log.
He's very near as old as I
    And ought to have more sense —
I've hammered him so many times
    Along the boundary-fence.

My mother says that boundary-fence
    Must surely be bewitched;
The old man says that through that fence
    The neighbours are enriched;
It's always down, and through the gaps
    Our stock all get them hence —
It takes me half my time to watch
    The doings of that fence.

But should you seek the reason
    You won't travel very far:
'Tis hid a mile away among
    The murmuring belar:
The Jones's block joins on to ours,
    And so, in consequence,
It's part of Polly's work to ride
    Their side the boundary-fence.

83. HENRY LAWSON

The Drover's Wife

The "house" contains two rooms; is built of round timber, slabs, and stringy bark, and floored with split slabs. A big bark kitchen stands at the end, and is larger than the house itself, verandah included.

Bush all round—bush with no horizon, for the country is flat. No ranges in the distance. The bush consists of stunted, rotten "native apple trees". No undergrowth. Nothing to relieve the eye, save the darker green of a few "she-oaks" which are sighing above the narrow, almost waterless creek. Nineteen miles to the nearest sign of civilisation—a shanty on the main road.

The drover—an ex-squatter—is away with sheep. His wife and children are left here alone.

Four ragged, dried-up-looking children are playing about the house. Suddenly one of them yells: "Snake! Mother, here's a snake!"

The gaunt, sun-browned bushwoman darts from the kitchen, snatches "the baby" from the ground, holds it on her left hip, and reaches for a stick.

"Where is it?"

"Here! gone into the wood-heap!" yells the eldest boy—a sharp-faced, excited urchin of eleven. "Stop there, mother! I'll have him. Stand back! I'll have the beggar!"

"Tommy, come here, or you'll be bit. Come here at once when I tell you, you little wretch!"

The youngster comes reluctantly, carrying a stick bigger than himself. Suddenly he yells, triumphantly:

"There it goes, under the house!" and darts away, with club uplifted. At the same time, the big, black, yellow-eyed dog-of-all-breeds, who has shown the greatest interest in the proceedings, breaks his chain and darts after that snake. He is a moment late, however, and his nose reaches the crack in the slabs just as the end of the snake's tail disappears.

Almost at the same moment the boy's club comes down and skins the aforesaid nose. The dog takes small notice of this and proceeds to undermine the building; but he is subdued after a struggle and chained up. They can't afford to lose him.

The drover's wife makes the children stand together near the dog-house while she watches for the snake. She gets two small dishes of milk and sets them down near the wall to tempt the snake out; but an hour goes by and it does not show itself.

It is near sunset, and a thunderstorm is coming. The children must be brought inside. She will not take them into the house, for she knows the snake is there and may at any moment come up through the cracks in the rough slab floor. So she carries several armfuls of firewood into the kitchen, and then takes the children there. The kitchen has "no floor", or rather an earthen one called a "ground floor" in this part of the bush. There is a large, roughly-made table in the centre of the place. She brings the children in and makes them get on this table. They are two boys and two girls—mere babies. She gives them some supper, and then, before it gets dark, she goes into the house, and snatches up some pillows and bed-clothes—expecting to see or lay her hand on the snake any minute. She makes a bed on the kitchen-table for the children and sits down beside it to watch all night.

She has an eye on the corner, and a green sapling club laid in readiness on the dresser by her side; also her sewing basket and a copy of the *Young Ladies' Journal*. She has brought the dog into the room.

Tommy turns in, under protest, and says he'll lay awake all night and smash that blinded snake.

His mother asks him how many times she has told him not to swear.

He has his club with him under the bed-clothes, and the child next to him protests:

"Mummy! Tommy's skinnin' me alive wif his club. Make him take it out."

Tommy: "Shet up, you little——! D'yer want to be bit with the snake?"

Jacky shuts up.

"If yer bit," says Tommy, after a pause, "you'll swell up, an' smell, an' turn red an' green an' blue all over till yer bust. Won't he, mother?"

"Now then, don't frighten the child. Go to sleep," she says.

The two younger children go to sleep, and now and then Jacky complains of being "skeezed". More room is made for him. Presently Tommy says: "Mother! listen to them (adjective) little possums. I'd like to screw their blanky necks."

And Jacky protests drowsily.

"But they don't hurt us, the little blanks!"

Mother: "There, I told you, you'd teach Jacky to swear." But Jacky's remark makes her smile. Jacky goes to sleep.

Presently, Tommy asks:—

"Mother! Do you think they'll ever extricate the (adjective) kangaroo?"

"Lord! How am I to know, child? Go to sleep."

"Will you wake me if the snake comes out?"

"Yes. Go to sleep."

Near midnight. The children are all asleep and she sits there still, sewing and reading by turns. From time to time she glances round the floor and wall-plate, and, whenever she hears a noise, she reaches for the stick. The thunderstorm comes on, and the wind, rushing thro' the cracks in the slab wall, threatens to blow out her candle. She places it on a sheltered part of the dresser, and fixes up a newspaper to protect it. At every flash of lightning, the cracks between the slabs gleam like polished silver. The thunder rolls, and the rain comes down in torrents.

"Alligator" (the dog) lies at full length on the floor, with his eyes turned towards the partition. She knows by this that the snake is there. There are large cracks in that wall opening under the floor of the dwelling-house.

She is not a coward, but recent events have shaken her nerves. A little son of her brother-in-law was lately bitten by a snake, and died. Besides, she has not heard from her husband for six months, and is anxious about him.

He was a drover and started squatting here when they were married. The drought of 18– ruined him. He had to sacrifice the remnant of his flock and go droving again. He intends to move his family into the nearest town when he comes back, and, in the meantime, his brother, who lives on the main road, comes over about once a month with provisions. The wife has still a couple of cows, one horse, and a few sheep. The brother-in-law kills one of the latter occasionally, gives her what she needs of it, and takes the rest in return for other provisions.

She is used to being left alone. She once lived like this for 18 months. As a girl she built, we suppose, the usual air-castles, but all her girlish hopes and aspirations are dead. She finds all the excitement and recreation she needs in the *Young Ladies' Journal*, and, Heaven help her! takes a pleasure in the fashion-plates.

Her husband is an Australian, and so is she. He is careless, but a good enough husband. If he had the means he would take her to the city and keep her there like a princess. They are used to being apart, or at least she is. "No use frettin'," she says. He may forget sometimes that he is married; but if he has a good cheque when he comes back he will give most of it to her. When he had money he took her to the city several times—hired a railway sleeping compartment, and put up at the best hotels. He also bought her a buggy, but they had to sacrifice that along with the rest.

The last two children were born in the bush—one while her husband was bringing a drunken doctor, by force, to attend to her. She was alone on this occasion, and very weak. She had been ill with a fever. She prayed to God to send her assistance. God sent "Black Mary,"—the "whitest" gin in all the land.

One of her children died while she was here alone. She rode nineteen miles for assistance, carrying the dead child.

*   *   *

It must be near one or two o'clock. The fire is burning low. Alligator lies with his head resting on his paws, and watches the wall. He is not a very beautiful dog to look at, and the light shows numerous old wounds where the hair will not grow. He is afraid of nothing on the face of the earth or under it. He will tackle a bullock as readily as he will tackle a flea. He hates all other dogs—except kangaroo dogs—and has a marked dislike to friends or relations of the family. They seldom call, however. He sometimes makes friends with strangers. He hates snakes and has killed many, but he will be bitten some day and die; most snake-dogs end that way.

Now and then the bushwoman lays down her work and watches, and listens, and thinks. She thinks of things in her own life, for there is little else to think about.

The rain will make the grass grow, and this reminds her how she fought a bush fire once while her husband was away. The grass was long, and very dry, and the fire threatened to burn her out. She put on an old pair of her husband's trousers, and beat out the flames with a green bough till great drops of sooty perspiration stood out on her forehead and ran in streaks down her blackened arms. The sight of his mother in trousers greatly amused Tommy, who worked like a little hero by her side; but the baby howled lustily to be taken up, and the fire would have mastered her but for four excited bushmen who arrived in the nick of time. It was a mixed up affair all round. When she went to take up the baby he screamed and struggled convulsively, thinking it was a "black man"; and Alligator, trusting more to the child's sense than his own instinct, charged furiously, and being old and slightly deaf did not in his excitement at first recognise his mistress's voice but continued to hang on to the moleskins until choked off by Tommy with a saddle-strap. The dog's sorrow for the mistake he so nearly made and his anxiety to let it be known that she was all a mistake, was as evident as his ragged tail and a six-inch grin could make it. It was a glorious time for the boys; a day to look back to, and talk about, and laugh over for many years.

She thinks how she fought a flood during her husband's absence. She stood for hours in the drenching downpour, and dug a drain to save the dam across the creek. But she could not save it. There are things that a bushwoman cannot do. Next morning the dam was broken, and her heart was nearly broken too, for she thought how her husband would feel when he came home and saw the result of months of labour swept away. She "cried" then.

She also fought the pleuro-pneumonia, dosed and bled the few remaining cattle, and wept again when her two best cows died.

Again, she fought a mad bullock that besieged the house for a day. She made bullets and fired at him thro' cracks in the slabs, with an old shotgun. He was dead in the morning. She skinned him, and afterwards got 7s. 6d. for the hide.

She also fights the crows and eagles that have designs on her chickens. Her plan of campaign is very original. The children cry "Crows, mother!" and she rushes out and aims a broomstick at the birds as though it were a gun, and says "Bung!" The crows leave in a hurry; they are cunning, but a woman's cunning is greater.

Occasionally a bushman in the "horrors", or a villainous-looking "sundowner", comes and scares the life out of her. She generally tells the suspicious-looking stranger that her "husband and two sons are at work below the dam", for he always cunningly enquires for "the boss".

Only last week a gallows-faced swagman—having satisfied himself or been informed that there were no men on the place—threw his swag down on the verandah, and demanded "tucker". She gave him something to eat, and then he expressed his intention of staying for the night. It was sundown then. She got a batten from the sofa, loosened the dog, and confronted the stranger—holding the batten in one hand and the dog's collar with the other. "Now you go!" she said. He looked at her and at the dog and said "All-right, mum," in a cringing tone, and left. She was a determined-looking woman, and Alligator's yellow eyes glared unpleasantly. Besides, the dog's chawing-up apparatus greatly resembled that of his namesake.

*   *   *

She has few pleasures to think of as she sits here alone by the fire, on guard against a snake. All days are much the same to her; but on Sunday afternoon she dresses herself, tidies the children, smartens-up baby, and goes for a lonely walk along the bush-track, pushing an old perambulator in front of her. She does this every Sunday. She takes as much care to make herself and the children "look smart" as she would if she were going to "do the block" in Sydney. There is nothing to see, however, and not a soul to meet. You might walk for 20 miles along this track without being able to fix a point in your mind, unless you are a bushman. It is because of the maddening, everlasting, sameness of the stunted trees—that monotony which makes a new-chum long to break away and travel as far as trains can go, and sail as far as ships can sail—and further.

But this bushwoman is used to the loneliness of it. As a girl-wife she hated it, but now she would feel strange away from it.

She is glad when her husband returns, but she does not gush or make a fuss about it. She gets him something good to eat and tidies up the children.

She seems contented with her lot. She loves her children, but has no time to show it. She seems harsh to them. Her surroundings are not favourable to the development of the "womanly" or sentimental side of nature.

*   *   *

It must be near morning now, but the clock is in the other room. Her candle is nearly done; she forgot that she is out of candles. Some more wood must be got to keep the fire up, and so she shuts the dog inside and hurries round to the woodheap. The rain has cleared off. She seizes a stick, pulls it out, and—crash! the whole pile collapses, and nearly frightens her to death.

Yesterday she bargained with a stray Blackfellow to bring her some wood, and while he was at work she went in search of a missing cow. She was absent an hour or so, and the Black made good use of his time. On her return she was astonished by seeing a great heap of wood by the chimney. She gave the Black an extra fig of tobacco, and praised him for not being lazy. He thanked her, and left with head erect. *But he built the woodheap hollow.*

She is hurt now, and tears spring to her eyes as she sits down again by the table. She snatches up a handkerchief to wipe the tears away, but pokes her eyes with her bare fingers instead. The handkerchief is full of holes, and she finds that she has put her thumb through one, and her forefinger through another.

This makes her laugh suddenly, to the surprise of the dog. She has a keen, very keen sense of the ridiculous; and sometime or another she will amuse bushmen by relating this incident.

She was amused once before in a manner similar in some respects. One day she sat down "to have a good cry", as she said—and the old cat rubbed against her dress and "cried, too". Then she "had to laugh".

*   *   *

It must be near daylight now. The room is very close and hot because of the fire. Alligator still watches the wall from time to time. Suddenly he becomes greatly interested; he draws himself a few inches nearer the partition, and a thrill runs through his body. The hair on the back of his neck begins to bristle, and the battle light is in his yellow eyes. She knows what this means, and lays her hand on the stick. The lower end of one of the partition slabs has a large crack on each side of it. An evil pair of small, bright, bead-like eyes glisten at one of these holes. The snake—a black one—comes slowly out, about a foot, and moves its head up and down. The dog lies still, and the woman sits as one fascinated. The snake comes out a foot further. She lifts her stick, and the reptile, as though suddenly aware of danger, sticks his head in through the crack on the other side of the slab, and hurries to get his tail round after him. Alligator springs, and his jaws come together with a snap. He misses this time, for his nose is large, and the snake's body close down in the angle formed by the slabs and the floor. He snaps again as the tail comes round. He has the snake now, and tugs it out eighteen inches. Thud, thud, comes the woman's club on the ground. Alligator pulls again. Thud, thud. Alligator pulls some more. He has the snake out now—a black brute, five feet long. The head rises to dart about, but the dog has the enemy close to the neck. He is a big, heavy dog, but as quick as a terrier. He shakes the snake as tho' he felt the curse of Toil in common with mankind. The eldest boy wakes up, seizes his stick, and makes to get out of bed, but his mother forces him back with a grip of iron. Thud, thud; the snake's back is broken in several places. Thud, thud; the head is crushed, and Alligator's nose skinned again.

She lifts the mangled reptile on the point of her stick, carries it to the fire, and throws it in. Then she piles on the wood and watches the snake burn. The boy and dog watch, too. She lays her hand on the dog's head, and all the fierce, angry light dies out of his yellow eyes. The younger children are quieted, and presently go to sleep. The dirty-legged boy stands for a moment in his shirt, watching the fire. Presently he looks at her. He sees the tears in her eyes, and, suddenly throwing his arms round her neck, exclaims:

"Mother, I won't never go drovin'; blast me, if I do!"

And she hugs him to her worn-out breast and kisses him, and they sit thus together while the sickly daylight breaks over the bush.

84. CHRISTOPHER BRENNAN

Fire in the heavens, and fire along the hills,
and fire made solid in the flinty stone,
thick-mass'd or scatter'd pebble, fire that fills
the breathless hour that lives in fire alone.

This valley, long ago the patient bed
of floods that carv'd its antient aplitude,
in stillness of the Egyptian crypt outspread,
endures to drown in noon-day's tyrant mood.

Behind the veil of burning silence bound,
vast life's innumerous busy littleness
is hush'd in vague-conjectured blur or sound
that dulls the brain with slumbrous weight, unless

some dazzling puncture let the stridence throng
in the cicada's torture-point of song.

85. JOSEPH FURPHY

THE GUMSUCKER'S DIRGE

Sing the evil days we see, and the worse that are to be,
   In such doggerel as dejection will allow,
We are pilgrims, sorrow-led, with no Beulah on ahead,
   No elysian Up the Country for us now.

For the settlements extend till they seem to have no end;
   Spreading silently, you can't tell when or how;
And a home-infested land stretches out on every hand,
   So there is no Up the Country for us now.

On the six-foot Mountain peak, up and down the dubious creek,
   Where the cockatoos alone should make a row,
There the rooster tears his throat, to announce with homely note,
   That there is no Up the Country for us now.

Where the dingo should be seen, sounds the Army tambourine,
   While the hardest case surrenders with a vow;
And the church-bell, going strong, makes us feel we've lived too long,
   Since there is no Up the Country for us now.

And along the pine-ridge side, where the mallee-hen should hide,
   You will see some children driving home a cow;
Whilst, ballooning on a line, female garniture gives sign,
   That there is no Up the Country for us now.

Here, in place of emu's eggs, you will find surveyors' pegs,
   And the culvert where there ought to be a slough;
There, a mortise in the ground, shows the digger has been round,
   And has left no Up the Country for us now.

And across this fenced-in view, like our friend the well-sung Jew,
   Goes the swaggy, with a frown upon his brow,
He is cabin'd, cribb'd, confin'd, for the thought is on his mind,
   That there is no Up the Country for him now.

And the boy that bolts from home has no decent place to roam,
   No region with adventure to endow,
But his ardent spirit cools at the sight of farms and schools,
   Hence, there is no Up the Country for him now.

Such a settling, spreading curse must infallibly grow worse,
    Till the saltbush disappears before the plough,
But the future, evil-fraught, is forgotten in the thought,
    That there is no Up the Country for us now.

We must do a steady shift, and devote our minds to thrift,
    Till we reach at length the standard of the Chow,
For we're crumpled side by side in a world no longer wide,
    And there is no Up the Country for us now.

Better we were cold and still, with our famous Jim and Bill,
    Beneath the interdicted wattle-bough,
For the angels made our date five-and-twenty years too late,
    And there is no Up the Country for us now.

In a Wet Season

It was raining—"general rain".

The train left Bourke, and then there began the long, long agony of scrub and wire fence, with here and there a natural clearing, which seemed even more dismal than the funereal "timber" itself. The only thing which might seem in keeping with one of these soddened flats would be the ghost of a funeral—a city funeral with plain hearse and string of cabs—going very slowly across from the scrub on one side to the scrub on the other. Sky like a wet, grey blanket; plains like dead seas, save for the tufts of coarse grass sticking up out of the water; scrub indescribably dismal—everything damp, dark, and unspeakably dreary.

Somewhere along here we saw a swagman's camp—a square of calico stretched across a horizontal stick, some rags steaming on another stick in front of a fire, and two billies to the leeward of the blaze. We knew by instinct that there was a piece of beef in the larger one. Small, hopeless-looking man standing with his back to the fire, with his hands behind him, watching the train; also, a damp, sorry-looking dingo warming itself and shivering by the fire. The rain had held up for a while. We saw two or three similar camps further on, forming a temporary suburb of Byrock.

The population was on the platform in old overcoats and damp, soft felt hats; one trooper in a waterproof. The population looked cheerfully and patiently dismal. The local push had evidently turned up to see off some fair enslavers from the city, who had been up-country for the cheque season, now over. They got into another carriage. We were glad when the bell rang.

The rain recommenced. We saw another swagman about a mile on struggling away from the town, through mud and water. He did not seem to have heart enough to bother about trying to avoid the worst mud-holes. There was a low-spirited dingo at his heels, whose sole object in life was seemingly to keep his front paws in his master's last footprint. The traveller's body was bent well forward from the hips up; his long arm—about six inches through his coat sleeves—hung by his sides like the arms of a dummy, with a billy at the end of one and a bag at the end of the other; but his head was thrown back against the top end of the swag, his hat-brim rolled up in front, and we saw a ghastly, beardless face which turned neither to the right nor the left as the train passed him.

After a long while we closed our book, and, looking through the window, saw a hawker's turn-out which was too sorrowful for description.

We looked out again while the train was going slowly, and saw a teamster's camp: three or four waggons covered with tarpaulins which hung down in the mud all round and suggested death. A long, narrow man, in a long, narrow, shoddy overcoat and a damp felt hat, was walking quickly along the road past the camp. A sort of cattle-dog glided silently and swiftly out from under a waggon, "heeled" the man, and slithered back without explaining. Here the scene vanished.

We remember stopping—for an age it seemed—at half-a-dozen straggling shanties on a flat of mud and water. There was a rotten weatherboard pub, with a low, dripping verandah, and three wretchedly forlorn horses hanging, in the rain, to a post outside. We saw no more, but we knew that there were several apologies for men hanging about the rickety bar inside—or round the parlour fire. Streams of cold, clay-coloured water ran in all directions, cutting fresh gutters, and raising a yeasty froth whenever the water fell a few inches. As we left, we saw a big man in an overcoat riding across a culvert; the tails of the coat spread over the horse's rump, and almost hid it. In fancy still we saw him—hanging up his weary, hungry, little horse in the rain, and swaggering into the bar; and we almost heard someone say, in a drawling tone: "'Ello, Tom! 'Ow are yer poppin' up?"

The train stopped (for about a year) within a mile of the next station. Trucking-yards in the foreground, like any other trucking-yards along the line; they looked drearier

than usual, because the rain had darkened the posts and
rails. Small plain beyond, covered with water and tufts of
grass. The inevitable, God-forgotten "timber", black in the
distance; dull, grey sky and misty rain over all. A small,
dark-looking flock of sheep was crawling slowly in across
the flat from the unknown, with three men on horseback
zig-zagging patiently behind. The horses just moved—that
was all. One man wore an oilskin, one an old tweed overcoat, and the third had a three-bushel bag over his head and
shoulders.

Had we returned an hour later, we should have seen the
sheep huddled together in a corner of the yards, and the
three horses hanging up outside the local shanty.

We stayed at Nyngan—which place we refrain from
sketching—for a few hours, because the five trucks of cattle
of which we were in charge were shunted there, to be taken
on by a very subsequent goods train. The Government allows one man to every five trucks in a cattle-train. We shall
pay our fare next time, even if we have not a shilling left over
and above. We had haunted local influence at
Comanavadrink, for two long, anxious, heart-breaking
weeks ere we got the pass; and we had put up with all the in-
dignities, the humiliation—in short, had suffered all that
poor devils suffer whilst besieging Local Influence. We only
thought of escaping from the bush.

The pass said that we were John Smith, drover, and that
we were available for return by ordinary passenger-train
within two days, we think—or words in that direction.
Which didn't interest us. We might have given the pass away
to an unemployed in Orange, who wanted to go Out Back,
and who begged for it with tears in his eyes; but we didn't
like to injure a poor fool who never injured us—who was an
entire stranger to us. He didn't know what Out Back meant.

Local Influence had given us a kind of note of introduction to be delivered to the cattle-agent at the yards that
morning; but the agent was not there—only two of his satel-
lites, a cockney colonial-experience man, and a scrub-town
clerk, both of whom we kindly ignore. We got on without
the note, and at Orange we amused ourself by reading it. It
said:

"Dear Old Man,—Please send this beggar on; and I hope

he'll be landed safely at Orange—or—or wherever the cattle go.—Yours,——."

We had been led to believe that the bullocks were going to Sydney. We took no further interest in those cattle.

After Nyngan the bush grew darker and drearier, and the plains more like ghastly oceans; and here and there the "dominant note of Australian scenery" was accentuated, as it were, by naked, white, ring-barked trees standing in the water and haunting the ghostly surroundings.

We spent that night in a passenger compartment of a van which had been originally attached to old No. 1 engine. There was only one damp cushion in the whole concern. We lent that to a lady who travelled for a few hours in the other half of the next compartment. The seats were about nine inches wide and sloped in at a sharp angle to the bare matchboard wall, with a bead on the outer edge; and as the cracks had become well caulked with the grease and dirt of generations, they held several gallons of water each. We scuttled one, rolled ourself in a rug, and tried to sleep; but all night long overcoated and comfortered bushmen would get in, let down all the windows, and then get out again at the next station. Then we would wake up frozen and shut the windows.

We dozed off again, and woke at daylight, and recognised the ridgy gum-country between Dubbo and Orange. It didn't look any drearier than the country further west—because it couldn't. There is scarcely a part of the country out west which looks less inviting or more horrible than any other part.

The weather cleared, and we had sunlight for Orange, Bathurst, the Blue Mountains, and Sydney. They deserve it; also as much rain as they need.

Extract from Such is Life [*The Lost Girl*]

"Where the (adj. sheol) do you reckon on bein' shoved into when you croak, Bob?" asked Donovan, with a touch of human solicitude.

"Well," replied Bob pointedly, as he unfolded his long angles to a perpendicular right line—"I got good hopes o' goin' to a place where there's no admittance for swearers. Ain't ashamed to say I repented eight or ten months ago. Guarantee you fellers ain't heard no language out o' my mouth since I set down here. Nor 'on't—never again. Well, take care o' yourselves, chaps." And, without further farewell, Bob removed his lonely individuality from our convention.

"Anointed (adj.) savage," remarked Donovan, as the subject of his comment receded into the hazy half-light of the plain, where his horse was feeding.

"Uncivilised (person)," added Baxter.

"Well—yes," conceded Thompson. "Same time, he's got the profit of his unprofitableness, so to speak. Hard to beat him in the back country. You'd have to be more uncivilised than he is. And I saw that very thing happen to him, four or five weeks ago, out on Goolumbulla." Thompson paused experimentally, then continued, "Yes, I saw him put-through, till he must have felt a lot too tall in proportion to his cleverness." Another tentative pause. "But it took the very pick of uncivilisation to do it." A prolonged pause, while Thompson languidly filled and lit his pipe. Still the dignified indifference of the camp remained unruffled. Thompson might tell his yarn, or keep it to himself. Once already during the evening his tongue had run too freely. "What I'm thinking about," he continued, in a tone of audible musing, "is that I forgot to tell Bob, when he was here, that I had a long pitch with Dan O'Connell, three or four nights ago."

"Boundary man on Goolumbulla," I suggested apathetically. "Got acquainted with Bob years ago, when he was making himself useful on Moogoojinna, and Bob was making himself obnoxious on Wo-Winya, or Boolka."

"No; they never met till four or five weeks ago," replied Thompson, with inimitable indifference, though now licensed to proceed without damage to his own dignity. "Dan's an old acquaintance of yours—isn't he? I heard your name mentioned over the finding of a dead man—George something—had been fencing on Mooltunya—George Murdoch. Yes."

Thompson told a story well. I verily believe he used to practise the accomplishment mentally, as he sauntered along beside his team. He knew his own superiority here; his acquaintances knew it too, and they also knew that he knew it. Hence they were reluctant to minister occasion to his egotism.

"Speaking of Bob," he continued listlessly; "I met him in the hut, at Kulkaroo, on the evening I got there with the load. He was on his way down from that new place of M'Gregor's, where he's been; and he had come round by Kulkaroo to see one of the very few friends he has in the world; but he lost his labour, for this cove had left the station more than a year before.

"However, he had been yarning for hours, and the station chaps were about turning-in, when we heard someone coming in a hurry. No less than Webster himself—first time he had been in the hut since it was built, the chaps told me afterward. He had a leaf of a memorandum-book in his hand; and says he:

"'Child lost in the scrub on Goolumbulla. Dan O'Connell's little girl—five or six years old. Anybody know where there's any blackfellows?'

"Nobody knew.

"'Well, raise horses wherever you can, and clear at once,' says he. 'One man, for the next couple of days, will be worth a regiment very shortly. As for you, Thompson,' says he; 'you're your own master.'

"Of course, I was only too glad of any chance to help in such a case, so I went for my horse at once. Bob had duffed his two horses into the ration paddock, on his way to the hut, and had put them along with my mare, so that he could find them at daylight by the sound of her bell. This started me and him together. He lent his second horse to one of the station chaps; and the three of us got to Goolumbulla just after sunrise—first of the crowd. Twenty-five mile. There was tucker on the table, and chaff for our horses; and, during the twenty minutes or so that we stayed, they gave us the outline of the mishap.

"Seems that, for some reason or other—valuation for mortgage, I'm thinking—the classer had come round a few days before; and Spanker had called in every man on the station, to muster the ewes. You know how thick the scrub is on Goolumbulla? Dan came in along with the rest, leaving his own place before daylight on the first morning. They swept the paddock the first day for about three parts of the ewes; the second day they got most of what was left; but Spanker wanted every hoof, if possible, and he kept all hands on for the third day.

"Seems, the little girl didn't trouble herself the first day, though she hadn't seen Dan in the morning; but the second day there was something peculiar about her—not fretful; but dreaming, and asking her mother strange questions. It appears that, up to this time, she had never said a word about the man that was found dead near their place, a couple of months before. She saw that her parents didn't want to tell her anything about it, so she had never showed any curiosity; but now her mother was startled to find that she knew all the particulars.

"It appears that she was very fond of her father; and this affair of the man perishing in the scrub was working on her mind. All the second day she did nothing but watch; and during the night she got up several times to ask her mother questions that frightened the woman. The child didn't understand her father going away before she was awake, and not coming back. Still, the curious thing was that she never took her mother into her confidence, and never seemed to fret.

"Anyway, on the third morning, after breakfast, her mother went out to milk the goats, leaving her in the house. When the woman came back, she found the child gone. She looked round the place, and called, and listened, and prospected everywhere, for an hour; then she went into the house, and examined. She found that the little girl had taken about a pint of milk, in a small billy with a lid, and half a loaf of bread. Then, putting everything together, the mother decided that she had gone into the scrub to look for her father. There was no help to be had nearer than the home-station, for the only other boundary man on that part of the run was away at the muster. So she cleared for the station—twelve mile—and got there about three in the afternoon, not able to stand. There was nobody about the station but Mrs. Spanker, and the servant-girl, and the cook, and the Chow slushy; and Mrs. Spanker was the only one that knew the track to the ewe-paddock. However, they got a horse in, and off went Mrs. Spanker to give the alarm. Fine woman. Daughter of old Walsh, storekeeper at Moogoojin-na, on the Deniliquin side.

"It would be about five when Mrs. Spanker struck the ewe-paddock, and met Broome and another fellow. Then the three split out to catch whoever they could, and pass the word round. Dan got the news just before sundown. He only remarked that she might have found her own way back; then he went for home as hard as his horse could lick.

"As the fellows turned-up, one after another, Spanker sent the smartest of them—one to Kulkaroo, and one to Mulppa, and two or three others to different fencers' and tank-sinkers' camps. But the main thing was blackfellows. Did anybody know where to find a blackfellow, now that he was wanted?

"Seems, there had been about a dozen of them camped near the tank in the cattle-paddock for a month past, but they were just gone, nobody knew where. And there had been an old lubra and a young one camped within a mile of the station, and an old fellow and his lubra near one of the boundary men's places; but they all happened to have shifted; and no one had the slightest idea where they could be found. However, in a sense, everyone was after them.

"But, as I was telling you, we had some breakfast at the station, and then started for Dan's place. Seven of us by this time, for another of the Kulkaroo men had come up, and there were three well-sinkers in a buggy. This was on a Thursday morning; and the little girl had been out twenty-four hours.

"Well, we had gone about seven mile, with crowds of fresh horse-tracks to guide us; and we happened to be going at a fast shog, and Bob riding a couple or three yards to the right, when he suddenly wheeled his horse round, and jumped off.

"'How far is it yet to Dan's place?' says he.

"'Five mile,' says one of the well-sinkers. 'We're just on the corner of his paddock. Got tracks?'

"'Yes,' says Bob. 'I'll run them up, while you fetch the other fellows. Somebody look after my horse.' And by the time the last word was out of his mouth, he was twenty yards away along the little track. No trouble in following it, for she was running the track of somebody that had rode out that way a few days before—thinking it was her father's horse, poor little thing!

"Apparently she had kept along the inside of Dan's fence—the way she had generally seen him going out—till she came to the corner, where there was a gate. Then she had noticed this solitary horse's track striking away from the gate, out to the left; and she had followed it. However, half-a-mile brought us to a patch of hardish ground, where she had lost the horse's track; and there Bob lost hers. Presently he picked it up again; but now there was only her little boot-marks to follow."

"A goot dog would be wort vivty men dere, I tink," suggested Helsmok.

"Same thought struck several of us, but it didn't strike Bob," replied Thompson. "Fact, the well-sinkers had brought a retriever with them in the buggy; a dog that would follow the scent of any game you could lay him on; but they couldn't get him to take any notice of the little girl's track. Never been trained to track children—and how were they going to make him understand that a child was lost? However, while two of the well-sinkers were persevering with their retriever, the other fellow drove off like fury to fetch Dan's sheep-dog; making sure that we would only have to follow him along the scent. In the meantime, I walked behind Bob, leading both our horses.

"Give him his due, he's a great tracker. I compare track-ing to reading a letter written in a good business hand. You mustn't look at what's under your eye; you must see a lot at once, and keep a general grasp of what's on ahead, besides spotting each track you pass. Otherwise, you'll be always turning back for a fresh race at it. And you must no more confine yourself to actual tracks than you would expect to find each letter correctly formed. You must just lift the general meaning as you go. Of course, our everyday tracking is not tracking at all.

"However, Bob run this little track full walk, mile after mile, in places where I would'n't see a mark for fifty yards at a stretch, on account of rough grass, and dead leaves, and so forth. One thing in favour of Bob was that she kept a fairly straight course, except when she was blocked by porcupine or supple-jack; then she would swerve off, and keep another middling straight line. At last Bob stopped.

"'Here's where she slept last night,' says he; and we could trace the marks right enough. We even found some crumbs of bread on the ground, and others that the ants were carrying away. She had made twelve or fourteen mile in the day's walk.

"By this time, several chaps had come from about Dan's place; and they were still joining us in twos and threes. As fast as they came, they scattered out in front, right and left, and one cove walked a bit behind Bob, with a frog-bell, shaking it now and then, to give the fellows their latitude. This would be about two in the afternoon, or half-past; and we pushed along the tracks she had made only a few hours before, with good hopes of overtaking her before dark. The thing that made us most uneasy was the weather. It was threatening for a thunderstorm. At this time we were in that unstocked country south-east of the station. Suddenly Bob rose up from his stoop, and looked round at me with a face on him like a ghost.

"'God help us now, if we don't get a blackfellow quick!' says he, pointing at the ground before him. And, sure enough, there lay the child's little copper-toed boots, where she had taken them off when her feet got sore, and walked on in her socks. It was just then that a tanksinker drove up, with Dan and his dog in the buggy."

"Poor old Rory!" I interposed. "Much excited?"

"Well—no. But there was a look of suspense in his face that was worse. And his dog—a dog that had run the scent of his horse for hundreds of miles, all put together—that dog would smell any plain track of the little stocking-foot, only a few hours old, and would wag his tail, and bark, to show that he knew whose track it was; and all the time showing the greatest distress to see Dan in trouble; but it was no use trying to start him on the scent. They tried three or four other dogs, with just the same success. But Bob never lost half-a-second over these attempts. *He* knew.

"Anyway, it was fearful work after that; with the thunderstorm hanging over us. Bob was continually losing the track; and us circling round and round in front, sometimes picking it up a little further ahead. But we only made another half-mile or three-quarters, at the outside—before night was on. I daresay there might be about twenty-five of us by this time, and eighteen or twenty horses, and two or three buggies and wagonettes. Some of the chaps took all the horses to a tank six or eight mile away, and some cleared off in desperation to hunt for blackfellows, and the rest of us scattered out a mile or two ahead of the last track, to listen.

"They had been sending lots of tucker from the station; and before the morning was grey everyone had breakfast, and was out again. But, do what we would, it was slow, slow work; and Bob was the only one that could make any show at all in running the track. Friday morning, of course; and by this time the little girl had been out for forty-eight hours.

"At nine or ten in the forenoon, when Bob had made about half-a-mile, one of the Kulkaroo men came galloping through the scrub from the right, making for the sound of the bell.

"'Here, Bob!' says he. 'We've found the little girl's billy at the fence of Peter's paddock, where she crossed. Take this horse. About two mile—straight out there.'

"I had my horse with me at the time, and I tailed-up Bob to the fence. He went full tilt, keeping the track that the horse had come, and this fetched us to where a couple of chaps were standing over a little billy, with a lump of bread beside it. She had laid them down to get through the fence, and then went on without them. The lid was still on the billy, and there was a drop of milk left. The ants had eaten the bread out of all shape.

"But Bob was through the fence, and bowling down a

dusty sheep-track, where a couple of fellows had gone before him, and where we could all see the marks of the little bare feet—for the stockings were off by this time. But in sixty or eighty yards this pad run into another, covered with fresh sheep-tracks since the little girl had passed. Nothing for it but to spread out, and examine the network of pads scattered over the country. All this time, the weather was holding-up, but there was a grumble of thunder now and then, and the air was fearfully close.

"At last there was a coo-ee out to the left. Young Broome had found three plain tracks, about half-a-mile away. We took these for a base, but we didn't get beyond them. We were circling round for miles, without making any headway; and so the time passed till about three in the afternoon. Then up comes Spanker, with his hat lost, and his face cut and bleeding from the scrub, and his horses in a white lather, and a black lubra sitting in the back of the buggy, and the Mulppa stock-keeper tearing along in front, giving him our tracks.

"She was an old, grey-haired lubra, blind of one eye; but she knew her business, and she was on the job for life or death. She picked-up the track at a glance, and run it like a bloodhound. We found that the little girl hadn't kept the sheep-pads as we expected. Generally she went straight till something blocked her; then she'd go straight again, at another angle. Very rarely—hardly ever—we could see what signs the lubra was following; but she was all right. Uncivilised, even for an old lubra. Nobody could yabber with her but Bob; and he kept close to her all the time. She began to get uneasy as night came on, but there was no help for it. She went slower and slower, and at last she sat down where she was. We judged that the little girl had made about seventeen mile to the place where the lubra got on her track, and we had added something like four to that. Though, mind you, at this time we were only about twelve or fourteen mile from Dan's place, and eight or ten mile from the home-station.

"Longest night I ever passed, though it was one of the shortest in the year. Eyes burning for want of sleep, and couldn't bear to lie down for a minute. Wandering about for miles; listening; hearing something in the scrub, and finding it was only one of the other chaps, or some sheep. Thunder and lightning, on and off, all night; even two or three drops of rain, toward morning. Once I heard the howl of a dingo, and I thought of the little girl, lying worn-out, half-asleep and half-fainting—far more helpless than a sheep—and I made up my mind that if she came out safe I would lead a better life for the future.

"However, between daylight and sunrise—being then about a mile, or a mile and a half, from the bell—I was riding at a slow walk, listening and dozing in the saddle, when I heard a far-away call that sounded like 'Dad-dee!'. It seemed to be straight in front of me; and I went for it like mad. Hadn't gone far when Williamson, the narangy, was alongside me.

"'Hear anything?' says I.

"'Yes,' says he. 'Sounded like 'Daddy!' I think it was out here.'

"'I think it was more this way,' says I; and each of us went his own way.

"When I got to where I thought was about the place, I listened again, and searched round everywhere. The bell was coming that way, and presently I went to meet it, leading my horse, and still listening. Then another call came through the stillness of the scrub, faint, but beyond mistake, 'Dad-de-e-e!'. There wasn't a trace of terror in the tone; it was just the voice of a worn-out child, deliberately calling with all her might. Seemed to be something less than half-a-mile away, but I couldn't fix on the direction; and the scrub was very thick.

"I hurried down to the bell. Everyone there had heard the call, or fancied they had; but it was out to their right—not in front. Of course, the lubra wouldn't leave the track, nor Bob, nor the chap with the bell; but everyone else was gone—Dan among the rest. The lubra said something to Bob.

"'Picaninny tumble down here again,' says Bob. 'Getting very weak on her feet.'

"By-and-by, 'Picaninny plenty tumble down.' It was pitiful; but we knew that we were close on her at last. By this time, of course, she had been out for seventy-two hours.

"I stuck to the track, with the lubra and Bob. We could

hear some of the chaps coo-eeing now and again, and call-ing 'Mary!'"——

"Bad line—bad line," muttered Saunders impatiently.

"Seemed to confuse things, anyway," replied Thompson. "And it was very doubtful whether the little girl was likely to answer a strange voice. At last, however, the lubra stopped, and pointed to a sun-bonnet, all dusty, lying under a spreading hop-bush. She spoke to Bob again.

"'Picaninny sleep here last night', says Bob. And that was within a hundred yards of the spot I had made-for after hearing the first call. I knew it by three or four tall pines, among a mass of pine scrub. However, the lubra turned off at an angle to the right, and run the track—not an hour old—toward where we had heard the second call. We were crossing fresh horse-tracks every few yards; and never two minutes but what somebody turned-up to ask the news. But to show how little use anything was except fair tracking, the lubra herself never saw the child till she went right up to where she was lying between two thick, soft bushes that met over her, and hid her from sight"——

"Asleep?" I suggested, with a sinking heart.

"No. She had been walking along—less than half-an-hour before—and she had brushed through between these bushes, to avoid some prickly scrub on both sides; but there happened to be a bilby-hole close in front, and she fell in the sort of trough, with her head down the slope; and that was the end of her long journey. It would have taken a child in fair strength to get out of the place she was in; and she was played-out to the last ounce. So her face had sunk down on the loose mould, and she had died without a struggle.

"Bob snatched her up the instant he caught sight of her, but we all saw that it was too late. We coo-eed, and the chap with the bell kept it going steady. Then all hands reckoned that the search was over, and they were soon collected round the spot.

"Now, that little girl was only five years old; and she had walked nothing less than twenty-two miles—might be nearer twenty-five."

There was a minute's silence. Personal observation, or trustworthy report, had made every one of Thompson's audience familiar with such episodes of new settlement; and, for that very reason, his last remark came as a confirmation rather than as an over-statement. Nothing is more astonishing than the distances lost children have been known to traverse.

"How did poor Rory take it?" I asked.

"Dan? Well he took it bad. When he saw her face he gave one little cry, like a wounded animal; then he sat down on the bilby-heap, with her on his knees, wiping the mould out of her mouth, and talking baby to her.

"Not one of us could find a word to say; but in a few minutes we were brought to ourselves by thunder and lightning in earnest, and the storm was on us with a roar. And just at this moment Webster of Kulkaroo came up with the smartest blackfellow in that district.

"We cleared out one of the wagonettes, and filled it with pine leaves, and laid a blanket over it. And Spanker gently took the child from Dan, and laid her there, spreading the other half of the blanket over her. Then he thanked all hands, and made them welcome at the station, if they liked to come. I went, for one; but Bob went back to Kulkaroo direct, so I saw no more of him till tonight.

"Poor Dan! He walked behind the wagonette all the way, crying softly, like a child, and never taking his eyes from the little shape under the soaking wet blanket. Hard lines for him! He had heard her voice calling him, not an hour before; and now, if he lived till he was a hundred, he would never hear it again.

"As soon as we reached the station, I helped Andrews, the storekeeper, to make the little coffin. Dan wouldn't have her buried in the station cemetery; she must be buried in con-secrated ground, at Hay. So we boiled a pot of gas-tar to the quality of pitch, and dipped long strips of wool-bale in it, and wrapped them tight round the coffin, after the lid was on, till it was two ply all over, and as hard and close as sheet-iron. Ay, and by this time more than a dozen blackfellows had rallied-up to the station.

"Spanker arranged to send a man with the wagonette, to look after the horses for Dan. The child's mother wanted to go with them, but Dan refused to allow it, and did so with a harshness that surprised me. In the end, Spanker sent Ward, one of the narangies. I happened to camp with them four nights ago, when I was coming down from Kulkaroo, and they were getting back to Goolumbulla. However," added Thompson, with sublime lowliness of manner, "that's what I meant by saying that, in some cases, a person's all the better for being uncivilised. You see, we were nowhere beside Bob, and Bob was nowhere beside the old lubra."

"Had you much of a yarn with the poor fellow when you met him?" I asked.

"Evening and morning only," replied Thompson, maintaining the fine apathy due to himself under the circumstances. "I was away all night with the bullocks, in a certain paddock. Didn't recognise me; but I told him I had been there; and then he would talk about nothing but the little girl. Catholic priest in Hay sympathised very strongly with him, he told me, but couldn't read the service over the child, on account of her not being baptised. So Ward read the service. His people are English Catholics. Most likely Spanker thought of this when he sent Ward. Dan didn't seem to be as much cut-up as you'd expect. He was getting uneasy about his paddock; and he thought Spanker might be at some inconvenience. But that black beard of his is more than half white already. And—something like me—I never thought of mentioning this to Bob when he was here. Absence of mind. Bad habit."

"This Dan has much to be thankful for," remarked Stevenson, with strong feeling in his voice. "Suppose that thunderstorm had come on a few hours sooner—what then?"

There was a silence for some minutes.

"Tell you what made me interrupt you, Thompson, when I foun' fault with singin'-out after lost kids," observed Saunders, at length. "Instigation o' many a pore little (child) perishin' unknownst. Seen one instance when I was puttin' up a bit o' fence on Grundle—hundred an' thirty-four chain an' some links—forty-odd links, if I don't disremember. Top rail an' six wires. Jist cuttin' off a bend o' the river, to make a handy cattle-paddick. They'd had it fenced-off with dead-wood, twelve or fifteen years before; but when they got it purchased they naterally went-in for a proper fence. An' you can't lick a top rail an' six wires, with nine-foot panels"——

"You're a bit of an authority on fencin'," remarked Baxter drily.

"Well, as I was sayin'," continued Saunders; "this kid belonged to a married man, name o' Tom Bracy, that was workin' mates with me. One night when his missus drafted the lot she made one short; an' she hunted roun', an' called, an' got excited; an' you couldn't blame the woman. Well, we hunted all night—me, an' Tom, an' Cunningham, the cove that was engaged to cart the stuff on-to the line. Decent, straightforrid chap, Cunningham is, but a (sheol) of a liar when it shoots him. Course, some o' you fellers knows him. Meejum-size man, but one o' them hard, wiry, deep-chested, deceivin' fellers. See him slingin' that heavy red-gum stuff about, as if it was broad palin'. Course, he was on'y three-an' twenty; an' fellers o' that age don't know their own strenth. His bullocks was fearful low at the time, on account of a trip he had out to Wilcanniar with flour; an' that's how he come to take this job"——

"Never mind Cunningham; he's dead now," observed Donovan indifferently.

"Well, as I was tellin' you," pursued Saunders, "we walked that bend the whole (adj.) night, singin' out 'Hen-ree! Hen-ree!' an' in the mornin' we was jist as fur as when we started. Tom, he clears-off to the station before daylight, to git help; an' by this time I'd come to the conclusion that the kid must be in the river, or out on the plains. I favoured the river a lot: but I bethought me o' where this dead-wood fence had bin burnt, to git it out o' our road, before the grass got dry. So I starts at one end to examine the line o' soft ashes that divided the bend off o' the plain—an' har'ly a sign o' traffic across it yet. Hadn't went, not fifteen chain, before I bumps up agen the kid's tracks, plain as A B C, crossin' out towards the plain. Coo-ees for Cunningham; shows him the tracks; an' the two of us follers the line o' ashes right to the other end, to see if the tracks come back. No (adj.) tracks. So we tells the missus; an' she clears-out for the plain, an' me after her. Cunningham, he collars his horse, an' out for the plain too. Station chaps turns-up, in ones an' twos; an' when they seen the tracks, they scattered for the plain too. Mostly young fellers, on good horses—some o' them good enough to be worth enterin' for a saddle, or the like o' that. Curious how horses was better an' cheaper them days nor what they are now. I had a brown mare that time; got her off of a traveller for three notes; an' you'd pass her by without lookin' at her; but of all the deceivin' goers you ever come across"——

"No odds about the mare; she's dead long ago," interposed Thompson.

"About two o'clock," continued Saunders cheerfully, "I was deadbeat an' leg-tired; an' I went back to the tent, to git a bite to eat; an', comin' back agen, I went roun' to have another look at the tracks. Now, thinks I, what road would that little (wanderer) be likeliest to head from here? An' I hitches myself up on a big ole black log that was layin' about a chain past the tracks, an' I set there for a minit, thinkin' like (sheol). You wouldn't call it a big log for the Murray, or the Lower Goulb'n, but it was a fair-size log for the Murrumbidgee. I seen some whoppin' red-gums in Gippsland too; but the biggest one I ever seen was on the Goulb'n. Course, when I say 'big', I mean measurement; I ain't thinkin' about holler shells, with no timber in 'em. This tree I'm speakin' about had eleven thousand two hundred an' some odd feet o' timber in her; an' Jack Hargrave, the feller that cut her"——

"His troubles is over too," murmured Baxter.

"Well, as I was tellin' you, I begun to fancy I could hear the whimper of a kid, far away. 'Magination, thinks I. Lis'ns fit to break my (adj.) neck. Hears it agen. Seemed to come from the bank o' the river. Away I goes; hunts roun'; lis'ns; calls 'Hen-ree!'; lis'ns agen. Not a sound. Couple o' the station hands happened to come roun', an' I told 'em. Well, after an hour o' searchin' an' lis'nin', the three of us went back to where I heard the sound. I hitches myself up on-to the log agen, an' says I:

"'This is the very spot I was,' says I, 'when I heard it.' An' before the word was out o' my mouth, (verb) me if I didn't hear it agen!

"'There you are!' says I.

"'What the (sheol) are you blatherin' about?' says they.

"'Don't you hear the (adj.) kid?' says I.

"'Oh, that ain't the kid, you (adj.) fool!' says they, lookin' as wise as Solomon, an' not lettin' on they couldn't hear it.

But for an' all, they parted, an' rode roun' an' roun', as slow
as they could crawl, stoppin' every now an' agen, an' listening for all they was worth; an' me settin' on the log, puzzlin'
my brains. At last I hears another whimper.

"'There you are again!' says I.

"An'one cove, he was stopped close in front o' the butt
end o' the log at the time; an' he jumps off his horse, an'
sticks his head in the holler o' the log, an' lets a oath out of
him. Fearful feller to swear, he was. I disremember his name
jis' now; but he'd bin on Grundle ever since he bolted from
his old man's place, in Bullarook Forest, on account of a
lickin' he got; an' it was hard to best him among sheep; an'
now I rec'lect his name was Dick—Dick—it's jist on the tip
o' my (adj.) tongue"——

"No matter hees name," interposed Helsmok; "he have
yoined der graat màyority too."

"Well, as I was sayin'," continued the patient Saunders,
"we lis'ned at the mouth o' the holler, an' heard the kid
whinin' inside; an' when we sung-out to him, he was as
quiet as a mouse. An' we struck matches, an' tried to see
him, but he was too fur along, an' the log was a bit crooked;
an' when you got in a couple o' yards, the hole was so small
you'd wonder how he done it. Anyhow, the two station
blokes rode out to pass the word; an' the most o' the crowd
was there in half-an-hour. The kid was a good thirty foot up
the log; an' there was no satisfaction to be got out of him.
He wouldn't shift; an' by-'n'-by we come to the impression
that he couldn't shift; an' at long an' at last we had to chop
him out, like a bees' nest. Turned out after, that the little
(stray) had foun' himself out of his latitude when night come
on; an' he'd got gumption enough to set down where he
was, an' wait for mornin'. He'd always bin told to do that, if
he got lost. But by-'n'-by he heard 'Hen-ree! Hen-ree!'
boomin' an' bellerin' back an' forrid across the bend in the
dark; an' he thought the boody-man, an' the bunyip, an' the
banshee, an' (sheol) knows what all, was after him. So he
foun' this holler log, an' he thought he couldn't git fur
enough into it. He was about seven year old then; an' that
was in '71—the year after the big flood—an' the shearin'
was jist about over. How old would that make him now?
Nineteen or twenty. He left his ole man three year ago, to

travel with a sheep-drover, name o' Sep Halliday, an' he's bin with the same bloke ever since. Mos' likely some o' you chaps knows this Sep? Stout butt of a feller, with a red baird. Used to mostly take flocks for truckin' at Deniliquin; but that got too many at it—like everything else—an' he went out back, Cooper's Creek way, with three thousand Gunbar yowes, the beginnin' o' las' winter, an' I ain't heard of him since he crossed at Wilcanniar"——

"No wonder," I observed; "he's gone aloft, like the rest."

There was a pause, broken by Stevenson, in a voice that brought constraint on us all:

"Bad enough to lose a youngster for a day or two, and find him alive and well: worse, beyond comparison, when he's found dead; but the most fearful thing of all is for a youngster to be lost in the bush, and never found, alive or dead. That's what happened to my brother Eddie, when he was about eight year old. You must remember it, Thompson?"

"Wasn't my father out on the search?" replied Thompson. "Tom's father, too. You were living on the Upper Campaspe."

"Yes," continued Stevenson, clearing his throat; "I've been thinking over it every night for these five-and-twenty years, and it seems to me the most likely thing that could have happened to him was to get jammed in a log, like that other little chap. Then after five years, or ten years, or twenty years, the log gets burned, and nobody notices a few little bones, crumbled among the ashes.

"I was three or four years older than Eddie," he resumed hoarsely; "and he just worshipped me. I had been staying with my uncle in Kyneton for three months, going to school; and Eddie was lost the day after I came home. We were out, gathering gum—four of us altogether—about a mile and a half from home; and I got cross with the poor little fellow, and gave him two or three hits; and he started home by himself, crying. He turned round and looked at me, just before he got out of sight among the trees; and that was the last that was ever seen of him, alive or dead. My God! When I think of that look, it makes me thankful to remember that every day brings me nearer to the end. The spot where he turned round is in the middle of a cultivation-paddock now, but I could walk straight to it in the middle of the darkest night.

"Yes; he started off home, crying. We all went the same way so soon afterward that I expected every minute to see him on ahead. At last we thought we must have passed him on the way. No alarm yet, of course; but I was choking with grief, to think how I'd treated the little chap; so I gave Maggie and Billy the slip, and went back to meet him. I knew from experience how glad he would be.

"Ah well! the time that followed is like some horrible dream. He was lost at about four in the afternoon; and there would be about a dozen people looking for him, and calling his name, all night. Next day, I daresay there would be about thirty. Next morning, my father offered £100 reward for him, dead or alive; and five other men guaranteed £10 each. Next day, my father's reward was doubled; and five other men put down their names for another £50. Next day, Government offered £200. So between genuine sympathy and the chance of making £500, the bush was fairly alive with people; and everyone within thirty miles was keeping a look-out.

"No use. The search was gradually dropped, till no one was left but my father. Month after month, he was out every day, wet or dry; and my mother waiting at home, with a look on her face that frightened us—waiting for the news he might bring. And, time after time, he took stray bones to the doctor; but they always turned out to belong to sheep, or kangaroos, or some other animal. Of course, he neglected the place altogether, and it went to wreck; and our cattle got lost; and he was always meeting with people that sympathised with him, and asked him to have a drink—and you can hardly call him responsible for the rest.

"However, on the anniversary of the day that Eddie got lost, my mother took a dose of laudanum; and that brought things to a head. My father had borrowed every shilling that the place would carry, to keep up the search; and there was neither interest nor principal forthcoming, so the mortgagee—Wesleyan minister, I'm sorry to say—had to sell us off to get his money. We had three uncles; each of them took one of us youngsters; but they could do nothing for my father. He hung about the public-houses, getting lower and lower, till he was found dead in a stable, one cold winter morning. That was about four years after Eddie was lost."

Stevenson paused, and restlessly changed his position, then muttered, in evident torture of mind:

"Think of it! While he was going away, crying, he looked back over his shoulder at me, without a word of anger; and he walked up against a sapling, and staggered—and I laughed!—Great God!—I laughed!"

That was the end of the tank-sinker's story; and silence fell on our camp. Doubtless each one of us recalled actions of petty tyranny toward leal, loving, helpless dependents, or inferiors in strength—actions which now seemed to rise from the irrevocable past, proclaiming their exemption from that moral statute of limitations which brings self-forgiveness in course of time. For an innate Jehovah sets His mark upon the Cain guilty merely of bullying or terrifying any brother whose keeper he is by virtue of superior strength; and that brand will burn while life endures. (Conversely—does such remorse ever follow disdain of authority, or defiance of power? I, for one, have never experienced it.)

Soon a disquietude from another source set my mind at work in troubled calculation of probabilities. At last I said:

"Would you suppose, Steve, that the finding of George Murdoch's body was a necessary incitement among the causes that led to the little girl's getting lost?"

"Domson's ascleep," murmured Helsmok. "I tink dey all ascleep. I wass yoos dropp'n off mineself."

And in two minutes, his relaxed pose and regular breathing affirmed a kind of fellowship with the rest, in spite of his alien birth and objectionable name. But I couldn't sleep. Dear innocent, angel-faced Mary! perishing alone in the bush! Nature's precious link between a squalid Past and a nobler Future, broken, snatched away from her allotted place in the long chain of the ages! Heiress of infinite hope, and dowered with latent fitness to fulfil her part, now so suddenly fallen by the wayside! That quaint dialect silent so soon! and for ever vanished from this earth that keen, eager, perception, that fathomless love and devotion! But such is life.

88. EDWARD DYSON

The Conquering Bush

Ned "picked up" his wife in Sydney. He had come down
for a spell in town, and to relieve himself of the distress of
riches—to melt the cheque accumulated slowly in toil and
loneliness on a big station in the North. He was a stockrider,
a slow, still man naturally, but easily moved by drink. When
he first reached town he seemed to have with him some of
the atmosphere of silence and desolation that surrounded
him during the long months back there on the run. Ned was
about thirty-four, and looked forty. He was tall and raw-
boned, and that air of settled melancholy, which is the certain result of a solitary bush life, suggested some romantic
sorrow to Mrs. Black's sentimental daughter.

Darton, taught wisdom by experience, had on this occasion taken lodgings in a suburban private house. Mrs.
Black's home was very small, but her daughter was her only
child, and they found room for a "gentleman boarder".

Janet Black was a pleasant-faced, happy-hearted girl of
twenty. She liked the new boarder from the start, she
acknowledged to herself afterwards, but when by some for-
tunate chance he happened to be on hand to drag a half-
blind and half-witted old woman from beneath the very
hoofs of a runaway horse, somewhat at the risk of his own
neck, she was enraptured, and in the enthusiasm of the moment she kissed the hand of the abashed hero, and left a tear
glittering on the hard brown knuckles.

This was a week after Ned Darton's arrival in Sydney.

Ned went straight to his room and sat perfectly still, and
with even more than his usual gravity watched the tear fade
away from the back of his hand. Either Janet's little
demonstration of artless feeling had awakened suggestions
of some glorious possibility in Ned's heart, or he desired to
exercise economy for a change; he suddenly became very
judicious in the selection of his drinks, and only took

enough whisky to dispel his native moodiness and taciturnity and make him rather a pleasant acquisition to Mrs. Black's limited family circle.

When Ned Darton returned to his pastoral duties in the murmuring wilds, he took Janet Black with him as his wife. That was their honeymoon.

Darton did not pause to consider the possible results of the change he was introducing into the life of his bride—few men would. Janet was vivacious, and her heart yearned towards humanity. She was bright, cheerful, and impressionable. The bush is sad, heavy, despairing; delightful for a month, perhaps, but terrible for a year.

As she travelled towards her new home the young wife was effervescent with joy, aglow with health, childishly jubilant over numberless plans and projects; she returned to Sydney before the expiration of a year, a stranger to her mother in appearance and in spirit. She seemed taller now, her cheeks were thin, and her face had a new expression. She brought with her some of the brooding desolation of the bush—even in the turmoil of the city she seemed lost in the immensity of the wilderness. She answered her mother's every question without a smile. She had nothing to complain of: Ned was a very good husband and very kind. She found the bush lonesome at first, but soon got used to it, and she didn't mind now. She was quite sure she was used to it, and she never objected to returning.

A baby was born, and Mrs. Darton went back with her husband to their hut by the creek on the great run, to the companionship of bears, birds, 'possums, kangaroos, and the eternal trees. She hugged her baby on her breast, and rejoiced that the little mite would give her something more to do and something to think of that would keep the awful ring of the myriad locusts out of her ears.

Man and wife settled down to their choking existence again as before, without comment. Ned was used to the bush—he had lived in it all his life— and though its influence was powerful upon him he knew it not. He was necessarily away from home a good deal, and when at home he was not companionable, in the sense that city dwellers know. Two bushmen will sit together by the fire for hours, smoking and mute, enjoying each other's society; "in mute discourse" two bushmen will ride for twenty miles through the most desolate or the most fruitful region. People who have lived in crowds want talk, laughter, and song. Ned loved his wife, but he neither talked, laughed, nor sang.

Summer came. The babe at Mrs. Darton's breast looked out on the world of trees with wide, unblinking, solemn eyes, and never smiled.

"Ned," said Janet, one bright, moonlight night, "do you know that that 'possum in the big blue gum is crazy? She has two joeys, and she has gone mad."

Janet spent a lot of her time sitting in the shade of the hut on a candle-box, gazing into her baby's large, still eyes, listening to the noises of the bush, and the babe too seemed to listen, and the mother fancied that their senses blended, and they both would some day hear something awful above the crooning of the insects and the chattering of the parrots. Sometimes she would start out of these humours with a shriek, feeling that the relentless trees which had been bending over and pressing down so long were crushing her at last beneath their weight.

Presently she became satisfied that the laughing jackasses were mad. She had long suspected it. Why else should they flock together in the dim evening and fill the bush with their crazy laughter? Why else should they sit so grave and still at other times, thinking and grieving?

Yes, she was soon quite convinced that the animals and birds, even the insects that surrounded her, were mad, hopelessly mad, all of them. The country was now burnt brown, and the hills ached in the great heat, and the ghostly mirage floated in the hollows. In the day-time the birds and beasts merely chummered and muttered querulously from the deepest shades, but in the dusk of evening they raved and shrieked, and filled the ominous bush with mad laughter and fantastic wailings.

It was at this time that Darton became impressed by the peculiar manner of his wife, and a great awe stole over him as he watched her gazing into her baby's eyes with that strange look of frightened conjecture. He suddenly became very communicative; he talked a lot, and laughed, and strove to be merry, with an indefinable chill at his heart. He failed to interest his wife; she was absorbed in a terrible thought. The bush was peopled with mad things—the wide wilderness of trees, and the dull, dead grass, and the cowering hills instilled into every living thing that came under the influence of their ineffable gloom a madness of melancholy. The bears were mad, the 'possums, the shrieking cockatoos, the dull grey laughing jackasses with their devilish cackling, and the ugly yellow-throated lizards that panted at her from the rocks—all were mad. How, then, could her babe hope to escape the influence of the mighty bush and the great white plains beyond, with their heavy atmosphere of despair pressing down upon his defenceless head? Would he not presently escape from her arms, and turn and hiss at her from the grass like a vicious snake; or climb the trees, and, like a bear, cling in·day-long torpor from a limb; or, worst of all, join the grey birds on the big dead gum, and mock at her sorrow with empty, joyless laughter?

These were the fears that oppressed Janet as she watched her sad, silent baby at her breast. They grew upon her and strengthened day by day, and one afternoon they became an agonizing conviction. She had been alone with the dumb child for two days, and she sat beside the hut door and watched the evening shadows thicken, with a shadow in her eyes that was more terrible than blackest night, and when a solitary mopoke began calling from the Bald Hill, and the jackasses set up a weird chorus of laughter, she rose, and clasping her baby tighter to her breast, and leaning over it to shield it from the surrounding evils, she hurried towards the creek.

Janet was not in the hut when Ned returned home half an hour later. Attracted by the howling of his dog, he hastened to the waterhole under the great rock, and there in the shallow water he found the bodies of his wife and child and the dull grey birds were laughing insanely overhead.

89. THOMAS SPENCER

HOW M'DOUGAL TOPPED THE SCORE

A peaceful spot is Piper's Flat. The folk that live around —
They keep themselves by keeping sheep and turning up the
     ground;
But the climate is erratic, and the consequences are
The struggle with the elements is everlasting war.
We plough, and sow, and harrow — then sit down and pray for
     rain;
And then we all get flooded out and have to start again.
But the folk are now rejoicing as they ne'er rejoiced before,
For we've played Molongo cricket, and M'Dougal topped the
     score!

Molongo had a head on it, and challenged us to play
A single-innings match for lunch — the losing team to pay.
We were not great guns at cricket, but we couldn't well say No,
So we all began to practise, and we let the reaping go.
We scoured the Flat for ten miles round to muster up our men,
But when the list was totalled we could only number ten.
Then up spoke big Tim Brady: he was always slow to speak,
And he said — "What price M'Dougal, who lives down at
     Cooper's Creek?"

So we sent for old M'Dougal, and he stated in reply
That he'd never played at cricket, but he'd half a mind to try,
He couldn't come to practise — he was getting in his hay,
But he guessed he'd show the beggars from Molongo how to
     play.
Now M'Dougal was a Scotchman, and a canny one at that,
So he started in to practise with a paling for a bat.
He got Mrs. Mac. to bowl him, but she couldn't run at all,
So he trained his sheep-dog, Pincher, how to scout and fetch the
     ball.

Now Pincher was no puppy, he was old, and worn, and grey;
But he understood M'Dougal, and — accustomed to obey —
When M'Dougal cried out "Fetch it!" he would fetch it in a
     trice,
But until the word was "Drop it!" he would grip it like a vice.
And each succeeding night they played until the light grew dim;
Sometimes M'Dougal struck the ball — sometimes the ball struck
     him!

Each time he struck, the ball would plough a furrow in the ground,
And when he missed the impetus would turn him three times
    round.

The fatal day at length arrived — the day that was to see
Molongo bite the dust, or Piper's Flat knocked up a tree!
Molongo's captain won the toss, and sent his men to bat,
And they gave some leather-hunting to the men of Piper's Flat.
When the ball sped where M'Dougal stood, firm planted in his
    track,
He shut his eyes and turned him round, and stopped it — with
    his back!
The highest score was twenty-two, the total sixty-six,
When Brady sent a yorker down that scattered Johnson's sticks.

Then Piper's Flat went in to bat, for glory and renown,
But, like the grass before the scythe, our wickets tumbled down.
"Nine wickets down for seventeen, with fifty more to win!"
Our captain heaved a heavy sigh, and sent M'Dougal in.
"Ten pounds to one you'll lose it!" cried a barracker from town;
But M'Dougal said "I'll tak' it, mon!" and planked the money
    down.
The he girded up his moleskins in a self-reliant style,
Threw off his hat and boots, and faced the bowler with a smile.

He held the bat the wrong side out, and Johnson with a grin
Stepped lightly to the bowling crease, and sent a "wobbler" in;
M'Dougal spooned it softly back, and Johnson waited there.
But M'Dougal, crying *"Fetch it!"* started running like a hare.
Molongo shouted "Victory! He's out as sure as eggs,"
When Pincher started through the crowd, and ran through
    Johnson's legs.
He seized the ball like lightning; then he ran behind a log,
And M'Dougal kept on running, while Molongo chased the
    dog!

They chased him up, they chased him down, they chased him
    round, and then
He darted through a slip-rail as the scorer shouted "Ten!"
M'Dougal puffed; Molongo swore; excitement was intense;
As the scorer marked down twenty, Pincher cleared a barbed-
    wire fence.
"Let us head him!" shrieked Molongo: "Brain the mongrel with
    a bat!"
"Run it out! Good old M'Dougal!" yelled the men of Piper's
    Flat.
And M'Dougal kept on jogging, and then Pincher doubled back,
And the scorer counted *"Forty"* as they raced across the track.

M'Dougal's legs were going fast, Molongo's breath was gone —
But still Molongo chased the dog — M'Dougal struggled on.
When the scorer shouted *"Fifty"* then they knew the chase could
  cease,
And M'Dougal gasped out *"Drop it!"* as he dropped within his
  crease.
Then Pincher dropped the ball, and as instinctively he knew
Discretion was the wiser plan, he disappeared from view;
And as Molongo's beaten men exhausted lay around
We raised M'Dougal shoulder-high, and bore him from the
  ground.

We bore him to M'Ginniss's, where lunch was ready laid,
And filled him up with whisky-punch, for which Molongo paid.
We drank his health in bumpers, and we cheered him three
  times three,
And when Molongo got its breath, Molongo joined the spree.
And the critics say they never saw a cricket match like that,
When M'Dougal broke the record in the game at Piper's Flat;
And the folk are jubilating as they never did before;
For we played Molongo cricket — and M'Dougal topped the
  score!

Notes on the Authors

In addition to biographical details, I have listed here the most useful editions of each author's work (where such editions exist) as well as a brief guide to bibliographical and critical material. A further, more general bibliography appears at the end of the book.

Adams, Arthur Henry (b. Lawrence, New Zealand, 1872 d. Sydney 1936) worked in New Zealand, Australia and England as a journalist, succeeding A.G. Stephens as editor of the *Bulletin*'s Red Page, from 1906 to 1909. Adams wrote eleven novels and several volumes of poetry and plays.

Bayldon, Arthur Albert Dawson (b. Leeds, England, 1865 d. 1958) published a novel was well as seven books of verse. His *Collected Poems* appeared in 1932.

Baynton, Barbara Jane Ainsleigh (b. Scone, N.S.W., 1857 d. Melbourne 1929) published only a handful of stories and one novel. *Bush Studies* (1902) has recently been reprinted and is now recognized as one of the key texts of the 1890s.

Boake, Barcroft Henry Thomas (b. Sydney 1866 d. Sydney 1892) published poems in the *Bulletin* before his early suicide. A.G. Stephens edited his work, *Where the Dead Men Lie and Other Poems* (2nd edition, 1913). See Clement Semmler, *Barcroft Boake* (1965).

Brennan, Christopher John (b. Sydney 1870 d. Sydney 1932) was the most distinguished Australian poet of the 1890s and the early years of this century. A graduate from the University of Sydney he studied in Berlin and became Associate Professor of Comparative Literature at Sydney university though he was later dismissed following a scandal. The standard editions of Brennan's work are edited by A.R. Chisholm and J.J. Quinn: *Verse* (1960) and *Prose* (1962). The *Verse* volume includes a substantial biography. See also Hugh Anderson and Walter Stone, *Christopher John Brennan: A Comprehensive Bibliography* (1959), James McAuley, *Christopher Brennan* (1963), and H.F. Chaplin, *A Brennan Collection* (1966).

Brereton, John le Gay (b. Sydney 1871 d. Sydney 1933) was a librarian and academic, becoming Professor of English at the University of Sydney. Brereton was the "cultured critic" of Lawson's verse. He published eight books of poetry together with plays, essays, and literary criticism. H.P. Heseltine, *John le Gay Brereton* (1965) includes a bibliography.

Daley, Victor James William Patrick (b. Navan, Ireland, 1858 d. Sydney 1905) was a journalist, poet, and prominent bohemian. *At Dawn and Dusk* (1898) was the only volume of Daley's verse published in his lifetime. *Wine and Roses* (1911) was followed by *Creeve Roe* (1947), edited by Muir Holborn and Marjorie Pizer. H.J. Oliver made the most recent selection, *Victor Daley* (1963). These last two volumes include many pieces previously uncollected.

Dorrington, Albert (b. Stratford on Avon, England, 1871 d. 1953) spent twenty years from 1887 in Australia where his stories, *Castro's Last Sacrament* (1900), were published by the *Bulletin*. Although he lived for the rest of his life in England, some of his many later novels draw upon his experiences in Australia.

Dyson, Edward George (b. Ballarat, Victoria, 1865 d. 1931) worked principally as a journalist. He published several novels as well as volumes of stories and verse. His "The Golden Shanty" is one of the best-known stories from the

1880s. It provided the title for the first *Bulletin* anthology, *A Golden Shanty: Australian Stories and Sketches. Prose and Verses by Bulletin Writers* (1890).

Evans, George Essex (b. London 1863 d. Toowoomba, Queensland, 1909) came to Australia in 1881 and worked on the land as well as at teaching and journalism. His *Collected Verse* appeared in 1928.

Farrell, John (b. Buenos Aires, Argentina, 1851 d. Sydney 1904) was brought to Australia during the gold rush of 1852. He worked principally as a journalist. The best selection of his work remains *How He Died and Other Poems* (1905).

Franklin, Stella Maria Miles (b. Talbingo, N.S.W., 1879 d. Sydney 1954) also wrote under the pseudonym "Brent of Bin Bin". *My Brilliant Career* (1901), her first novel, was followed by numerous others of country life. See Ray Mathew, *Miles Franklin* (1963) and Marjorie Barnard, *Miles Franklin* (1967).

Furphy, Joseph ("Tom Collins") (b. Yarra Glen, Victoria, 1843 d. Claremont, Western Australia, 1912) began *Such is Life* in the early 1890s though it was not published till 1903. His own experiences as a bullocky provided much of the background for the book. Two lengthy excisions from the original manuscript appeared as *Rigby's Romance* (1921) and *The Buln-Buln and the Brolga* (1948). See Walter Stone, *Joseph Furphy: An Annotated Bibliography* (1959), Miles Franklin and Kate Baker, *Joseph Furphy: The Legend of a Man and His Book* (1944), and John Barnes, *Joseph Furphy* (1963). John Barnes (ed.), *The Writer in Australia: A Collection of Literary Documents, 1856 to 1964* (1969) reprints some of the correspondence between Furphy and A.G. Stephens about the publication of *Such is Life* as well as Furphy's own "review" of the novel.

Gay, William (b. Scotland 1865 d. Bendigo, Victoria, 1897) arrived in Australia in 1888. Like Bernard O'Dowd he was a great admirer of Walt Whitman. Gay's *Poetical Works* appeared in 1911.

Gilmore, Mary Jean (b. Goulburn, N.S.W., 1865 d. Sydney

1962) worked as a teacher before joining William Lane's Utopian settlement in Paraguay in 1896. After her return to Australia in 1902 she worked in journalism for many years, particularly with *The Worker* in Sydney. Her first book, *Marri'd and Other Verses* (1910) was followed by a dozen others. Mary Gilmore was created a Dame of the Order of the British Empire in 1936 in recognition of her services to literature. Her *Selected Verse* (1948) and *Selected Poems* (1963) remain the best editions. See Dymphna Cusack and others (eds.), *Mary Gilmore: A Tribute* (1965) and W.H. Wilde, *Three Radicals* (1969).

Goodge, William Thomas (b. 1862 d. 1909) published a single volume, *Hits! Skits! and Jingles!* (1899). A second edition (1904) was illustrated by the young Norman Lindsay.

Lane, William ("John Miller") (b. Bristol, England, 1861 d. New Zealand 1917) worked in Australia in the 1880s and early 1890s as a journalist and political activist. He was editor of the Brisbane *Boomerang* when A.G. Stephens and Henry Lawson were on the staff (1891). Lane led the "New Australia" group to Paraguay in 1893. Gavin Souter's *A Peculiar People* (1968) is an account of this extraordinary undertaking. See also Lloyd Ross, *William Lane and the Australian Labor Movement* (1937).

Lawson, Henry Archibald (b. Grenfell, N.S.W., 1867 d. Sydney 1922) was the great Australian short story writer of the 1890s. Though his literary career spanned forty years almost all his best work belongs to the 1890s and the first few years of this century. See George Mackaness, *An Annotated Bibliography of Henry Lawson* (1951), Walter Stone, *Henry Lawson: A Chronological Checklist of his Contributions to "The Bulletin"*. 1887–1924 (2nd edn., 1964), and H.F. Chaplin, *Henry Lawson: His Books, Manuscripts, Autograph Letters and Association Copies* (1974). The best biography of Lawson remains Denton Prout's *Henry Lawson: The Grey Dreamer* (1963). Colin Roderick has edited the major edition of Lawson's work: *Collected Verse* (3 volumes, 1967–69), *Short Stories and Sketches* and *Autobiographical and Other Writings* (1972). There is also a companion volume of *Henry Lawson*

Criticism (1972). The best single volume selection of Lawson is that edited by Brian Kiernan, *Henry Lawson* (in the University of Queensland Press's Portable Australian Authors series, 1976). See also Brian Matthews, *The Receding Wave: Henry Lawson's Prose* (1972).

Lawson, Louisa (b. Guntawang, N.S.W., 1848 d. Sydney 1920) was the mother of Henry Lawson. She edited and managed *The Dawn*, a monthly magazine for women, from 1888 to 1905. *The Lonely Crossing* was her only book of verse.

McCrae, Hugh Raymond (b. Melbourne 1876 d. Sydney 1958) worked as an actor, journalist, and illustrator. *Story Book Only* (1948) is the best collection of his prose. There are two selections of his verse: by R.G. Howarth, *The Best Poems of Hugh McCrae* (1961), and Douglas Stewart, *Hugh McCrae: Selected Poems* (1966).

Morant, Henry Harbord ("Harry", "The Breaker") (b. Bideford, England, 1865 d. South Africa 1902) worked up country in Australia before journeying to the Boer War. He was executed after a court-martial concerning the shooting of a prisoner. A selection of Morant's verse appears in Frank Renar, *Bushman and Buccaneer* (1902) and in F.M. Cutlack, *Breaker Morant* (1962). Kit Denton has written a historical novel, *The Breaker* (1973).

Neilson, John Shaw (b. Panola, South Australia, 1872 d. Melbourne 1942) began publishing verse in the early 1890s though his first book did not appear till 1916. Most of his life was spent as an itinerant labourer. The best edition of Neilson's work, though far from complete, is that edited by A.R. Chisholm, *The Poems of Shaw Neilson* (2nd edn., 1973). See also Hugh Anderson, *Shaw Neilson: An Annotated Bibliography and Checklist* (1956) and Hugh Anderson and L.J. Blake, *John Shaw Neilson* (1972).

O'Dowd, Bernard Patrick (b. Beaufort, Victoria, 1866 d. Melbourne 1953) graduated from the University of Melbourne in Arts and Law and worked as a legal librarian and a parliamentary draftsman. His several books of verse were collected as *Poems* (3rd edn., 1944). A selection has been edited by A.A. Phillips, *Bernard O'Dowd* (1963). See Hugh Anderson, *Bernard O'Dowd (1866–1953): An Annotated Bibliography* (1963), Nettie Palmer and Victor Kennedy, *Bernard O'Dowd* (1954), W.H. Wilde, *Three Radicals* (1969), and Hugh Anderson, *The Poet Militant* (1969).

Ogilvie, William Henry (b. Kelso, Scotland, 1869 d. 1963) spent the 1890s in Australia, his numerous ballads being collected in two volumes published by the *Bulletin: Fair Girls and Gray Horses* (1898) and *Hearts of Gold* (1903). In later life he continued his prolific output. His Australian experiences are recounted in *My Life in the Open* (1908).

O'Hara, John Bernard (b. Bendigo, Victoria, 1862 d. Melbourne 1927), an Arts graduate from the University of Melbourne, worked as a teacher for most of his life. He published nine books of verse.

Paterson, Andrew Barton ("Banjo") (b. Narrambla, N.S.W. 1864 d. Sydney 1941) qualified as a solicitor but worked much of his life as a journalist. He was perhaps the most popular balladist of the 1890s. His "Waltzing Matilda" is part of our folklore. See Clement Semmler, *The Banjo of the Bush* (2nd edn., 1974).

Quinn, Roderic Joseph (b. Sydney 1867 d. Sydney 1949) worked as a journalist. In addition to several books of verse he published a novel and numerous short stories.

"Rudd, Steele" (Arthur Hoey Davis) (b. Drayton, Queensland, 1868 d. Brisbane 1935) produced twenty-four volumes of short stories, though none of the later ones recaptured the popularity of his first collection, *On Our Selection* (1899). See Eric Davis, *The Life and Times of Steele Rudd* (1976).

Spencer, Thomas Edward (b. London 1845 d. 1910) published several novels as well as volumes of stories and verse.

Stephens, Alfred George (b. Toowoomba, Queensland, 1865 d. Sydney 1933) worked throughout his life as a journalist and publisher, being in charge of the *Bulletin*'s literary activities from 1894 to 1906. Stephens's Red Page was a major force in Australian writing during that time. See Vance Palmer, *A.G. Stephens, His Life and Work* (1941). The most recent selection of his work is that edited by Leon Cantrell, *A.G. Stephens: Selected Writings* (1977).

Stephens, James Brunton (b. Borrowstowness, Scotland, 1835 d. Brisbane 1902) graduated from the University of Edinburgh and arrived in Australia in 1866. He worked as a teacher and then for twenty years in the Queensland Chief Secretary's Department. His *Poetical Works* appeared in 1902. See Cecil Hadgraft, *James Brunton Stephens* (1969).

"Warung, Price" (William Astley) (b. Liverpool, England, 1855 d. Sydney 1911) published five volumes of stories during the 1890s, mainly about the convict days. There have been two modern selections: *Convict Days* (1960) and B.G. Andrews, ed., *Tales of the Convict System: Selected Stories of Price Warung* (1975).

Textual Sources

All the pieces in this anthology were written in Australia during the 1890s. Most of the stories and verses were initially published in magazines or newspapers and later collected into book form. My copy text has been this later book appearance on the grounds that such publication is more likely to be an accurate account of the author's intentions than is publication in the columns of a journal. Where possible, I have then collated my copy text with earlier published texts. This editorial policy means that some pieces appear here in a slightly different version to that encountered elsewhere (Lawson, for instance, later revised much of his earlier work), but they are as their authors first issued them in permanent form. They are as the nineties knew them. Each piece (with the exception of the novel extracts) is a complete work. The only changes I have made have been to correct obvious typographical errors.

Each item is numbered as in the contents and the sources are as follows:

Adams, Arthur, 9, 11, 39: *Maoriland, and Other Verses*. Sydney: *Bulletin* Newspaper Company, 1899.
Bayldon, Arthur, 17: *Poems*. Brisbane: W.H. Wendt, 1899.
Baynton, Barbara, 80: *Bush Studies*. London: Duckworth, 1902.
Boake, Barcroft, 27, 58, 81, 82: *Where the Dead Men Lie and Other Poems*. Sydney: Angus and Robertson, 1897.
Brennan, Christopher, 28–37, 84: *Poems*. Sydney: G.B. Philip, 1913.
Brereton, John le Gay, 20: *Sweetheart Mine: Lyrics of Love and Friendship*. Sydney: Angus and Robertson. 1897. 22: *The Song of Brotherhood and Other Verses*. London: Allen, 1896.
Daley, Victor, 2, 6, 13, 14, 26, 59: *Wine and Roses*. Sydney: Angus

and Robertson, 1911. 3, 46, 54: *Creeve Roe.* Sydney: Pinchgut Press, 1947. 19, 24: *At Dawn and Dusk.* Sydney: Angus and Robertson, 1898.

Dorrington, Albert, 75: *Castro's Last Sacrament and Other Stories.* Sydney: *Bulletin* Newspaper Company, 1900.

Dyson, Edward, 61: *Rhymes From the Mines and Other Lines.* Sydney: Angus and Robertson, 1896. 88: *Below and On Top.* Melbourne: George Robertson, 1898.

Evans, George Essex, 52: *The Repentance of Magdalenè Despar and Other Poems.* London: Sampson Low, 1891.

Farrell, John, 44: *Australia to England.* Sydney: Angus and Robertson, 1897.

Franklin, Miles, 68: chapter 5 of *My Brilliant Career.* Edinburgh: Blackwood, 1901.

Furphy, Joseph, 85: *The Poems of Joseph Furphy.* Melbourne: Lothian, 1916. 87: part of chapter 5 of *Such is Life.* Sydney: *Bulletin* Newspaper Company, 1903.

Gay, William, 49: *Sonnets.* Bendigo: William Gay, 1896.

Gilmore, Mary, 16, 23: *Marri'd and Other Verses.* Melbourne: George Robertson, 1910.

Goodge, W.T., 76: *Hits! Skits! and Jingles!* Sydney: *Bulletin* Newspaper Company, 1899.

Lane, William, 15: chapter 4 of *The Workingman's Paradise: An Australian Labour Novel.* Sydney: Edwards, Dunlop, 1892.

Lawson, Henry, 1: *Bulletin,* 21 January 1899, Red Page. 4, 41, 47, 62, 64, 67, 73: *In the Days When the World Was Wide and Other Verses.* Sydney: Angus and Robertson. 1896. 5: *Verses Popular and Humorous.* Sydney: Angus and Robertson, 1900 (special large paper edition). 7, 45: *Verses Popular and Humorous.* Sydney: Angus and Robertson, 1900. 12, 86: *While the Billy Boils.* Sydney: Angus and Robertson, 1896. 43: *For Australia and Other Poems.* Melbourne: Standard Publishing, 1913. 51, 83: *Short Stories in Prose and Verse.* Sydney: Louisa Lawson, 1894. 72: *In the Days When the World Was Wide and Other Verses.* Sydney: Angus and Robertson, 1900 (new edition). 74: *Over the Sliprails.* Sydney: Angus and Robertson, 1900.

Lawson, Louisa, 77: *The Lonely Crossing and Other Poems.* Sydney: *The Dawn,* 1905.

McCrae, Hugh, 21: *The Bulletin Reciter.* Sydney: *Bulletin* Newspaper Company, 1901.

Morant, Harry, 56: F.M. Cutlack, *Breaker Morant: A Horseman Who Made History.* Sydney: Ure Smith, 1962.

Neilson, John Shaw, 18: *The Bulletin Reciter.* Sydney: *Bulletin* Newspaper Company, 1901.

O'Dowd, Bernard, 10, 38, 50: *Dawnward?* Sydney: *Bulletin* Newspaper Company, 1903.

Ogilvie, Will, 60, 69, 78: *Fair Girls and Gray Horses: With Other Verses*. Sydney: *Bulletin* Newspaper Company, 1898.

O'Hara, John Bernard, 42: *Songs of the South*. London: Ward, Lock, 1891.

Paterson, A.B. "Banjo", 55, 57, 63, 66, 70, 79: *The Man From Snowy River and Other Verses*. Sydney: Angus and Robertson, 1895.

Quinn, Roderic, 25: *The Hidden Tide*. Sydney: *Bulletin* Newspaper Company, 1899. 48: *The Circling Hearths*. Sydney: *Bulletin* Newspaper Company, 1901.

"Rudd, Steele", 65, 71: chapters 1 and 5 of *On Our Selection!* Sydney: *Bulletin* Newspaper Company, 1899.

Spencer, Thomas, 89: *The Bulletin Reciter*. Sydney: *Bulletin* Newspaper Company, 1901.

Stephens, A.G., 8: From *The Bulletin Story Book*. Sydney: *Bulletin* Newspaper Company, 1901.

Stephens, James Brunton, 53: *The Poetical Works of Brunton Stephens*. Sydney: Angus and Robertson, 1902.

"Warung, Price", 40: *Tales of the Old Regime and The Bullet of the Fated Ten*. Melbourne: George Robertson, 1897.

Select Bibliography

Adams, Francis. *The Australians: A Social Sketch*. London: Unwin, 1893.

Barnes, John, ed. *The Writer in Australia: A Collection of Literary Documents, 1856 to 1964*. Melbourne: Oxford University Press, 1969.

Cantrell, Leon, ed. *Bards, Bohemians, and Bookmen: Essays in Australian Literature*. St. Lucia: University of Queensland Press, 1976. Includes essays on Lawson, Furphy, Brennan, and A.G. Stephens as well as on the nineties generally.

Crowley, F.K., ed. *A New History of Australia*. Melbourne: Heinemann, 1974.

Dixson, Miriam. *The Real Matilda: Women and Identity in Australia 1788 to 1975*. Harmondsworth: Penguin, 1976.

Dutton, Geoffrey, ed. *The Literature of Australia*. 2nd edition. Ringwood: Penguin, 1976.

Gould, Nat. *On and Off the Turf in Australia*. London: Routledge, 1895.

Green, H.M. *A History of Australian Literature*. Sydney: Angus and Robertson, 1961.

Hadgraft, Cecil H. *Australian Literature: A Critical Account to 1955*. London: Heinemann, 1960.

Johnston, Grahame, ed. *Australian Literary Criticism*. Melbourne: Oxford University Press, 1962. Includes G.A. Wilkes, "The Eighteen Nineties".

Jones, Joseph. *Radical Cousins: Nineteenth Century American and Australian Writers*. St. Lucia: University of Queensland Press, 1976.

Jose, A.W. *The Romantic Nineties*. Sydney: Angus and Robertson, 1933.

Lawson, Ronald. *Brisbane in the 1890s: A Study of an Australian Urban Society*. St. Lucia: University of Queensland Press, 1973.

Lindsay, Norman. *Bohemians of the Bulletin*. Sydney: Angus and Robertson, 1965.

McQueen, Humphrey. *A New Britannia: An Argument Concerning the Social Origins of Australian Radicalism and Nationalism*. 2nd edition. Harmondsworth: Penguin, 1975.

Mackaness, George, and Stone, Walter. *The Books of "The Bulletin", 1880–1952. An Annotated Bibliography*. Sydney: Angus and Robertson, 1955.

Nesbitt, Bruce. "Literary Nationalism and the 1890s". *Australian Literary Studies* 5 (1971): 3–17.

Palmer, Vance. *The Legend of the Nineties*. Melbourne: Melbourne University Press, 1954.

Phillips, A.A. *The Australian Tradition: Studies in a Colonial Culture*. 2nd edition. Melbourne: Cheshire, 1966.

Semmler, Clement, ed. *Twentieth Century Australian Literary Criticism*. Melbourne: Oxford University Press, 1967. As well as pieces generally on the nineties it includes essays on Quinn, O'Dowd, Furphy, Boake, Lawson, Brennan, and others.

Taylor, George. *Those Were the Days: Being Reminiscences of Australian Writers and Artists*. Sydney: Tyrrell, 1918.

Turner, H.G., and Sutherland, A. *The Development of Australian Literature*. Melbourne: Robertson, 1898.

Wallace-Crabbe, Chris, ed. *The Australian Nationalists: Modern Critical Essays*. Melbourne: Oxford University Press, 1971. The most important collection of criticism of the nineties period. Includes Ken Levis, "The Role of the *Bulletin* in Indigenous Short-story Writing during the Eighties and Nineties", together with essays on Brennan, Paterson, Lawson, Baynton, Furphy, and others.

Ward, Russel. *The Australian Legend*. Melbourne: Oxford University Press, 1958.

Wilkes, G.A. "Going Over the Terrain in a Different Way: An Alternative View of Australian Literary History". *Southerly* 35 (1975): 141–56.

Wilding, Michael. "A New Colonialism?" *Southerly* 35 (1975): 95–102.

Woodward, Judith M. "Urban Influences on Australian Literature in the late Nineteenth Century". *Australian Literary Studies* 7 (1975): 115–29.

Wright, Judith. *Preoccupations in Australian Poetry*. Melbourne: Oxford University Press, 1966.